Heterodox Islamic Economics

The fields of morality and ethics have been left out significantly from socio-scientific study in economics and finance in particular. Yet this book argues that, in this age of post-modernist analytical inquiry, the study of morality and ethics is an epistemological requirement.

Heterodox Islamic Economics illustrates the delimiting nature of mainstream economic reasoning in treating morality and ethics, and highlights the potential contribution of analytical monotheism, as typified by the Islamic concept of *Tahwid*. This book asks the burning question: Is a revolutionary and/or evolutionary new methodological worldview possible in science in general and economics in particular? It also investigates the emergent nature of meta-science and the socio-scientific epistemology of the monotheistic unity of knowledge. The principal purpose of this book is to undertake an introductory exploration of the critical area of comparative economic thought in order to place the nature and emergence of ethico-economic theory in its proper context. It is ultimately argued that such a post-orthodoxy revolutionary methodological worldview can be presented by Islamic political economy, Islamic economics, and finance.

This volume is of great interest to those who study political economy, economic theory, and philosophy, as well as economics in the Middle East.

Masudul Alam Choudhury is Professor of Islamic Economics and Finance, Faculty of Economics, Trisakti University, Jakarta, Indonesia. Presently he is Visiting Professor in the Department of Shari'ah and Economics, Academy of Islamic Studies, University of Malaya, Kuala Lumpur, Malaysia.

Ishaq Bhatti is Reader, Islamic Finance Program, LaTrobe University, Melbourne, Australia.

Routledge Frontiers of Political Economy

Heterodox Islamic Economics

The emergence of an ethico-economic theory

**Masudul Alam Choudhury and
Ishaq Bhatti**

LONDON AND NEW YORK

First published 2017 by Routledge

2 Park Square, Milton Park, Abingdon, Oxfordshire OX14 4RN
52 Vanderbilt Avenue, New York, NY 10017

Routledge is an imprint of the Taylor & Francis Group, an informa business

First issued in paperback 2019

Copyright © 2017 Masudul Alam Choudhury and Ishaq Bhatti

The right of Masudul Alam Choudhury and Ishaq Bhatti to be identified as authors of this work has been asserted by them in accordance with sections 77 and 78 of the Copyright, Designs and Patents Act 1988.

All rights reserved. No part of this book may be reprinted or reproduced or utilised in any form or by any electronic, mechanical, or other means, now known or hereafter invented, including photocopying and recording, or in any information storage or retrieval system, without permission in writing from the publishers.

Notice:
Product or corporate names may be trademarks or registered trademarks, and are used only for identification and explanation without intent to infringe.

British Library Cataloguing in Publication Data
A catalogue record for this book is available from the British Library

Library of Congress Cataloging in Publication Data
Names: Bhatti, Ishaq, 1957- author.
Title: Heterodox Islamic economics: the emergence of an ethico-economic theory / Ishaq Bhatti and Masudul Alam Choudhury.
Description: New York: Routledge, 2016.
Identifiers: LCCN 2016010191| ISBN 9781138960831 (hardback) | ISBN 9781315660172 (ebook)
Subjects: LCSH: Economics–Religious aspects–Islam. | Islamic ethics. | Knowledge, Theory of (Islam) | Islamic philosophy.
Classification: LCC BP173.75.B49 2016 | DDC 330.917/67–dc23
LC record available at https://lccn.loc.gov/2016010191

ISBN: 978-1-138-96083-1 (hbk)
ISBN: 978-0-367-32195-6 (ebk)

Typeset in Times New Roman
by Sunrise Setting Ltd., Brixham, UK

Contents

Figures

Tables

Foreword

It is evident that the human condition in the world today is unacceptable morally and ethically. The world may be richer in terms of material wealth, conventionally measured, but a rising tide of operational renunciation of moral and ethical principles seems to have accompanied the increase in material wealth. There is systemic injustice and poverty. The potential for large armed conflict has not been eradicated and there exists sufficient stock of weapons of mass destruction to wipe out the human race many times over. There has been an unstoppable increase in carbon dioxide emission in the world and, with it, a likely increase in global surface temperature change. Clearly, the status quo is not acceptable. The received socio-scientific-philosophical paradigms have to change.

But where must one begin practically? The basic, pragmatic method of decision-making in the mobilization and use of socio-politico-economic resources of society must change to a method that respects the morality and ethics embedded in the "monotheistic unity of knowledge and the unified nature of the world-system induced by the episteme of unity of knowledge" (p. 83). This is where Masudul Alam Choudhury and Ishaq Bhatti make a contribution. In nine chapters of the book, they lay what might be the essential first development of a philosophical-scientific foundation of heterodox Islamic economics that may lead to the emergence of ethico-economic theory.

Pragmatism is individualistic, embodying as it does separation not only in connection with human welfare, but also in the empirical world of reality. It denies the totality of factors in a choice situation and the completeness of knowledge for a proper decision. It is oriented to a short time horizon—whatever choice provides the highest benefits here and now, do it. It is, importantly, directed to the materialistic benefits of this world alone, denying, or at best having a neutral attitude toward, the existence of God and the benefits of the Hereafter. It believes in the efficacy of conventional science to increase human welfare, denying itself the a priori knowledge contained in the holy books of God—most importantly, the *Qur'an*. Pragmatism may be considered to be the practical model of 'de-knowledge' (rationalism) by the *Tawhidi* (monotheistic) String Model.

The philosophical ideas of Emanuel Kant are consistent with pragmatism:

> A clear exposition of morality of itself leads to the belief in God. Belief in this philosophic connexion means not trust in a revelation, but trust arising

from the use of the reason, which springs from the principle of practical morality.

(Kant, 1963)

Thus people in capitalist regimes may believe in a personal God, but such a belief excludes application of the words of God in the public sphere.

Heterodox Islamic economics, founded on the principle of the monotheistic law of knowledge ontologically, epistemologically, and phenomenologically, may, in time, put back God and His words where they functionally belong—and that is everywhere that the human mind can comprehend. Practically, this civilizational change has to happen in Indonesia, having, as it does, the Belief in the One God as the very first and foremost of five principles of her Constitution. The monotheistic methodology of unity of knowledge needs to be applied to the functional interpretations of the other four for consistent applications in the multiverse field of human experience.

This book is an essential step in that direction. A lot of research needs to be done, not only to further refine the new technology for operational use, but also to make research results acceptable to users in order for it to be implemented. The research program will have to consist of two broad categories: managing the world-system, or parts thereof, based on the pragmatic philosophy; and managing the world-system based on the monotheistic methodology. The monotheistic methodology may take us nearer to the truth and allow us to be more consistent in our strategies with our human goals—but absolute truth remains with God.

Sayuti Hasibuan
Professor of Economics
Al Azhar University
Jakarta, Indonesia

Reference

Kant, I. (1963). "Natural religion: Prayer," in *Kant's Lectures on Ethics*, trans., I. Infeld, Indianapolis, IN: Hackett.

Epigraph

Qur'an and meta-science

In praise of God:

> And if all the trees on earth were pens and the ocean (were ink), with seven oceans behind it to add to its (supply), yet would not the words of Allah be exhausted (in the writing): for Allah is Exalted in Power, full of Wisdom.
>
> (*Qur'an*, 31:27)

In renunciation of rationalism:

> Woe to the false-mongers, – those who (flounder) heedless in floods of confusion.
>
> (*Qur'an*, 51:10–11)

In quest of meta-science:

> No falsehood can approach it from before or behind it: It is sent down by One Full of Wisdom, worthy of all praise.
>
> (*Qur'an*, 41:42)

Introduction

The objective (and contribution) of this research work is to raise the consciousness among the global socio-scientific community of a new vista of scientific possibility that has not been inquired into in recent times. This assertion is not to discount the great works of learning that were produced during the times of Islamic scholasticism and in Europe pre- and post-Enlightenment in the field of science and society. Yet the truly analytical framework of socio-scientific intellection and application of the ontological and epistemological field of monotheistic law as methodology in unity of knowledge and its governance over the generality and particulars of the world-system, also referred to as "consilience," has not been undertaken.

Contrarily, the present work is among the building blocks of the meta-scientific inquiry and discovery of the substantive monotheistic role in socio-scientific extension and application. The emergent methodology is merged with formalism, methodical groundwork, and the vast number of applications. In the process, the emerging perspective of the meta-science of the monotheistic law of unity of knowledge is taken away from a garb of religiosity. Instead, it is placed where it appropriately ought to be to encompass all learning and wellbeing. This particular context is one of deriving knowledge and its constructive potentiality on the basis of unity of knowledge arising from the completeness of the monotheistic law as a supercardinal topological entity. Rucker (1982) refers to such cardinalities as "large cardinalities." This yields a mathematical formalism.

This work nonetheless refers to the *Qur'an* as the primal ontology of the super-cardinal knowledge premise, and to the *sunnah*, the teaching of the Prophet Muhammad, as the functional ontology used to map the incomprehensibly vast knowledge of the *Qur'an* by bits into the world-system. The circular, multi-causal interrelationship between the *Qur'an*, the *sunnah*, and the world-system (*a'lameen*) in the continuity of the evolutionary learning processes of the unity of knowledge thereby forms a system and cybernetic mathematical study. It carries with it substantively comparative ontological and epistemological implications within an analytical and mathematical socio-scientific worldview.

This work refers to such a nature of the new meta-scientific ontology immersed in its analytical, mathematical, and applied features as "epistemic analytic (mathematics)." Thus, even though God is not configurative and commensurate, the divine law of monotheism as the supercardinal topological domain of a complete, unbounded, yet investigative universe encompassing multiverses is a field of resilient socio-scientific enterprise. God cannot be symbolized according to the *Qur'an*, yet the monotheistic law can be symbolized for socio-scientific study across a never-ending, evolutionary learning socio-scientific multiverse.

Some analytical and mathematical properties of the ontology of the monotheistic multiverse (*a'lameen*) need to be established outright to pave the way for the acceptance of the monotheistic law as meta-science of creation. Those that we will consider in this work are: (1) the universality and unique nature of the monotheistic ontology; (2) the operations of supercardinal topology, which are established in the multiverse overarching the monotheistic law; and (3) the self-referencing nature of the monotheistic law, which is a corollary to the first property and proves the closure in the meta-socio-scientific multiverse. The closure in the small and the very large and ultimate multiverse forms the self-referencing property of the meta-science in reference to meta-mathematics (Choudhury, 1993). We will avoid mathematical treatment in this Introduction.

The property of universality of the monotheistic law is proved by its inclusion of both Truth (T) and Falsehood (F). The uncertain categories of undecidability as temporary states become well determined, even as T and F become well determined and are sorted into their respective categories. The undecidable category disappears as evolutionary learning continues to sort out the states between truth and falsehood ultimately. Because T and F are mutually disjoint, therefore, either T or F belongs to the primal ontology of the monotheistic law, denoted by Ω. In the set-theoretic sense, $T \cup F = \Omega$; $T \cap F = \Phi \in \Omega$.

The uniqueness of the nature of unity of knowledge arising from the monotheistic law is proved by its holistic relationship of unification between the a priori and a posteriori domains of reasoning—that is, between *noumenon* and phenomenon, or deductive and inductive arguments of the socio-scientific, mind–matter space. The property of uniqueness along these directions annuls the heteronomy and dualism that form the permanent *problematique* of science as we know it. Unity of knowledge in its full manifestation thus remains the only reality of moral construction in the monotheistic universe at the mutual exclusion of heteronomous thinking. The *Qur'an* opens up the search for universality and uniqueness with the assertion: There exists nothing other than the *Qur'an* as the primal knowledge.

On the property of supercardinality, note that, while T and F are both explained by the monotheistic law in Ω, so also the null set between T and F belongs to Ω. All monotonic positive mappings by "S," signifying certainty of these two categories, preserve the two properties of T and F in Ω. Consequently, both Ω and $S(\Omega) \subset \Omega$ form topologies. Since "S" is order-preserving and monotonic positive on the open and unbounded monotheistic universe of complete knowledge, therefore, both primal ontology of the monotheistic law and the specified mappings on it are respectively supercardinal and functional topologies. By the same kind of arguments applied to the world-system and its sub-systems, all of which are described by the nature of unity of knowledge of the primal ontology, the resulting sub-systems of the world-system are also topological spaces.

They are described by their own functional ontologies that are primarily derived in terms of unity of knowledge arising from the primal ontology of Ω.

The self-referencing property of the *Qur'an* is proved by way of the circular causation in unity of knowledge, whereby every representative variable out of a vector of variables is causally related to the rest of the variables for reasons of explaining the paired (unified) nature of the universe. Thereby, every representative variable proves to be circularly referenced. Circular causation is therefore the property of the paired or complementary universe of endogenously learning variables, their relations, and between the inherent entities (Sztompka, 1974).

The emergence of ethico-economics in heterodox economic thought

Because the monotheistic law forms the primal ontology of unity of knowledge and the demarcation of "de-knowledge" concerning "everything" as topologies, in the age of heterodox thinking the meta-science of the monotheistic universe encompasses the socio-scientific field of economics and society—of science, nature, and man. The nature of the universal law as the monotheistic law establishes morality and ethics to be the endogenously embedded factors of mind–matter reality.

Thus ethics as consciousness derived from the primal ontology of Ω in unity of knowledge presents the field of ethico-economics. In reference to the building blocks of the meta-science of the monotheistic law, the dynamics, explanation, formalism, and applications of the new heterodox thinking in ethico-economics rests on the methodological worldview of its ontology. That is to make consciousness by morality and ethics rest on unity of knowledge explained as pervasive complementarities between the good things of life. Likewise, the monotheistic law that defines and rejects the bad things of life in its moral and ethical fold explains the continued failure of economics either in traditional or heterodox thought.

The foundation of new epistemological thought against traditional thought in both the Islamic and Occidental cases is constructed on the moral and ethical worldview of unity of knowledge between the good things of life. Orthodox and heterodox economic theories are critically evaluated in the light of the ethical foundation of unity of knowledge. In this way, this work discusses, formalizes, and applies the newly emergent ethico-economic theory based on ethical consciousness as the yardstick of the emergent theory of heterodox economic theory. The consequence also critically annuls the orthodox, mainstream, and selected heterodox economic theories that do not rest on the ethical episteme.

Critique of Islamic economics as orthodox and mainstream economics contra the heterodox paradigm

The present work wrests into its portfolio of criticism the remnant of a once-self-proclaimed field of Islamic economics. This work shows that Islamic economics has remained simply an offshoot of orthodox and mainstream economics without any different way of thinking along scientific lines. An example of this is the practice of interest-free banking without the development of the theory of interest, trade, money, and spending in the ontological light of the *Qur'an* and the *sunnah*.

The present work will examine some empirical cases and some institutional cases in this respect under the methodological worldview of the monotheistic law. The formal model of the "paired" universe of the *Qur'an*, exemplified by pervasive complementarities between the good things of life and rejection of the bad and differentiated things of life, is based on a circular causation model of wellbeing. This is studied in reference to consciousness as the ethics of multi-causal complementarities.

Islamic economics has not been able to develop any similar consistent idea that would otherwise contribute to the world of new heterodox economic thought. The project of exegesis of the *Qur'an* and *sunnah* forming the ontological basis of the morally reconstructed socio-economic world-system never occurred in the traditional project of Islamic economics, then or now.

Such failures in orthodox, mainstream, heterodox, and Islamic economic thought have caused the critical reinvestigation of the field of Islamic economics in this book. The methodological issues examined here form the premise of construction of the meta-science of "everything." The emergent formalism reflects the methodical nature of the new meta-science. The applications of the methods highlight samples of the vast relevance of the new ethico-economic theory in the socio-scientific world-system arising from heterodox Islamic economics. In these respects, the present book is both a research book and a contribution to the world of learning. Its methodological content is bereft of undue religiosity and parochial thinking. Readers are considered here as the subjects of fresh learning to launch critical thinking within a project of the common weal of wellbeing for all.

Contents of this book

The various chapters in this book establish the scope of the extension of the monotheistic law to meta-science in the vastly socio-scientific field. Especial attention is given to ethico-economics and heterodox Islamic economics within the comprehensive theory of "everything."

In Chapter 1, the important preliminary concepts related to terminology, methodological orientation, and the development of meta-science are introduced. The requirement and opportunity for an extension of existing scientific enterprise into the meta-science of the monotheistic methodological worldview are introduced. The problems of orthodox, mainstream, and heterodox economics are pointed out. Islamic economics as it presently exists is argued to be part and parcel of these schools of economic thought. The new heterodox economic theory and its applications are discussed for inclusion as a particular pursuit within the generalized methodological worldview of meta-science arising from the monotheistic law. The episteme of unity of knowledge and its induction of the generality and particulars of the diverse world-systems are thus shown to articulate the conscious role of morality and ethics in unified reasoning concerning God, the world-system, and mind–matter realism. Through all of these means, the gateway of novel intellection in this book is opened up.

In Chapter 2, an original socio-scientific theory is developed out of a contrast with the paradigm of rationalism. The new methodological worldview arises from the epistemology of unity of knowledge and its *functional* ontological implication of unity of the world-system. The Kantian epistemological meaning of heteronomy is shown to be one of the permanent socio-scientific problems of rationalism.

The formalism arising from the methodology is of the nature of topological mathematics by virtue of the complex problems and forms that inhere in the criticism of Kantian heteronomy and the project of rationalism. The emergence of the new epistemological worldview of unity of knowledge and the knowledge-induced world-system is formalized. Several theoretical constructs and applications of the episteme of unity of knowledge are pointed out in diverse fields.

Chapter 3 introduces the nature and critique of selected major approaches to non-orthodox economic and scientific thought. Heterodoxy in socio-scientific thought is thereby examined in its tradition and new meanings. The principal focus of heterodox thought is formalized and used to introduce the formalism that would represent the post-orthodoxy and prevalent heterodoxy in the indispensable fold of ethico-economics. The critique of some standing ideas in heterodox economic theory is followed by the introduction of the idea of the "epistemic analytic (mathematics)" approach of the new field of meta-science. It rests on the foundational ontology of the monotheistic law of unity of knowledge and the induced world-system in general and in particular. Selected applications are presented in order to bring out the most central, yet missing, roles of ethics and consciousness in all of orthodox and received heterodox socio-scientific thought. Its source in the monotheistic methodology of unity of knowledge is raised as the challenge of the ultimate possibility for a global meta-science of "everything."

Chapter 4 explores the premise that, in Islamic socio-scientific inquiry, the *primal* ontology on which the entire Islamic worldview rests in generality and in particular is the monotheistic Oneness of God and the unity of the consequential world-system created by the ontological precept. The equivalent meaning of "oneness" in its cognitive and applicable form in the context of the world-system must be based on the episteme of unity of knowledge. This ensues from the divine law, and then finds its relevant explanatory space in explaining the generality and specifics of the world-system. The generality of the worldview is established by the organically unified form of the world-system existing by virtue of knowledge, agency, and potentiality. The example of a specific sub-system of the generalized world-system is the field of Islamic financial economics.

This chapter studies the following specific problem of Islamic financial economics taken up in its epistemological context: How is economic and financial reasoning actualized in the context of unity of knowledge (formalism) and unity of the world-system? This is exemplified by the evolutionary learning model caused by interaction and integration between money, finance, and the real economy. There are many other ones.

Chapter 5 investigates the current status of intellection in Islamic economics to discover whether this field, as it has developed in contemporary times, has any epistemological basis that can render a revolutionary contribution to academia.

The extensively reviewed inquiry into the field of economic orthodoxy, and within it of Islamic economics, reveals that the latter field remains contained wholly in mainstream economic reasoning. Islamic economics has thereby missed the opportunity to project its distinctively new methodology and the emanation of methodical formalism from the methodology. Mainstream economics comprising neoclassical, Keynesian, monetarist, Austrian, and evolutionary institutional paradigms are examined in this work against the backdrop of a freshly new heterodox economic structure. It shows that Islamic economics rightly conceived and developed has the potential to render its true epistemological foundations and applications. But, over the many years that Islamic economics has tried to cut a space out for itself, this has not happened.

The predicament of Islamic economics is true only as it presently stands without an explained episteme and no agreed-upon definition. Contrarily, if Islamic economics were to be studied on the basis of its foundational epistemology of the monotheistic worldview and by the methodical formalism that arises from it, then one can see a tremendous possibility for Islamic economics in the field of a truly socio-scientific revolution. Islamic economics would become a fresh, socio-scientific theory with profound analytics and applications. It could then be retained in the intellectual annals by its universality and uniqueness.

Chapter 6 accumulates the meta-scientific concepts of the previous chapters into a structure of generality and particularism of the methodology of the monotheistic law as the science of consilience (unity of knowledge). A certain degree of mathematical rigor is employed to draw out the nature of logical mathematics that is used in the building of the "epistemic analytic (mathematics)" of the meta-science of unity of knowledge and its induction into the world-system. In specifying to Islamic economics and heterodox economics with the fusion of ethical consciousness in them some conceptual topics are examined.

Chapter 7 comprises an empirical version of the properties of interaction, integration, and evolutionary learning according to the monotheistic law that reflects the episteme of unity of knowledge in these properties. A simple approach is adopted, while the theory underlying the complex nature of evaluating historical paths of evolutionary learning is provided. The example of Islamic financing instruments is used in order to prove the need for a unified way of addressing Islamic financing, rather than the mutually separable ways of using financing instruments as independent entities. The unified portfolio of Islamic financial instruments implies the principle of unity of knowledge adopted in the choice of the good things of life. The separate use of financing instruments is a way of providing methodological individualism in the nature of the combined complementary portfolio. The conclusion thereby evidently points toward the problem of Islamic financing in promoting Islamic values, rather than the trillions of dollars of commercial financing on which Islamic financing thrives today. Many thanks to my student, Dr Ari Pratiwi of the Postgraduate Program in Islamic Economics and Finance, Faculty of Economics, Trisakti University and IBM Indonesia, for assisting with the empirical work in this chapter.

Chapter 8 looks at the approach of the scientific research program and its overarching system and cybernetic worldview; such is the nature of the meta-science built on the foundation of the monotheistic law of unity of knowledge and its induction of the world-system. The systemic worldview also presents the complex nature of the holistic evolutionary learning process. Nonetheless, the extreme degree of systemic complexity is reduced to computability by means of the method of circular causation relations that underlie the wellbeing criterion function representing degrees of complementarities between the variables characterizing the varied sub-systems of the world-system. The approach here is a generalized one in its formal framework. Within such a framework, the particular case of heterodox Islamic economics can be studied without change in conception and application. The only difference is in the socio-economic and financial problem at hand. These can be legion in diversity.

Chapter 9 is yet another institutional application of heterodox Islamic economics in the field of pedagogy in terms of how heterodox Islamic economics ought to be taught and researched in order to establish the building blocks of meta-science of the monotheistic law. Some examples of comparative economic theory are reinvestigated in the light of heterodox Islamic economics and its interactive, integrative, and evolutionary learning properties. The concluding statement is that regarding the phenomenological methodology of meta-science. It applies to both the advent of science beyond the present days' approach to scientific inquiry.

The conclusion highlights the importance of ethico-economics as a revolutionary, methodological worldview in heterodox Islamic economics. Its due place in the world of learning is thus elaborated upon. Some specific examples are briefly covered to show the historical approach of heterodox Islamic economics, in contrast to what it presents today as a mainstream and orthodox venture. As a concluding chapter, this brings together the contrasting nature of the monotheistic epistemic nature of reality with those that exist both in science and economics of the mainstream type that is embedded in Islamic economics. The contrary process of understanding heterodox Islamic economics is presented.

Significant contribution of this work

This research work is of an original nature, both in the field of heterodox socio-scientific thought and in terms of the epistemic orientation of heterodox Islamic economics. By its ontological and epistemological approach, the emergent methodology of meta-science arising from the monotheistic principle of unity of knowledge provides a significantly new understanding of the socio-scientific enterprise. This is true for all of science taken in its generalized form and its particulars. The study of economics, finance, science, and society is embodied in the generality of the socio-scientific space by the uniqueness of methodology and its "epistemic analytic (mathematics)."

The emergent field of the science of monotheistic law in respect of the episteme of unity of knowledge is proved to be conceptually rich, formal in nature, and applied both nationally and globally. The central message projected in this work is that heterodox Islamic economics needs to be practiced as an exclusive field of economics with diverse congeries of interdisciplinary synergy; the pursuit is for the nature and discovery of the meta-scientific theme of the monotheistic law of unity of knowledge that explains "everything." Heterodox Islamic economics is treated as a particular discipline within the meta-scientific methodology. There is no change in methodology and formal method of empirical application, except for the diversity of problems under study in the field of economics. Heterodox Islamic economics thereby presents a deeply epistemological re-origination of the science of economics within the universal and unique methodology of unity of knowledge in meta-science.

To provide a brief definition: Heterodox Islamic economics is the thoroughly ingrained, analytical study of the epistemological foundations of the monotheistic law of unity of knowledge in the congeries of disciplines, factors, and problems that interactively affect the holistic economic experience. We have therefore named the analytical and epistemological nature of the monotheistic law in its functional formalism as "epistemic analytics (mathematics)." Such a study is rare in the domain of socio-scientific inquiry and heterodox thought. It confronts the fields of Islamic classification that have entered the contemporary academic showcase. Examples are the received mainstream and orthodox heritages of Islamic economics, Islamic finance, and Islamic social studies.

This entire work is not meant to be confined to religious dogmatism. The common pursuit of academia is ultimate truth and methodological rightness. The pursuit of humankind is the common good of wellbeing for all—nature and humanity—in the present and the future. Surrounding such impending questions is the ultimate source of knowledge and its applications that can establish universal and unique truth in the sciences by research, discourse, analytics, and discovery. In social experience, the goal is the common brotherhood of humanity. It shares common heritage and wellbeing from conscious recognition of that which unifies. It rejects that which differentiates. This is the project of unity of knowledge arising from its surest root. That is the monotheistic law as the common human heritage. In the living domain, the axiom of the monotheistic law expresses itself by the methodology of complementarity—that is, participatory "pairing" of dynamics in the good things of life and the abandonment of the things that are not recommended for human wellbeing. The pairing dynamics unravel the organic unity of being and becoming in the order and scheme of "everything." The *Qur'an* (49:13) declares in this regard:

> O mankind! We created you from a single (pair) of a male and a female, and made you into nations and tribes, that ye may know each other (not that ye may despise (each other). Verily the most honoured of you in the sight of *Allah* is (he who is) the most righteous of you. And *Allah* has full knowledge and is well acquainted (with all things).

The attribute of the project of meta-science as potentiality encompassing the subjective and the objective realities is that of unifying the hitherto discordant existences of the a priori and a posteriori realms of rationalism as the principal existing nature of the *problematique* of science. Indeed, as Heidegger and Husserl separately have pointed out, the ultimate project of meta-science will be to dismantle the heteronomous *problematique* into the formation of one seamless holism.

On this objective potentiality of meta-science, Heidegger (1962: 414) writes:

> In the mathematical projection of Nature, moreover, what is decisive is not primarily the mathematical as such; what is decisive is that this projection discloses something that is *a priori*. Thus the paradigmatic character of mathematical natural science does not lie in its exactitude or in the fact that it is binding for 'Everyman'; it consists rather in the fact that the entities which it takes as its theme are discovered in it in the only way in which entities can be discovered – by the prior projection of their state of Being.

In the area of search and discovery of the meta-science of the monotheistic law of unity of knowledge, this rare book forms a rigorous study in the underlying ontology and epistemology. The formalism is then carried into analytical rigor. Application is presented in the light of the emergent phenomenological question. The conclusion is then actualized in characterizing the emergent theory of ethico-economics as the content of heterodox Islamic economics beyond its failure within the mainstream and orthodox leaning (Mahomedy, 2013).

An important intellectual distinction to note: the primacy of monotheistic law over *maqasid as-shari'ah*

The importance of this work is in the primal ontology of the monotheistic law of unity of knowledge and its induction of the unity of the world-system taken in general and in particular. The resulting worldview is a strictly methodological one. Thus the monotheistic law as methodology is indispensably framed in either the explanation or the rigor of formalizing the underlying "monotheistic analytic (mathematics)" formalism. The inferences derived from this methodological approach are of a logical nature arising from the primal ontology of the *Qur'an* and the *sunnah*. The inferences are also established analytically by the principle of acceptance and continuity of the emerging phenomenological consequences over the totality of knowledge, space, and time dimensions. The result is a thoroughly evolutionary learning multiverse formalism in unity of knowledge in the domain of what we refer to as the great closure of the open and unbounded terminal points enclosing within it the smaller closures as open sub-systems of topologies of the world-system.

When the monotheistic methodological worldview is so conceptualized in its primacy, then the logical conclusion is that the oft-spoken role of primacy of the objective and purpose of the Islamic law, termed *maqasid as-shari'ah*, is rejected. The *maqasid as-shari'ah* forms an ever-changing bundle of legal rules that are derived from the fundamental premise of the monotheistic law. The *maqasid as-shari'ah* cannot then be taken as the law par excellence; only the divine monotheistic law, *Tawhid*, represented through *Sunnat Allah*, forms the primal law. It is therefore mandatory for Islamic intellection over the socio-scientific space to derive every time and continuously new vistas of the total multiverse intellectual interpretations by repeatedly returning to the primal ontological beginning. This experience is then followed by reformulations of *maqasid as-shari'ah* in the spirit of inquiry revolving around the *Qur'an* and the *sunnah*. Such an experience is referred to as *ijtihad*. The practice of reinvestigating facts in the light of the *Qur'an* and the *sunnah*, and in the light of the monotheistic law, is referred to as *fiqh al-Qur'an*. The consensus based on the inferences drawn out of *ijtihad* is the consultative process called the *shura* process. All of these together form the institutionalized aspects of evolutionary learning in the monotheistic unity of knowledge with the inner properties of interaction and integration in systemic sense. In all of these, there remains no necessity to subscribe wholly to the opinions of the earlier learned ones (*mujtahid*). The *Qur'an* and the *sunnah* being the primal ontology,[1] all other sources of knowledge remain relative in the interpretation of the edicts of the monotheistic law.

The intellectual implications of the primacy of the monotheistic law, to which belongs *maqasid as-shari'ah* as a topological subset of freshly generated and discoursed rules, introduces a greater degree of dynamics to the now-dormant and often contentious nature of the *shari'ah*. This is to expand the domain of intellectual investigation concerning wellbeing between the heavens and the earth and all between, on and below the earth. In the present state of the *shari'ah*, ignoring the greater potentiality of the *maqasid as-shari'ah*, the bounded limit is the domain of worldly matters (*muamalat*), whereas, truly, the expanded domain of the *maqasid as-shari'ah* is the interactive, integrative, and evolutionary learning multiverse of the heavens and the earth, including all that is in between and below the earth.

An example of such a systemic organic holism is to be found in chapter 13 of the *Qur'an*, named *Ra'd* (Thunder), verses 1–5. In terms of the intellectual overarching comprehension of the monotheistic law now giving dynamic and expanded shape and meaning to the *maqasid as-shari'ah*, we deduce:
Sustainability=*maslaha*, [W]ellbeing(Cosmology, Earth)

$$\text{Sustainability} = maslaha, \ [\text{W}]\text{ellbeing(Cosmology, Earth)}[\theta \hat{I}(\Omega, S)], \ dW/d\theta > 0,$$

with the property of systemic interrelations {Cosmology} $\cap$ {Earth} $\neq \phi$
implying the existence of organic interrelations.

An example is conveyed by denoting,

$$\text{Cosmology} = \{\text{energy } x_1, \text{ scientific study of energy } x_2, \text{ meta-scientific reality } x_3\}$$
$$\text{Earth} = \{\text{vegetation } x_4, \text{ cybernetics of heaven and earth interrelations } x_5, \text{ energy } x_6\}$$

Thereby, evaluate $W=W(x_1, x_2, x_3, x_4, x_5, x_6)[\theta]$, with the vector $\{x_1, x_2, x_3, x_4, x_5, x_6, \theta\}$, subject to the formal relations (f_i) of multi-causal interrelations implying continuous complementarities between the variables as the sign of the monotheistic unity of knowledge (sign of God). Such a system of organic interrelations between the variables and the knowledge parameter is called the "circular causation system of relations":

$$x_1 = f_1(x_2, x_3, ..., x_6, \theta)$$
$$x_2 = f_2(x_1, x_3, ..., x_6, \theta)$$

$$...$$

$$x_6 = f_1(x_1, x_2, ..., x_5, \theta)$$
$$\theta = F(x_1, x_2, ..., x_6)$$

which again is the measured form of the wellbeing (*maslaha*) function conveying an attained or targeted level of sustainability.

The extension of the *maqasid as-shari'ah* as the derivation of the monotheistic law is thus attained by the circular causation evaluation of the wellbeing function (*maslaha*) in terms of measuring the degree of unity of relations that exists between inter-variables to convey the monotheistic law of unity of knowledge and unity of the world-system.

A warning is thus placed in this work regarding the extent to which the origin of knowledge and worldly actions and responses can be vested in the *shari'ah*. Since the *shari'ah* is a discoursed extract of the monotheistic law, which forms the primal ontology, the *shari'ah* remains subjected to discursive practice in the light of the primacy of *fiqh al-Qur'an*. It is not correct, therefore, to raise a catchword that is often floated among orthodox adherents of the *shari'ah*—that is, to announce that everything that is not rejected clearly or accepted clearly by the *shari'ah* can remain acceptable or rejected, respectively. This is shallow judgment. Take the example of the gold standard of monetary aggregates. Imam Ghazali said that any coin that did not have at least some weight of gold in it was not to be considered an acceptable Islamic currency. Such a pronouncement would suggest that all forms of alternative ways of holding money would be rejected according to the *shari'ah*. Yet it can be argued for a 100 percent reserve requirement system that a small amount of gold can support a huge amount of trade. Therefore paper currency can be backed by a small amount of gold stored with the central bank, while circulation of paper money in this sense can be seen as representing the value of the gold. Such kinds of equivalent ways of denominating currency valuation can be inferred from the nature of financial contract in the *Qur'an* (2:282).[2] Likewise, cost-plus mark-up pricing, called *murabaha*, is declared to be acceptable under *shari'ah*. Yet such a pronouncement is debated unless *murabaha* is changed into a market-determined fair contract. It is not so presently under the ad hoc mark-up pricing rule and the unilateral determination of the mark-up rate.

The above treatment of *maqasid as-shari'ah*, contra the monotheistic law in all Islamic determinations, opens up serious discourse in heterodox Islamic economic theory. The role of law in heterodox Islamic economics has changed substantially from the present-day treatment of the *shari'ah* compliance rule that has entered, lock, stock, and barrel, the entire body of Islamic economics as a catchword of Islamic legitimacy.

Notes

1 *Qur'an* (6:59): "And with Him are the keys of the unseen; none knows them except Him. And He knows what is on the land and in the sea. Not a leaf falls but that He knows it. And no grain is there within the darknesses of the earth and no moist or dry [thing] but that it is written] in a clear record."
2 *Qur'an* (2:282): "O You who have attained to faith! Whenever you give or take credit for a stated term, set it down in writing. And let a scribe write it down equitably between you; and no scribe shall refuse to write as God has taught him: thus shall he write. And let him who contracts the debt dictate; and let him be conscious of God, his Sustainer, and not weaken anything of his undertaking."

References

Choudhury, M.A. (1993). *Unicity Precept and the Socio-scientific Order*, Lanham, MA: University Press of America.

Heidegger, M. (1962). *Being and Time*, trans. Macquarrie, J. and Robinson, E., London: SCM Press.

Mahomedy, A.C. (2013). "Islamic economics: Still in search of an identity," *International Journal of Social Economics*, 46, 6: 556–578.

Rucker, R. (1982). "Large cardinals," in *Infinity and the Mind*, New York: Bantam Books.

Sztompka, P. (1974). "Systemic models in functional analysis," in *System and Function: Towards a Theory of Society*, New York: Academic Press, pp. 47–57.

1 The way forward

The background and objective of this original work

This book features three interconnected debates. First, it examines the contrasting economic and social views between heterodox economics and mainstream economics. Second, there is a similar analysis of the prevalent nature of Islamic economics in particular, and in the broader field of study of diverse pertinent issues and problems within epistemological, analytical, and applied inquiries. Third, it focuses on the converging views between prevalent socio-scientific knowledge in Islamic socio-scientific study and mainstream and heterodox socio-scientific inquiries.

In the end, the emergent conflicting, different, and also somewhat converging methodological viewpoints interactively relate to chart the path of a revolutionary development of a structure of scientific investigation in the socio-scientific domain. But the emergent implications are larger in claiming an analytical meaning of methodological universality and uniqueness. The emergent domain of investigation encompasses the study of the interplay between moral law, ethicality, and the applied details of world-system studies. All such areas of study remain premised on distinctive values and their induction of the material order. Deep epistemological investigations and congeries of methodical approaches comprising mathematical and other analytical concepts abound.

How would this research work contribute to the world of socio-scientific originality and learning? Some seventy-plus (or thirty) years[1] since its inception, the field of Islamic economics has today withered away to become the remnant of a disinherited scholarship. Nothing original has been left behind for the world of learning in general. This "fallen" situation happened despite the fact that Islamic economic and socio-scientific reasoning can indeed be based on a revolutionary methodology in the socio-scientific field. The scholarly predicament of Islamic economics came about because it failed to be a scientific study on epistemological grounds regarding the critical foundation of the monotheistic law in its endogenous inter-causal relationship with the world-system. This is the message of the *Qur'an* in the first place. It is the project of ontology interrelating with epistemology toward understanding, with deep and rigorous knowledge regarding the centricity of the "praises" of God as the conscious recognition of the Oneness of God. Thereby, the unity of knowledge enabled by the monotheistic law and the unity of the world-system that is induced by the law in the meaning of "praises" of God conveys the signs of oneness in the order and scheme of the monotheistic law. Such a worldview of inter-causal relationship between knowledge and the world-system prevails in generality and in particular. The *Qur'an* refers to the emergent phenomenology (the nature and study of consciousness) as the *a'lameen*. The *a'lameen* is the world-system induced by the episteme of the monotheistic unity of knowledge.[2]

It looms as real fear that the currently emulated scope of Islamic finance, steeped in the pursuit of the shareholding model and all the neoclassical ramifications that this holds, will melt away without leaving behind a distinctive legacy of contribution to the world of learning (Boatright, 2010; Sen, 1977). This vacuum of scholarship will be all the more felt when the world needs something substantive in erudition and practice to rescue it from its complex volatility.

The result of such uncontrollable volatility is today extending adversity to the field of human deprivation and entitlement failure. The need for ethics to be included in subtle ways in the conceptualization and realization of financial stabilization will rest on a new epistemological approach that views financial economy and society under the lens of a unified way of understanding the nature and structure of our world-system. This is where the recently debated schools of thinking between Shiller's (2012) ideas of ethical finance and Fama's (1965, 2012) ideas on efficient financial markets will have to be re-formulated within a distinctive revisiting of the epistemological worldview of a unified methodology between equity and efficiency and similar apparent contrasts with the existing way of thinking in financial economics. Islamic economics and finance will remain deficient in providing the answer, owing to the absence of understanding of the functional principle of the monotheistic unity of knowledge in relationship with the reality of the unified world-system in its generality and detail. Presently, neither mainstream financial economics nor its replication in, and through, Islamic financial economics can bestow the new methodological worldview that is to be presented in this book.

Definitions of selected technical terms

Ontology

In this work, we will refer to the meaning of ontology in two ways. First, by "*primal ontology*" we mean the most reduced foundation of existence of the contextual law of unity of knowledge. In respect of the field of heterodox Islamic economics, the primal ontology is the axiom of the monotheistic law. This establishes and explains the ultimate premise of unity of knowledge as the ontology of the monotheistic law. Its formal derivations are used in formalizing the nature and construction of the unified world-system in its model of generality and details.

Besides the existence of primal ontology as the axiomatic foundation of the design of unity of knowledge and unification of the world-system, there are internal functions interrelating sequences of evolutionary learning to the transformation of the unified world-system in its various details. Such derived sequences of unity of knowledge denote "*functional* ontologies" (Gruber, 1993) of existences of unity of knowledge that are derived from the primal ontology. Just as the primal ontology establishes the generalized theory of unity of knowledge, so also the functional ontologies explain the occurrence of the particulars in the unified world-system. The particulars form inherent sub-systems. Thus the sub-systems are the particulars derived from the generality, but are governed by invariance of the axiomatic foundation of the monotheistic law of unity of knowledge that is conveyed by the primal ontology.

Epistemology

In the ontological foundations of unity of knowledge, epistemology explains the method of deriving unity of knowledge from the ontological origin for construction of the unified world-system. In the diversity of particulars that so arises, there are sequences of epistemologies, yet by the unique reference to the ontology of unity of knowledge. In this book, we will formalize the sequences of epistemologies emerging from evolutionary learning in unity of knowledge by showing how such sequences of knowledge of unity of being and becoming are determined across evolutionary learning processes. The difference between the meaning of epistemology as the theory of knowledge and ontology as the theory of existence and being is the knowledge derivation and continuity of processes of evolutionary learning in unity of knowledge; ontology means the simultaneous origination of the unified world-system, along with its particulars.

Phenomenology

Phenomenology, as the theory of consciousness, explains the evaluation of the impact of the ontological and epistemological phenomena in creating the explanatory contents of the knowledge-induced world-system. Thus primal ontology is the theory of the original existence of the monotheistic law of the oneness of knowledge. Functional ontology is the functional way of regenerating knowledge-induced particulars of the world-system. Epistemology is the derivation of knowledge from each of the ontological particulars. Phenomenology explains the analytical understanding of the knowledge-induced constructs in the domain of the general and the particular.

The ontological and epistemological, combined with the end result of phenomenological study and formalism of the monotheistic unity of knowledge and unity of the consequential world-system, thus assumes a scientific project that transcends a constricted scope of reality existing in dualism and the ill-defined dichotomy of reasoning. Islamic scholarship in general, and Islamic economics as a particular field of socio-scientific pursuit premised on the substantive foundations of ontology, epistemology, and phenomenology, have not been reopened in the present era of Islamic economics. Yet such was the meta-scientific nature of inquiry among Islamic scholars (Nasr and Leaman, 1996).

The relationship of ontology, epistemology, and phenomenology will be formalized in this book as the foundation of heterodox Islamic economic methodology along the lines of the following construct:

1   Primal ontology → Epistemology → General theory of unity of knowledge
2   Functional ontology → Epistemology → Particular sub-systems in unity of knowledge
3   Primal ontology → Epistemology → Functional ontology → Generality and particulars
4   Phenomenology: Analytical study of the knowledge-induced contents of generality and particulars of epistemological determination of ontological forms
5   Sequences of (1)–(4) exist for every given process of learning and are continued in evolutionary learning processes.

These sequences will be formalized substantially in the following way, to show how the limits of a heteronomous science can be rigorously extended to include the functionalism of the monotheistic law of unity of knowledge.

Episteme[3]

> Primal ontology → Epistemology → Functional ontology → Phenomenology → Recursive continuity

This representation of the project of unity of knowledge and unity of the corresponding world-system and its particulars highlights the point that there is recursive continuity between the concepts of ontology and epistemology. This book will argue that such groundwork for project of reasoning is foundational in the scientific understanding of a unified world-system and its consequences, integrating essence, mind, and matter in reasoning.

By combining the sequentially determined evolutionary learning dynamics of (1)–(5), this work becomes a critical study and methodological reconstruction of Islamic economics within the general formalism of the unified worldview of the monotheistic law and its unified world-system dynamics.

The monotheistic primal ontology of the law of unity of knowledge

Since God is non-corporeal and non-dimensional, the precept to understand the Oneness of God is to reflect upon the unity of knowledge (consilience) conveyed by the divine law and used as rules derived from the primal ontology and encompassed by the epistemic process that this work will establish in a formal way. Such is the methodological meaning of monotheism and divine Oneness conveyed by the *Qur'an*.[4]

In this work, the scientific explanation of unity of knowledge in the monotheistic law inducing the generality and particulars of the world-system rests on the super-cardinal topology of the primal ontology and the recursively continuous relationship between epistemology and functional ontology. This book will point out the mathematical results of Fixed Point Theorems and self-referencing of evolutionary learning in the domains of supercardinal knowledge in a closed, but unbounded, universe of knowledge at the primal ontology in the beginning and at the end completing in primal ontology once again. Both of these terminal points are the domains of unbounded knowledge, defining the topological closure of the beginning and the end. Thus the totality of ontological and epistemological inter-causal relations between knowledge and the world-system prevails in epistemic completeness.

Within the scope of science, the precept of the monotheistic law as the supercardinal topology of unity of knowledge becomes an analytical study. Despite this, the monotheistic law assumes the ultimate axiomatic premise of socio-scientific construction in a new epistemic way of understanding reality that is extended and holistic in the realm of explanatory phenomena.

The socio-scientific world-system

The world-system encompasses the domain of "everything," which, in the epistemic foundation of this work, will comprise the cognitive and extensive reality spanning knowledge, space, and time dimensions. The meaning of the world-system complies with the generalized theory of unity of knowledge in everything *res cogitans* and *res extensa*. Therefore, as there exists the treatment of particulars within the general theory, so also there are topologically imitated sub-systems of the world-system in its entirety. But, as will be formalized in this work, the world-system existing in generality and sub-systems of the world-system as particulars manifest their properties identically as topologies, albeit with differences in specific problems. Such an understanding of the concept of the world-system and its topological sub-systems, and thereby of generality and particulars, will be shown to enrich the socio-scientific theory resting on the monotheistic law to explain multiverse systems.

Thus there arises the meaning of "socio-scientific" as the emergence of diverse multi-systems and their treatment under the scientific lens of a universal epistemic theory. Likewise, the sub-systems of the generalized world-system—being topologies—are governed by the same universal and unique theory of unity of knowledge of the monotheistic law. Society, economics, and science are not differentiated areas of investigation; they are unified by the same universal law. Reasoning is thus a unified experience between religion and science. Chapter 2 in this book constructs the model and application of the process-oriented system model of monotheistic phenomenology.

The overarching meaning of the monotheistic law as ontology spanning the socio-scientific world-system in unity of knowledge will draw on a truly *qur'anic* meaning of the objective and purpose of the Islamic law (*maqasid as-shari'ah*) as not the primal law, but an extract from the primal ontology of the divine law of Oneness (*sunnat Allah* in the *Qur'an*). Diverse systems of knowledge and socio-scientific particularities are unified by the same unique and universal law of monotheistic primal ontology. This is a belief in all religions and abstractions. The difference, though, lies in the absence of formal logic and methodology of the monotheistic characterization of the primal ontology governing the entirety of socio-scientific world-systems. Our assertion of this monotheistic concept principle existing between the heavens and the earth can thus be found cross-culturally. Kant (1949: 261) writes in this regard:

> Two things fill the mind with ever new and increasing awe and admiration the more frequently and continuously reflection is occupied with them; the starred heaven above me and the moral law within me. I ought not to seek either outside my field of vision, as though they were either shrouded in obscurity or were visionary. I see them confronting me and link them immediately with the consciousness of my existence.

Wellbeing

In the context of the monotheistic primal ontology prevailing prior to our contested view of primacy usually given to the *shari'ah* (*maqasid as-shari'ah*), the wellbeing function stands for the functional and dynamic role of evolutionary learning and its induction of the world-system. Such an evolutionary dynamics in respect of the ontological meaning evaluates the degree to which complementarities, produced by organic pairing, exist between possibilities. Deficiency in such pairing is next simulated to projected higher levels of potentiality via further organic pairing. The wellbeing function will be used extensively in this work as the objective criterion of conceptualizing and numerical evaluation of the degree of complementarities representing unity of knowledge. This conception is drawn out by the nature of the primal ontology of unity of knowledge that is addressed in the very first place.

The evolutionary learning properties of the wellbeing function will show that this objective criterion is contrary to the conceptual meaning of maximization of utility, welfare, profits, output etc., as so-called objective functions in mainstream economics. Sustained and continuously evolutionary learning does not allow any optimal and steady-state conditions of resource to occur. This is a substantive issue to contend with. It changes all of mainstream economic theory. The end result that we will be led to formalize in terms of the wellbeing function is that the cause and effect of this evolutionary, knowledge-centered criterion are both knowledge and its transformation in respect of interacting and endogenously circular relations between participatory and complementary epistemic consequences of knowledge.

Circular causation

Circular causation combines with the evaluation of the wellbeing criterion by applying the imminent primal ontology (axiom) of the monotheistic unity of knowledge to practical (ontic) particulars of world-system studies. Being such a derivation, the large system of equations in the circular causation method arising out of the methodology of unity of knowledge endogenously relates each variable to the other variables. This is a process method of evaluating the nature of paired—that is, participatory or complementary—interrelations between the selection of the good things of life as presented by the generic foundation of the monotheistic law. This work will bring several real-world examples to the construct, meaning, and inferences drawn from applying the circular causation method to the participatory worldview arising from the episteme of unity of knowledge.

Like the episteme of the monotheistic unity of knowledge and the world-system, circular causation is shown to apply to the evaluation of both organically unified things and organically differentiated things. The study of society, which includes economics, is shown to encompass both kinds of developments with their distinct implications in moral and ethical reconstruction. This book will use the empirical cases of structural equation models to simulate the way in which the wellbeing function is subject to circular causation relations.

Like the case of the universality of the monotheistic ontological origin across cultures, wellbeing and circular causation are used distinctively in important theories. Examples of the latter cases are Sen (1992), Dasgupta (1987), Myrdal (1958), and Toner (1999). The same idea was found among philosophers such as Kant (1964) and Hume (1988),[5] and upheld by scientists such as Hawking and Mlodinow (2010).

The new methodology of the project of meta-science

On the erudite search for the ultimate nature of scientific inquiry and its discovery, Hawking (1988: 15–16) writes:

> The eventual goal of science is to provide a single theory that describes the whole universe. However, the approach most scientists actually follow is to separate the problem into parts. First, there are the laws that tell us how the universe changes with time. ... Second, there is the question of the initial state of the universe. Some people feel that science should be concerned with only the first part; they regard the question of the initial situation as a matter for metaphysics or religion. They say that God, being omnipotent, could have started the universe off any way he wanted. That may be so, but in that case he also could have made it develop in a completely arbitrary way. Yet it appears that he chose to make it evolve in a very regular way according to certain laws. It therefore seems equally reasonable to suppose that there are also laws governing the initial state.

Our present work is also focused on establishing that the premise of the universal and unique methodological worldview of socio-scientific inquiry rests upon the episteme of unity of knowledge or consilience (Wilson, 1998), and across the systemic diversity of thought and disciplinary fields of application. This is the substantive difference between the socio-scientific methodological worldviews of Hawking and the concurrent scientific school of thought. This difference in the methodology and science of unity of knowledge as the foundation of emergent socio-scientific thought, inclusive of economics, finance, science, and society, is initiated in the project highlighted by Choudhury (1991: 25–26). Choudhury responded to the above conception of the initial state and the unification principle of universal laws in the following words (edited):

> The quest for the uniquely common and primal sources of knowledge is the essential character of the revolutionary (*qur'anic*) worldview. That unique knowledge is manifested as the truth in all things in the animate and inanimate worlds. It presents itself as the incessant and unfailing quest for the most irreducible level of truth. That irreducible truth is the reality of divine oneness perceived as the Creator, Absolute Owner, Cherisher and Sustainer of the universes. This is the meaning of the *Tawhidi* precept as presented in the *Qur'an*. All meanings or reality are derived from Him and return to Him. Thus, in this fold of knowledge acquisition, there cannot be any acquiescence to dualism, multiplicity, individualism and non-interactivity between knowledge domains.

A glimpse at the methodological aspects of the work

While studying the comparative and contrasting nature of heterodox Islamic economics, mainstream economics, and heterodox economics in general, the substantive debating groundwork will be the epistemological nature of inquiry, followed by the distinction in application and ethical reconstruction of the social economy that follows. It is therefore accepted that each of these areas of economic erudition has its substantive epistemology and resulting phenomenological model of applied nature upon which the comparative and contrasting perspectives rest. Besides, to investigate the scope of the general theory and the derived particulars in respect of specific applications, it will be necessary to know whether there exists, and if so, then in what perspective there exists, a general theory in terms of the overarching meanings of universality and uniqueness of the emergent model. This is a substantive worldview and will involve an explanation of the underlying self-referencing theorem given by Godel (1965).

The emergence of a theory of heterodox Islamic economics would thereby be explained by several factors. These are, namely, the universality and uniqueness of the emergent epistemological foundation regarding the nature and application of the epistemic theory to the entire domain of economic, financial, scientific, and social domains arising from the process-oriented interaction, unification, and dynamic evolution by the self-same formal methodology. In addition, there is also the underlying scientific nature of the comparative epistemology in terms of its explanatory power in the over-encompassing way for all of the competing theoretical alternatives and disciplines. It is noted and explained analytically that neither the quest for meta-reality to explain scientific understanding nor the Kantian form of heteronomy or antinomy between the categorical imperative of a priori reason and the Humean kind of a posteriori reasoning as the initiating domain of scientific knowledge can afford in providing a complete methodology for socio-scientific reasoning. That is, the possibility for unification of knowledge and to understand the function of unity of knowledge in actualizing a unified world-system of organic interrelations of the inter-causal variables is ruptured in the framework of heteronomous dichotomy between the a priori and the a posteriori domains of reasoning. Thereby the meaning of reasoning and the consequences of this form of reasoning cause heteronomous dichotomy in the real world as well.

This *problematique* in the epistemology of science denies unity of knowledge and the consequential unity of the knowledge-induced world-system. On the other hand, the new emergent theory of ethico-economics and the critique of the received nature of Islamic and mainstream economics in the light of heterodox economic theory are premised on the replacement of the dichotomous nature of reasoning in all socio-scientific study by the epistemological unification of the domains of reasoning. This analysis of the unified organic relationship between the a priori and a posteriori domains of a unified meaning of reasoning will be shown to emerge from the ultimate, unique, and universal nature of the epistemological challenge by the new field of heterodox Islamic economics.

On the theme of the heteronomous *problematique* of the prevalent nature of socio-scientific reasoning, Bhaskar (2002: 146) writes: "So long as there is any element of heteronomy, any unfulfilled intentionality, any attachment, any fixation within you, your freedom will be to that extent restricted."

On the subject of the dualism in reasoning that follows from heteronomy, Bhaskar (ibid.: 154) continues: "So long as we are talking about the physically embodied world, then we must always think in terms of having to use things which will involve dualistic mode."

The above remarks together lead to the fact that the scientific *problematique* of heteronomy, and the resulting dualistic consequences on the reasoning front between a priori and a posteriori reasoning, on the one hand, and in the physical world-system, on the other hand, can provide the possibility of the epistemic unity of knowledge as the epistemological challenge. This immediately explains the organically unified nature of abstraction in building the formal epistemology that redefines the meaning of reasoning as an integrated worldview. This accomplishment will also provide the possibility of attaining the organically unified nature of inter-causal relations between the variables that enter the epistemological formalization of circular causation model.

This research work is, ultimately, a search and inquiry for the socio-scientific epistemological foundation enabling the discovery of a unity of knowledge; in turn, this brings about the generality and particulars of the world-system and unifies them by organic formalism. The work then applies the imminent formal model of unity of knowledge and its induction of the unified world-system by generality and particulars empirically, and by redesign of the prevailing institutions and instruments being practiced in Islamic economics of the mainstream genre. The methodological design of socio-scientific thought under the principle of unity of knowledge, carrying with it unity of the knowledge-induced world-system, liberates scientific reasoning from heteronomy of the a priori domain of pure reason from the a posteriori domain of practical reason. In other words, the truth of God and the moral law and the ethicality emanating from this premise, and which are included in the a priori domain of categorical imperative, are explained to establish inter-causal relations and the meaning of sustainability in a substantive sense of wellbeing as a function of the variables and entities of the a posteriori domain, while deriving ontological meaning in the a priori domain of reasoning.

God, the moral law of unity of being, and becoming are endogenously embedded and circularly causal in the sense of organic interrelations between essence, quality, and materiality. Each emergent domain reinforces the other by recursive inter-causality between the variables and attributes of the moral and material domains of one integrated construct of reasoning. Thereby, religion and science, morality, ethicality, and the material concrescence are ontologically unified. On this idea of the analytical redesigning of scientific reasoning, Whitehead (1979: 46) writes:

> Accordingly the general potentiality of the universe must be somewhere; since it retains its "proximate relevance" to actual entities for which it is unrealized. This "proximate relevance" reappears in subsequent concrescence as final causation regulative of the emergence of novelty. This "somewhere" is the non-temporal actual entity. Thus 'proximate relevance' means 'relevance as in the primordial mind of God.

Along these lines, Whitehead explains the idea of knowledge as the perpetual search for the premise of the primal ontology of unity of knowledge through the discursive process of symbiotic relations between knowledge and knowledge-induced potentiality. On this point, Whitehead (ibid.: 43) writes:

> The ontological principle asserts the relativity of decision; whereby every decision expresses the relation of the actual thing, for which a decision is made, to an actual thing by which that decision is made. It constitutes the very meaning of actuality. An actual entity arises from decisions for it, and by its very existence provides decisions for other actual entities which supersede it. Thus the ontological principle is the first stage in constituting a theory embracing the notions of "actual entity," "giveness," and "process."

Converging on the emergent theory of ethico-economics

Similar to the investigation of the new ontological origin of economic thought (Lawson and Pesaran, 1985)—and the general ontological meaning of being and becoming based on the symbiotic learning nature of the evolutionary, knowledge-induced world-system—our theory runs along the same lines. While it refers to the generalized methodological worldview in the light of the evolutionary learning process and reality, it is specific for the similar study of the process orientation of economic and social reality that is ontologically sensitized by its foundational primal ontology. This is of God's order of consilience—that is, of unity of knowledge and its organic, inter-causal relations with the knowledge-induced interactive, integrative, and evolutionary world-system (Choudhury, 2014).

This book thus contributes to the wider field of new epistemological inquiries in economics, science, and society that have been initiated by leading heterodox economic thinkers today and in the recent past. Among them is Sraffa (1963), with his evolutionary ideas of general economic equilibrium. Sraffa was a front-runner and critique of the orthodox economic theory of neoclassicism (Pasinetti, 2001).[6] Sraffa's towering contribution to economic theory will be used to explain how, with pertinent changes of concept and methodology, his conception can be applied, or not, to the evolutionary learning processes of unity of knowledge and the consequential knowledge-induced world-system.

In this regard, we also note Lawson's (1997: 25) view that: "In short, knowledge must be recognized as a produced means of production (of further knowledge) and science as an ongoing transformative social activity. Knowledge is a social product, activity, produced by means of antecedent social products."

Keynes (1963)[7] contributed to the field of ethics, epistemology, and economic reasoning with his general equilibrium framework. Edel (1970), of the Vienna School, contributed to the understanding of the conscious nature of ethics in socio-scientific formalism.[8] Recently, the works of Lawson (2006) have opened up serious debates on economic theory revolving around heterodox economic reasoning.[9]

Questions central to these kinds of inquiry form the vital undertaking of the search for, and discovery of, the essential nature of scientific discovery. This is premised on the methodological worldview of new heterodox ontology. Its epistemological implications of unity of knowledge make the heterodox Islamic economic and socio-scientific project a significant investigation into this broad area. The result is significant and vast. The effect of this heterodox shift causes profound changes in the way we re-interpret the economic and socio-scientific worldview as a world-system of interactively integrated domains with evolutionary learning dynamics. The nature of the underlying meaning, the emergent epistemological context of reasoning, and the world-system study with the induction of unity of knowledge changes the nature of economic inquiry in the field of ethico-economics. The resulting changes that arise for intellection and applications can be understood from the work of Lee and Lavoie (2013: 109):

> Since the economy is an emergent system with various sub-systems, the heterodox theory of the social provisioning process is also an emergent theoretical system with various theoretical sub-systems. This implies that it cannot be divided into disjointed sub-systems of microeconomics and macroeconomics, which in turn are based on quite different theoretical arguments.

The critical structure and emergent issues of heterodox Islamic economic reasoning

The structure of scientific revolution is, as Kuhn (1970) noted, the development of science to such a level of advancement that it has no cumulative record. The process of development towards discovery is altogether novel: "[S]cientific revolutions are here taken to be those non-cumulative developmental episodes in which an older paradigm is replaced in whole or in part by an incompatible new one." (Kuhn, ibid.: 152),

With regard to all such arguments, the first step towards the great advance in thought is the discovery of the foundation of consilience (unity of knowledge) premised on the ultimate law of monotheistic oneness. The first step leads to the second, which is to derive flows of knowledge from the monotheistic ontological beginning of unity of knowledge. The process at work in this derivation of worldly knowledge gives rise to rigorously formal methods. Such a step is referred to as the epistemological path arising from the primal ontology of the monotheistic beginning. Yet the emergent knowledge-flows are carried into material reality by relational correspondences. Such mediums of transmission are functional ontologies. They are ways of deriving worldly knowledge-flows from the primal ontology through the epistemological medium for the construction of the world-system of unity of knowledge in the generality and particulars of theory. In the third step, the emergent knowledge-flows are ready for construction, explanation, and material applications in relation to the order and scheme of things. The point of application and analysis now establishes the emergent material concrescence in the dimensions of knowledge, space, and time. In these dimensions, events happen continuously and within the evolutionary learning framework. Such an actualized design of cognitive concrescence marks the generality of theory and the details of its applications. The fourth step of the methodological development establishes epistemic completion in any one complete process of learning pertaining to any systemic learning along a single or multi-systemic and collective body of issues and problems of a practical nature (concrescence). The fifth step marks the development of the methodological worldview of monotheistic consilience in relation to the primal ontology via the epistemological derivation of knowledge-flows. This is actualized by the choice of inter-causal analytical relations termed here as functional ontology. The resulting completion of a process is subsequently continued on into emergent processes of similar kinds. The continuity of such emergent processes of similar, but not identical, forms in the diverse domains of knowledge, space, and time marks the description and explanation of the historical processes of the epistemic totality (Hubner, 1985).

The totality of the path of episteme is the trajectory of understanding the purpose, course and continuity of historical consciousness (Lucaks, 1968; Hegel, 1956; Ibn Khaldun, in Mahdi, 1964) of socio-scientific events happening in the dimensions of knowledge, space, and time. The epistemic ensemble of events summarizes the inter-causal relationship between ontology, epistemology, and phenomenology. The world-system and its particulars such as economics, science, and society start from and return to the primal ontological foundation of the monotheistic law of unity of knowledge and the unity of the knowledge-induced particulars under study.[10]

The emergence, nature, and potentiality of the heterodox challenge to mainstream economics, and of heterodox Islamic economics to the mainstream nature of the prevalent field of Islamic economics, thus revolve around the universal status of the relationship between primal ontology, epistemology, and the characterization of the emergent particular problems of specific world-systems. This totality constitutes the episteme. The nature of heterodox Islamic economic theory thus finds its indispensable axiomatic beginning in the primal ontology of the monotheistic law.

It thereby formalizes and derives the nature and discovery of the unified world-system by systems of particulars on the basis of the primal ontology. Mainstream economics, and thereby its emulation by mainstream-related Islamic economics, must inescapably accept the specter of methodological individualism, and its consequences of self-interest and independence from any trace of inter-causality. The latter property otherwise denotes the sure sign of unity of knowledge and the organic unity of knowledge-induced particulars. This long-standing nature of today's Islamic economics has caused its ultimate demise and only a remnant now remains. Islamic economics of mainstream learning failed to contribute anything academic to the world of learning while it was unable to articulate a profound axiom and a methodological universality. The entire domain of ontological, epistemological, and phenomenological consequences has escaped the study of Islamic economics in its existing mainstream garb.

This academic neglect gives rise to the birth of heterodox Islamic economics as a foundational scholarly enterprise, together with its substantive application—along with empirical sophistication—to practical issues and problems—that is, the epistemic approach to problem-solving. Heterodox Islamic economics rejects the validity of Islamic thought as a methodological worldview premised on mainstream Islamic economics. It renders an alternative rigorous worldview that is premised on the ontology and epistemology of the monotheistic unity of knowledge, its intellection, and construction of particulars.

Thus the emergent nature of methods derived from this epistemological foundation is quite different. In fact, mainstream Islamic economics has no epistemology of its own; it borrows axioms, methodology, and the consequential methods of formalism and analysis. Even the scope and nature of applications of the methods are different between the contrary two schools of thinking in Islamic economics. This is proof of the scientific fact that was pointed out by Einstein to his friend, Niels Bohr (1985): "Science without epistemology is – insofar as it is thinkable at all – primitive and muddled." The importance of the epistemological element in the construction of scientific thought is equivalent to giving due attention to the scientific project of endogenously embedding morality and ethics into materiality. This again is equivalent methodologically to establishing the inter-causal relations between the domain of a priori reason and a posteriori reason. That is doing away with heteronomy and allowing the due foundational inter-causal relations between ethics and economics to abide, as the particular case is the nature of unity in reasoning between the a priori and the a posteriori domains of a unified reality. This high scientific enterprise is not possible in the mainstream methodology of heteronomy and, therefore, in Islamic economics of the mainstream genre.

Along with the independence of Islamic economics, with its mainstream leaning away from scientific epistemology and thereby moving onwards, this field has failed to develop that resilient knowledge-induced structure of the epistemic consilience of unity of knowledge for which it has the potential. With the absence of the epistemological question in Islamic economics, this field has also missed out the methodology of monotheistic oneness of being and becoming upon which the entirety of Islamic belief rests. Thus the prevalent nature of Islamic economics has neither the methodology nor the perspective to study the process-oriented essential structure of the *qur'anic* worldview. The heterodox Islamic economic approach to the rediscovery of Islamic economics is premised on the distinctive moorings of *qur'anic* epistemology.

Focus on the convergence between unity of knowledge, unity of the world-system, and process orientation of socio-scientific inquiry

This book will provide space to discuss and formalize the process orientation of economic and social phenomena. In the epistemological sense of its methodology, this book will explain that the episteme of unity of knowledge and the emergent process orientation of heterodox Islamic economics are multi-causal in nature. This book will draw out the fact that the organic nature of unity of knowledge, and thereby of the knowledge-induced unified issues of particularities causes the emergence of an evolutionary learning world-system. The internal properties of such an evolutionary learning world-system explain the inter-causal mingling between economics, society, science, and ethics. Consequently, the attributes of interaction leading to integration and followed by evolutionary learning as historistic dynamics also mark the fundamental epistemic nature of organic unity of knowledge. Such attributes will be derived from the Islamic epistemological roots of the *Qur'an*, the *sunnah* (as the teachings of the Prophet Muhammad), and the further interpretive exegesis of the foundational sources by the learned authority. This book will formalize the methodological structure that is caused by the convergence of the foundational ontology and epistemology relationship of monotheistic consilience as axiomatic of unity of knowledge arising from the moral law. The epistemic model is then followed by the emergence of the processes explained by the attributes of interaction, integration, and evolutionary learning (IIE). Such emergent attributes are followed by the phenomenological stage of application empirically, institutionally, or otherwise.

This book will also discuss the nature of mainstream economics as being without process orientation. This, however, is not overwhelming in the case of heterodox economics. Schumpeterian growth and development dynamics, Georgescu-Roegen's (1981) process orientation of market entropy, Marxist-Hegelian dialectical methodology, and, in some senses, both Keynesian and post-Keynesianism (Lawson, 2003) are recent examples of heterodox economic and social theories that rest on the process of dialectical methodology. Likewise, Islamic economics, without the essential ontological and epistemological approach of unity of knowledge, is a scientific error. It leaves no contribution to the world of learning as long as it remains tied to mainstream economics. Besides, such a failure of insensitivity to foundational issues also misses the great watershed of the *qur'anic* worldview. The *Qur'an* (65:11) declares on this point: "A Messenger, reciting *Allah's* clear verses to you to bring those who believe and do right actions out of the darkness into the Light. Whoever believes in *Allah* and acts rightly, We will admit him into Gardens."

Without establishing the ontological and epistemological relations between the monotheistic law and the world-system so as to establish a pervasively unified holism by unity of knowledge and the knowledge-induced world-system, systemic dualism remains. The idea of the monotheistic unity of knowledge as methodology is not known to the nature of Islamic economics today in its mechanistic copying of mainstream methodology. Consequently, an extended possibility of combining science with the monotheistic foundation remains distanced by the mainstream approach of Islamic economics. On the other hand, the extended possibility of science under the monotheistic ontological and epistemological methodology can prove to be a true actualization of meta-science, if the profoundly foundational meaning were understood and the groundwork recognized. This has not happened in Islamic economic and socio-scientific inquiry. As it stands today, the possibility of regaining the lost ground in its present mainstream content remains distanced.

The possibility of the universal reach of holistic meta-scientific theory is premised on the foundational unification of knowledge and its power in cognition, theory, and application. On this point, Laclau and Mouffe (see http://ethicalpolitics.org/seminars/neville.htm) write:

> [E]ven if we assume that there is a strict equation between the social and the discursive, what can we say about the natural world, about the facts of physics, biology or astronomy that are not apparently integrated in meaningful totalities constructed by men? The answer is that natural facts are also discursive facts. And they are so for the simple reason that the idea of nature is not something already there, to be read from the appearances of things, but itself is the result of a slow and complex historical and social construction.

> Here they move between epistemology and ontology without even recognising the difference. They raise a question about the natural world (an ontological issue) but then give an answer about ideas about the natural world (an epistemological issue) as if it were the same thing. Given the point that they suppose themselves to be making here all they do in fact is beg the question.

The integrated and foundational worldview gained from interrelated ontological and epistemological connectivity implies the extension of the intrinsic learning processes between God, knowledge, materiality, and the universe. This book will outline a rigorous model, explaining the interrelations of systemic processes between cognition and materiality. This socio-scientific inference will then be extended to the domain of understanding the philosophy underlying the purpose and objective of Islamic law (*maqasid as-shari'ah*) arising out of the primal ontology of the monotheistic law and the epistemology of socio-scientific consequences. With regard to the primacy of the divine law in "everything," the *Qur'an* (45:36) declares: "Then praise be to *Allah*, Lord of the heavens and Lord of the earth, the Lord of the Worlds." Thus this book argues that the starting point of Islamic erudition concerning Islamic law and its jurisprudential interpretation is based on the divine law (*Sunnat Allah*), while treating all other developments in *maqasid as-shari'ah* as relative and subject to critical discourse and development. The domain of meta-science, comprehending both science and society, is to be included in the overarching study of *maqasid as-shari'ah* while studying the connection between ontology and epistemology as an inter-causal precept of holistic scientific knowledge.

The nature of ethics and ethico-economics

The research underlying this book will derive the meaning of ethics from processes of interaction, integration, and evolutionary learning (IIE) and from the source of the monotheistic unity of knowledge and its worldly induction to establish a unified world-system of learning. The entire field of learning and its consequences, as premised and reconstructed on the basis of the law of unity of knowledge, will represent the meaning of ethics and its potentiality. And while evolutionary learning explains the meaning of sustainability premised on unity of knowledge and its progressive dynamics, ethics will be explained in formal ways based on its phenomenological endogenous relationship with the generality and particularity of the world-system. This entire domain comprehends economics, finance, science, and society in collective and multi-causal ways. How such ethical dynamics are conceptualized and their applications are explained will form the rigorous sections on formalism in this work.

Thus this book brings out in rigorous terms the methodology of multi-causal circular relations between the diversity of the multiverse entities existing as a holistic reality. Such reality exists in terms of the intrinsic unity of the worldview between systemic processes, ontology, epistemology, phenomenology, and the regeneration of these elements via evolutionary learning as the ethics of unity of knowledge progresses. The emergent evolutionary meaning of ethics in the regenerative world-system of the monotheistic unity of knowledge grounds the theory of endogenous ethics. Ethics, as an endogenous phenomenon acquiring the meaning of evolutionary learning in unity of knowledge, becomes the cause and effect of a self-regenerative conceptual and explanatory enterprise.

Yet the primal origin of learning in the monotheistic unity of knowledge is circularly caused and re-established in formalism by morality and ethics as the ultimate, given law resting on the primal ontology of being and existence (Nasr, 1996). Thus morality, like ethics, which is derived from the monotheistic law, now has a meaning. It is equivalent to the entire episteme caused by the monotheistic law of unity in content and applications. Hence morality marks the definition of the totality of the primal ontology leading to epistemology, phenomenology, and sustainability of this process by the continuous reappearance of the primal monotheistic law of unity of knowledge in evolutionary learning. History is thus created, regenerated, and continued in this way—the primal relationship of morality conveying the meanings of either a unified or a heteronomous evolutionary world-system. This book will bring out these substantive issues in its critique of the existence and the potentiality of emergence of the methodology and continuity of a world-system in science and society. The rupture of the endogenous relationship in mainstream economics, which is copied by Islamic economics (Sardar, 1984), leads to the new methodological worldview for economics as mankind's great entrepreneurial endeavor. A saying of Prophet Muhammad (*Hadith*, narrated by Anas ibn Malik) is about planting a tree at the moment of announcement of the coming doomsday: "Anas ibn Malik reported that the Prophet said, 'If the Final Hour comes while you have a palm-cutting in your hands and it is possible to plant it before the Hour comes, you should plant it'."

The *Qur'an* sets the model for the moral and ethical society in the following verses: "Have you not considered how Allah presents an example, [making] a good word like a good tree, whose root is firmly fixed and its branches [high] in the sky?" (*Qur'an*, 14:24).

The nature of ethico-economics

What, then, is the nature of ethico-economics? Economics as that great endeavor of man is seen as the interaction, integration, and inter-causal evolutionary learning therefrom—of the endogenous treatment of ethics and economic reasoning and applications. Heterodox Islamic economics is essentially ethico-economics. It is methodologically relevant in terms of the interactive, integrative, and evolutionary interrelations created by inter-causality between primal ontology, epistemology, phenomenology, and sustainability over paths of evolutionary learning. The totality of such epistemic ethico-economic behavior arises from the epistemic moral foundation of the monotheistic unity of knowledge that provides the functional nature of the unified economy within the widest expanse of the world-system and its congeries of sub-systems. Choudhury (2007) referred to this as the study of political economy and the world-system according to the monotheistic moral foundation of unity of knowledge.

In this book, the substantive difference (in the epistemic sense) between the originative foundations of morality that yield the meaning and nature of ethico-economics will be explained. On the other hand, the exogenous meaning of ethics is shown to be the permanent nature of behavioral economics and mainstream Islamic economics owing to their methodology premised on the heteronomous treatment of ethics and economics.

Conclusion

In this chapter, as throughout this book, we open up the topic of the scientific nature of heterodox economics in general and heterodox Islamic economics in particular. The epistemic foundation of the heterodox worldview in meta-science is to extend the nature, domain, and inferences premised on the existing scope of scientific inquiry to that of the monotheistic worldview. This book thereby raises questions about the new epistemic understanding of scientific inquiry. It thus emulates the *res extensa* and *res cogitans* scope of scientific inquiry, as pointed out in the *Qur'an* (13:31) regarding itself thus:

> If there were a *Qur'an* with which mountains were moved, or the earth were cloven asunder, or the dead were made to speak, (this would be the one!) but,

truly, the command is with *Allah* in all things! Do not the Believers know, that, had *Allah* (so) willed, He could have guided all mankind (to the right)? But the Unbelievers, never will disaster cease to seize them for their (ill) deeds, or to settle close to their homes, until the promise of *Allah* come to pass, for, verily, *Allah* will not fail in His promise.

In the words of Wilson (1998: 264):

Looked at in proper perspective, God subsumes science, science does not subsume God. ... Scientific research is not designed to explore all of the wondrous varieties of human experience. The idea of [God] in contrast, has the capacity to explain everything, not just measurable phenomena, but phenomena personally felt and sublimely sensed, including revelation that can be communicated solely through spiritual channels.

What is true of the vista of difference between heterodox economics and mainstream economics is equally true of existing ideas in Islamic economics as a mainstream offshoot. The great and substantive difference between heterodox Islamic economics and existing Islamic economics is the missing intellection of the meta-science of the monotheistic unity of knowledge in the latter. This is equivalent to the independence of existing Islamic mainstream economic reasoning from the epistemic understanding of the dynamic working of the monotheistic law, its use in the construction of socio-scientific thought, and its application in the moral reconstruction of the world-system with the force of universality and uniqueness for the world of learning.

This work will establish the extended epistemic nature of socio-scientific generality. Within this general theory rests the rigorous nature of the heterodox and substantive theory of Islamic economics. The book will thereafter bring out certain applications and the background empirical and institutional ramifications of these. It thereby lays down the outlook of a new episteme in holistic socio-scientific inquiry.

Furthermore, this chapter has laid down the other important coterminous focus of this work—that is, to establish the nature of ethics derived from its moral foundation. Ethics is construed as an evolutionary learning process that reflects the endogenous quality of participative relations between possibilities and agencies. The emergent theory of endogenous ethics lays down the epistemic foundation of the theory of ethico-economics. It forms the principal nature of heterodox economics contra mainstream economics and Islamic economics of the mainstream genre.

Notes

1 The study of Islamic economics dates back seventy-plus years if its beginnings are to be traced back to the efforts that were made by individual and research groups. On the other hand, the record of the beginning of Islamic economics dates back thirty years, to the time of the first conference on Islamic economics in Makkah, Saudi Arabia.

2 The *Qur'an* (1:2) declares: "Praise be to *Allah*, the Cherisher and Sustainer of the worlds."

3 Foucault (1972: 191) defines the word "episteme" as follows:

By *episteme* we mean ... the total set of relations that unite, at a given period, the discursive practices that give rise to epistemological figures, sciences, and possibly formalized systems ... The episteme is not a form of knowledge (*connaissance*) or type of rationality which, crossing the boundaries of the most varied sciences, manifests the sovereign unity of a subject, a spirit, or a period; it is the totality of relations that can be discovered, for a given period, between the sciences when one analyses them at the level of discursive regularities.

4   i   The *Qur'an* on totality or supercardinality of the divine law in "everything": God is the Lord of the Heavens and the Earth and all this between.

     ii   The *Qur'an* defines the paired entities of the world-system in the good things of life (*halal at-tayyabah*) as signs of God arising from the God-conscious world-system (*a'lameen*). The *Qur'an* also characterizes the heteronomous nature of the differentiated world of falsehood. The *Qur'an* makes the pairing principle the universal design of the participatory and complementary processes signifying unity of knowledge as the meaning conveyed by the divine law.

     iii   The *Qur'an* explains the re-originative (thus evolutionary learning) model of reality existing universally in cognition and observation by the principle of unity in diversity.

5   Immanuel Kant, quoted in Ledger and Pickard (2004: 8): "'Critique of Judgment': 'Parts bind themselves mutually into the unity of a whole in such a way that they are mutually cause and effect of one another'."

6   Pasinetti (2001) wrote regarding the Sraffian critique of neoclassical economic theory. Four themes that appear as poison-arrows in Piero Sraffa's critique of economic theory are:

1   the marginalist theory of production and distribution;
2   the theory of value (which marginalists call price theory);
3   the theory of marginal utility;
4   the theory of interest, when interest is presented as a reward for abstinence.

7   Keynes wrote, in his *Essays on Persuasion* (1963: 369), on the topic of the conscious interrelationship between ethics and economics:

> The love of money as a possession – as distinguished from the love of money as a means to the enjoyments and realities of life – will be recognized for what it is, a somewhat disgusting morbidity, one of those semi-criminal, semi-pathological propensities which one hands over with a shudder to the specialists in mental disease.

8   Abraham Edel (1970) writes: "Thus a question like the existence and properties of God may be considered in terms of the scientific study of the ways in which these ideas function in the ethical process in the lives and thoughts of men."

9   Lawson (1997: 238–246) writes: "A commitment to (ontological) realism combined with epistemological relativism sustains a judgmental rationality, and from this perspective the practice of contemporary economic modeling are found to be wanting."

10   Whitehead (1979: 48) focuses on the ultimate nature of the primal ontology. This establishes the general theory as universally above the relative nature of particulars in the a posteriori world-system, which is seen to be heteronomous with the a priori domain of the fundamental origin, but is circularly connected with the a posteriori domain:

> The notion of a universal is of that which can enter into the description of many particulars; whereas the notion of a particular is that it is described by universals, and does not itself enter into the description of any other particular.

References

Bhaskar, R. (2002). *Reflections on Meta-reality, Transcendence, Emancipation and Everyday Life*, New Delhi: Sage Foundation, p. 146.

Boatright, J.R. (2010). *Finance Ethics: Critical Issues in Theory and Practice*, New York: Wiley.

Bohr, N. (1985). "Discussions with Einstein on epistemological issues," in Folse, H. (ed.), *The Philosophy of Niels Bohr: The Framework of Complementarity*, Amsterdam: North Holland Physics.

Choudhury, M.A. (1991, reprinted). "The *Tawhidi* precept in the sciences," in Iqbal, M. (ed.), *Studies in the Islam and Science Nexus*, London: Ashgate, pp. 25–26.

Choudhury, M.A. (2007). *The Universal Paradigm and the Islamic World-System: Economics, Ethics, Science and Society*, Singapore: World Scientific.

Choudhury, M.A. (2014). *Tawhidi Epistemology and its Applications: Economics, Finance, Science, and Society*, Cambridge: Cambridge Scholars.

Dasgupta, A.K. (1987). *Epochs of Economic Theory*, Oxford: Basil Blackwell.

Edel, A. (1970). "Science and the structure of ethics," in Neurath, O., Carnap, R., and Morris, C. (eds.), *Foundations of the Unity of Science*, Chicago, IL: University of Chicago Press.

Fama, E.F. (1965). "Portfolio analysis in a stable Paretian market," *Management Science*, 11, 3: 404–419.

Fama, E.F. (2012). "Capital structure choices," *Critical Review*, 1, 1: 59–101.

Foucault, M. (1972). *The Archeology of Knowledge and the Discourse on Language*, trans. Sheridan, A.M., New York: Harper Torchbooks.

Georgescu-Roegen, N. (1981). *The Entropy Law and the Economic Process*, Cambridge, MA: Harvard University Press.

Godel, K. (1965). "On formally undecidable propositions of *Principia Mathematica* and related systems," in Davis, M. (ed.), *The Undecidable*, Hewlett, NY: Raven Press.

Gruber, T.R. (1993). "A translation approach to portable ontologies," *Knowledge Acquisition*, 5, 2: 199–200.

Hawking, S.W. (1988). *A Brief History of Time*, New York: Bantam Books, pp. 15–16.

Hawking, S.W. and Mlodinow, L. (2010). *The Grand Design*, New York: Bantam Books.

Hegel, G.W.F. (1956). *The Philosophy of History*, trans. by Sibree, J., New York: Dover Books.

Hubner, K. (1985). "Foundations of a universal historistic theory of the empirical sciences," trans. Dixon, P.R. Jr. and Dixon, H.M., *Critique of Scientific Reason*, Chicago, IL: University of Chicago Press, pp. 105–122.

Hume, D. (1988). *An Enquiry Concerning Human Understanding*, Buffalo, NY: Prometheus Books.

Kant, I. (1949). *The Philosophy of Kant*, Friedrich, C. J. (ed.), New York, NY: Modern Library.

Kant, I. (1964). *Groundwork of the Metaphysics of Morals*, trans. Paton, H.J., New York: Harper & Row.

Keynes, J.M. (1963 [1930]). "Economic possibilities for our grandchildren," in *John Maynard Keynes Essays in Persuasion*, New York: W.W. Norton, pp. 358–373.

Kuhn, T.S. (1970). *The Structure of Scientific Revolution*, Chicago, IL: University of Chicago Press, p. 152.

Lawson, T. (1997). *Economics and Reality*, London: Routledge, p. 25.

Lawson, T. (2003). "Competing theories and policies within post-Keynesianism," in *Reorienting Economics*, London: Routledge.

Lawson, T. (2006). "The nature of heterodox economics," *Cambridge Journal of Economics*, 30, 4: 483–505.

Lawson, T. and Pesaran, H. (1985). *Keynes' Economics: Methodological Issues*, London: Routledge.

Ledger, C. and Pickard, S. (eds.) (2004). *Creation and Complexity: Interdisciplinary Issues in Science and Religion*, Adelaide: ATF Press.

Lee, F.S. and Lavoie, M. (2013). *In Defense of Post-Keynesian and Heterodox Economics*, Abingdon, Oxford: Routledge, p. 109.

Lucaks, J. (1968). *Historical Consciousness*, New York: Harper & Row.

Mahdi, M. (1964). *Ibn Khaldun's Philosophy of History*, Chicago, IL: University of Chicago Press.

Myrdal, G. (1958). "The principle of cumulation," in Streeten, P. (ed.), *Value in Social Theory: A Selection of Essays on Methodology by Gunnar Myrdal*, New York: Harper & Brothers, pp. 198–205.

Nasr, S.H. (1996). "Mulla Sadra: His teachings," in Nasr, S.H. and Leaman, O. (eds.), *History of Islamic Philosophy I & II*, London and New York: Routledge, pp. 643–662.

Nasr, S.H. and Leaman, O. (1996). *History of Islamic Philosophy I & II*, London and New York: Routledge.

Pasinetti, L.F. (2001). "Continuity and change in Sraffa's thought," in Cozzi, T. and Marchionatti, R. (eds.), *Piero Sraffa's Political Economy*, London: Routledge.

Sardar, Z. (1984). "Islamisation of knowledge or the westernisation of Islam?" *Inquiry*, 1, 7.

Sen, A. (1977). "Rational fools: A critique of the behavioural foundations of economic theory," *Philosophy and Public Affairs*, 6: 317–344.

Sen, A. (1992). "Conduct, ethics and economics," in *On Ethics and Economics*, Oxford: Basil Blackwell, pp. 88–89.

Shiller, R. (2012). *Finance and the Good Society*, Princeton, NJ: Princeton University Press.

Sraffa, P. (1963). *Production of Commodities by Means of Commodities: Prelude to a Critique of Economic Theory*, Bombay: Vora & Co.

Toner, P. (1999). "Gunnar Myrdal (1898–1987): Circular and cumulative causation as the methodology of the social sciences," in *Main Currents in Cumulative Causation: The Dynamics of Growth and Development*, Houndmills: Macmillan, Chapter 5.

Whitehead, A.N. (1979). *Process and Reality*, in Griffin, D.R. and Sherburne, D.W. (eds.), New York: The Free Press, p. 46.

Wilson, E.O. (1998). *Consilience: The Unity of Knowledge*, New York, NY: Vantage Books.

2 Contrasting economic epistemology with and without heteronomy

Background and objective

The objective of this chapter is to explain the nature of the new scientific epistemology that extends the bounds of a posteriori and a priori knowledge in their existing form of dichotomy and forms them into a harmonized continuity in unity of knowledge. Upon the transformation of scientific reasoning including monotheism rests a dynamic, creative way of understanding reality. This extension of God and monotheism as the foundational reality in the scheme and order of things breaks down the heteronomy between a priori and a posteriori knowledge. As a result, science is formalized as the integrated and inter-causal study of reality in the light of scientific and analytical explanation.

Some of the great scientists and philosophers of science have written on the holistic meaning of the entirety of scientific potentiality. This chapter will use the underlying potentialities of the vastness of scientific intellection to extend monotheistic law, thus explaining "everything" as the analytical reality. As analytical monotheism encompasses the overarching domain of the "cosmic envelope," this is an idea similar to that identified by Bhaskar (2002: 12): "The principle of connectivity of the cosmic envelope enables us to define the next major distinguishing feature of the philosophy of meta-reality." The idea of the ultimate freedom from heteronomous reasoning marks the liberation of the unity of being as the primal ontology of divine Oneness and the induced unity of the generality and particulars of the world-system. The imminent scientific methodology marks the liberation from what Bhaskar (ibid.: 13) called the:

> ... unfulfilled and split intentionality, [which] describe two forms in which human beings contain elements of heteronomy which block and check their freedom. When we are free of all such heteronomy, when we contain nothing inconsistent with our ground states, that is we have eliminated negative incompleteness, we may be said to be "enlightened" or "realized."

Husserl (1965) writes on a similar note regarding the aesthetically fallen state of science by missing out the foundational role of a primal ontology that extends the boundary of modernity towards its true goal, ends, and potentiality. Husserl (1965) wrote in this regard:

> Blinded by naturalism the practitioners of humanistic science have completely neglected even to pose the problem of a universal and pure science of the spirit and to seek a theory of the essence of spirit as spirit, a theory that pursues what is unconditionally universal in the spiritual order with its own elements and its own laws. Yet this last should be done with a view to gaining thereby scientific explanations in an absolutely conclusive sense.

Kant (1949) was a forerunner in the approach to upholding heteronomy between a priori and a posteriori segmentations of reasoning. The consequence of heteronomous thinking regarding the monotheistic law as the foundation of the extension of science into a new horizon of intellection and the domain of reason—as the a posteriori segmentation of human intellection—can be read in his writing. Kant (1963: 80–81) wrote on the relationship between God and the moral law from a perspective that interrelated will and reason by invoking exclusively the a posteriori domain of reasoning:

> A clear exposition of morality of itself leads to the belief in God. Belief in this philosophic connexion means not trust in a revelation, but trust arising from the use of the reason, which springs from the principle of practical morality.

Kant (1949: 25), writing on his dichotomous perception of pure reason and practical reason, further intensifies his assertion of scientific heteronomy in the following words:

> This, then, is a question which at least calls for closer examination, and does not permit any off-hand answer: whether there is any knowledge that is thus independent of experience and even of all impressions of the senses. Such knowledge is entitled *a priori*, and is distinguished from the empirical, which has its sources *a posteriori*, that is, in experience.

Kant's a priori knowledge denotes pure reason and identifies his domain of freedom. The nature of heteronomy between the a priori and a posteriori nature of reasoning is cast thus in Kant's words (ibid.: 25):

> In what follows, therefore, we shall understand by *a priori* knowledge, no knowledge independent of this or that experience, but knowledge absolutely independent of all experience. Opposed to it is empirical knowledge, which is knowledge possible only *a posteriori*, that is through experience.

Now, when the function of freedom and human will, premised in pure reason as the moral law, is combined with the above-mentioned dichotomous nature of the origin of knowledge, we obtain the following relation within Kantian analysis. This heteronomous partition contradicts the possibility of discovering the tenets that can make holistic knowledge possible and meta-science capable of extending into the domain of the methodological understanding of the monotheistic law via the episteme of unity of knowledge.

The possibility of science without heteronomy

This chapter, contrary to heteronomous views in the constrained domain of science, will propound the unified methodological worldview of the monotheistic law and holistic science. The analytical nature of this extension of the holistic scientific project will be explored to develop a quantitative concept in complex system modeling that is embedded in monotheistic holism. Its foundation will rest on an epistemic approach of unity of knowledge that is contrasted with the notion of heteronomy. The latter foundation abounds in mainstream socio-scientific thought. These two contrasting concepts are explained as follows: Heteronomy manifests the mainstream epistemological concept of demarcation between a priori and a posteriori reasoning (Carnap, 1966). The philosophy of rationalism means experience premised on the separation (dualism) of the a priori domain of the monotheistic law from its inseparably endogenous relationship with the affairs of the world. Such heteronomy is argued to be an unwanted part of reasoning according to unity of knowledge, which otherwise rationalism harbors within it.

On the contrary, unity of knowledge as episteme means continuous and inseparable unity through the organic relationship between foundational moral and ethical law and the socio-scientific world-system. In the new socio-scientific episteme of unity of knowledge, the methodical approach is characterized by complex systems along with the inherent non-linear and pervasively endogenous relations that exist between variables and their relations in such systems (Choudhury, 2013). Such is the analytical approach of understanding the rightful meta-scientific extension of the monotheistic law of unity of knowledge.

As a specific example of the generalized worldview, we define the socio-scientific perspective of economic theory in relation to the endogenous moral and ethical value of the portfolio of economic, financial, and social elements. In mathematical terms, to allow for analysis and empiricism, the imminent models for studying the analytics of the monotheistic episteme are cast in terms of symbolized variables. The variables are represented in the form of knowledge induction and are pervasively multi-causal to draw out the organic nature of unity of knowledge arising from the monotheistic socio-scientific episteme. Moral and ethical values are embedded into human choices by the text of the divine law in terms of consilience as its attribute. Upon such choices and the multi-causal relations of endogenously embedded variables induced by the law of monotheistic consilience, the consequentialist epistemic nature of the moral law embedded in the multi-causal relations caused by emergent consilience results in the definition and evaluation of social wellbeing. The immanent wellbeing function, as the objective criterion, becomes the cause and effect circularly reproduced between the selected variables in the framework of monotheistic consilience. The emanation of socio-scientific choices (and consequential social evaluation) commences and repeats in the framework of the monotheistic episteme. General and particular choices are explained in the context of the methodological universality and uniqueness of the law and analytics of the emergent monotheistic episteme. All inter-systemic, social and scientific phenomena, and individual, institutional, and social choices, and their analytical studies, are carried out accordingly.

The derived socio-scientific criterion arising from the episteme of the monotheistic law is called the social wellbeing function (SWF). This is an evaluative criterion premised on the universality and uniqueness of unity of knowledge as the methodology and the consequentialist unity of the world-system. Within the world-system, we will particularize economic theory. The immanent formalism is an undertaking in analytical ethics. Edel (1970) has written emphatically about such analytical ethical methodology in science.

Because of the complex nature of the imminent epistemological investigation of monotheistic consilience leading to a new theoretical perspective on the understanding of our unified world-system, we will draw on the results of certain stated theorems. Edel's methodological approach will be combined with the original approach in this chapter. We refer to Edel's approach as the existentialist praxis (EP).

The heterodox methodological worldview of Islamic economics in respect of the episteme of unity of knowledge and the unified world-system for the generality of socio-scientific study in this chapter and the whole book entirely invokes the monotheistic foundation of the moral law in the *Qur'an*. The dynamic nature of the monotheistic law in the understanding and working of the world-system is drawn out by the following verses of the *Qur'an* (2:255):

> God! There is no god but He,—the Living, the Self-subsisting, Eternal, no slumber can seize Him nor sleep. His are all things in the heavens and on earth. Who is there to intercede in His presence except as He permits? He knows what (appears to His creatures as) before or after or behind them. Nor shall they encompass aught of His knowledge except as He wills. His Throne does extend over the heavens and the earth, and He feels no fatigue in guarding and preserving them for He is the Most High, the Supreme (in glory).

The above verses draw out the supremely creative command and act of God, who has thus created reason in the first place. But since God incessantly creates, governs, and guides the universes (*a'lameen*) by his law, the relationship of essence to creation is forever renewed. Reason is thereby created spontaneously by such renewed relationships. These relationships are dynamic and encompassed by human understanding, social action, and response, involving the material and cognitive worlds. They are manifested in and through the knowledge-flows that God bestows as He wills at the spontaneous *moment* of the emanating relations.

Similar concepts of the vast scope of meta-science were expressed by Einstein (n.d.). On this issue of extending the bounds of science, Einstein (1960) writes:

> It is the privilege of man's genius, impersonated by inspired individuals, to advance ethical axioms which are so comprehensive and so well founded that

men will accept them as grounded in the vast mass of their individual emotional experiences. Ethical axioms are founded and tested not differently from the axioms of science. Truth is what stands the test of experience.

Barrow (1990) writes on the universality and unique potentiality of science:

> The current breed of candidates of the title of a "Theory of Everything" hope to provide an encapsulation of all the laws of nature into a simple and single representation. The fact that such unification is even sought tells us something important about our expectations regarding the Universe. These we must have derived from an amalgam of our previous experience of the world and our inherited religious beliefs about its ultimate Nature and significance. Our monotheistic traditions reinforce the assumption that the Universe is at root a unity that is not governed by different legislation in different places, neither the residue of some clash of Titans wrestling to impose their arbitrary wills upon the Nature of things, nor the compromise of some cosmic committee.

Theorems: monotheistic methodology of unity of knowledge and the unified world-system

> *Theorem 1: There exists a "universal" mathematical topology from which the universal EP is derived and formalized in the functional ontological form.*

Let T denote the Truth (Ethical) set, F denote the Falsehood set (ethically neutral), and M denote the Undetermined set between Truth and Falsehood sets. The properties of these sets are $T \cap F = \phi$, when T and F are fully determined. But $T \cap M \neq \phi$; $F \cap M \neq \phi$ in the presence of evolutionary knowledge between T, F, and M.

Let $\{\theta\} \in T$ denote the set of knowledge-flows, such that, as learning towards gaining knowledge is acquired, then, in the limiting case, $\{\theta\} = T$. Likewise, there exists the Falsehood category of "de-knowledge" flows. Let the Falsehood "de-knowledge" flows be denoted by the set $\{\theta\sim\}$ as the mathematical opposite of the set $\{\theta\}$. Consequently, as $\{\theta\} \to T$, then $\{\theta\sim\} \to F$, and $M \to \phi$, the null set. Thus, for either case, $\{\theta\} = T$ or $\{\theta\sim\} = F$, $M \to \phi$ in these limiting conditions of convergence resulting in the determination of M into either T or F as the case may be.

With the above descriptions of the sets T and F, we can write, for the limiting case of knowledge acquisition (or "de-knowledge" acquisition), $\{\theta\} \cup \{\theta\sim\} \subseteq T \cup F$.

Let us define the topology (Ω, S) by the usual properties of a topology (Maddox, 1970), where Ω denotes the universal set and S denotes the well-defined mapping (relational correspondence) that preserves the properties of the topology. These properties are namely, $(\Omega, S) \supseteq T \cup F$; $(\Omega, S) \supseteq T \cap F = \phi$. Thus (Ω, S) includes itself. This means that (Ω, S) self-references. Thereby, all combinations of T and F, denoted by (T, F), like $\cup \cap (T, F) \subset (\Omega, S)$.

Consequently, any positive monotonic continuous and compact mapping on $\cup \cap (T, F) \subset (\Omega, S)$[1] preserves the properties of the topology. In other words, every proper set of mappings on $U \cap (T,F)$ belongs to (Ω,S), and is thereby a sub-topology within the universal topology.

Let us formulate such a well-defined continuous and bounded mapping '*f*' on (Ω, S). '*f*' converts into the following correspondence in (Ω,S), $f(\Omega,S) = f(T) + f(F)$, in the limit of $M \rightarrow \phi$, or likewise a similar $g(.)$-correspondence causes, $g(T,F,M) = g(T) + g(F) + g(M)$, with the result arising from mathematical opposite (complementation) on the (T,F,M)-set that states as $(\theta\uparrow \Rightarrow \theta\sim\downarrow$ and vice versa$) \Rightarrow M \rightarrow \phi$, etc.

The mathematical phenomenological model of $\{\Omega,S,\theta,x(\theta)\}$ in continuity and continuums of the evolutionary processes explains both Truth and Falsehood in terms of their organic property of unity of being and the differentiated world-system, respectively.

Theorem 2: (Ω,S) as supercardinal topology is unique in its determination of (T,F,M).

To prove this, we simply note the result of self-referencing mentioned above as a logical property derived from the topological definition. Hence $f(\Omega,S) = (\Omega,S)$, together with the compound functions of $f(.)$. The exception is the case of the Falsehood domain, $\{F\}$, over which a demarcation of ethical values from scientific inquiry occurs (Popper, 2004), otherwise emulating Edel's methodology of EP. Systemic differentiation occurs both between T and F $(T \cap F = \phi)$, as well as in the limit of evolutionary processes, $\cap\{F\} \rightarrow \phi$.

T and F, as topological subsets governed by (Ω,S), have their distinctly unique equilibrium points of the evolutionary kind in evolutionary sets of T,F,M, leading to their ultimate null intersection. This is denoted by evolutionary neighborhoods of $h(\theta) = \{x(\theta)\}$ around the initial Identity map, (I), relating to the existence of equilibrium for the relationship, $I.\theta = f(\{x(\theta)\})$; f as vector of topological mapping defined over $\{x(\theta)\}$ in the domain of $\{\theta\} \in (\Omega,S)$.[2] Hence all subsets as sub-topologies of the self-referenced (Ω,S) are evolutionary in the learning sense of θ-ethical induction, but are order-preserving in respect of (T,F,M). The same kinds of method of deduction can be repeated to prove how (Ω,S) defines uniquely: $\forall\theta\sim\in F$, etc. This is the meaning of uniqueness of (Ω,S) in characterizing (T,F,M).

Unity of knowledge is impossible in the Falsehood (rationalist) system. It is central to the epistemology of $\{\Omega,S,\theta,x(\theta)\}$ explaining both Truth and Falsehood, $\{\Omega,S,\theta\sim,x(\theta\sim)\}$, in continuity across continuums. Hence the epistemology of unity of knowledge is uniquely universal across all verities of systems.

The supercardinal representation of (Ω,S) in respect of (T,F,M)

Note that T by itself cannot imply F; F by itself cannot imply T. That is because, for each $\theta \in T$, there exists $\theta\sim$, for which $\{\theta\} \cap \{\theta\sim\} = \phi$. Hence there is no correspondence between T and F. It requires a supercardinal topology that will include T, F, and M. M is sifted into either T or F, as the case may be, as knowledge advances to its limiting values in each of these cases in the learning system categorizing (T,F,M)-relations, so as to explain these sets by their respective properties. Therefore (Ω,S) is the topology that defines reality universally according to the mutually disjoint nature of T and F and the limiting M, by using the functional ontological correspondence (mapping), S. All this is formalized as follows.

$[T \cap F \cap M][\theta] \subseteq f(\Omega,S)$ denotes an imperfect determination of M by T or F, as $lim \ (\theta \rightarrow \theta^*)[f(\Omega,S) \rightarrow {}_S(\Omega,S)] \supseteq [T \cap F \cap M][\theta] = \phi$. Hence each of T, F, and M is contained in its differentiated topological representation. Therefore (Ω,S) denotes the supercardinal topological space that gives definition to all categories.

A consequentialist socio-scientific extension of the EP formalism

In the socio-scientific system that arises from the one-to-one correspondence between knowledge formation and its representation in the revealed socio-scientific variables, these are induced by the knowledge-flows $\{\theta\}$. It is oppositely true of the prevalence of "de-knowledge-flows," a system marked by the differentiated sub-systems of absence of unity of knowledge, $\{\theta\sim\}$. Examples of "de-knowledge" systems are methodological individualism, ethically benign economic theory, and rationalism that gives rise to the postulates of economic rationality via an economic system that remains differentiated by marginalism.

In note 2, we explain the relationships that continue on to compound into extensively interactive, integrative, creatively evolutionary forms by the learning dynamics based on the induction of knowledge-flows derived from the monotheistic ontology. The argument presented is that only organic unity of being and becoming can manifest the properties of unification in the cognitive and real world-system. Such organic unity establishes the meaning of monotheistic consilience of mind and matter. In this regard, the *Qur'an* points out the pairing truth between "everything" in the domains of Truth (unity) and Falsehood ("de-knowledge" by differentiation).[3]

Thus $\theta \rightarrow {}_h x(\theta)$ yields $h(\theta)=\{x(\theta)\}$ and its monotonic transformation is denoted by $(g \bullet h)(x(\theta));=f(x(\theta))$, say, with $(g \bullet h)=f$, for each element, $x(\theta) \in \{x(\theta)\}$. Bold letters represent vectors. An example is this: Knowledge of organizing organic unity of the financial system with the real economy results in a definitive way, represented by the identity map, 'I', such that, $I.\theta = \{x_1,x_2\}[\theta]$. Let $x=\{x_1,x_2\}[\theta]$. Likewise, by the monotonic mapping $f(.)$, we obtain $I.\theta = f(\{x=x_1,x_2\})[\theta]$, $x=\{x_1,x_2\}[\theta]$.

As an example, let x_1 be the vector of financial variables; x_2 is the vector of real-economy variables, both being induced by the knowledge of organizing the economy along lines of pervasive complementarities or systemic participation between finance and the real economy. Over this initial organizing experience, further positive monotonic transformations can be induced by $h(.)$, etc., as monotonic transformations forming topological mappings.

The simplified result is, $\{x(\theta)\}=I.\theta$. This means that the monotonic positive transformation, $f(x(\theta))=I.\theta$, evolves into compound functions, $I.\theta= f[(.) \bullet g(.) \bullet h (.) \bullet ....]$, across intra- and inter- evolutionary learning processes. Such functional forms are defined over the continuously compact set of θ-values. The implication then is of the existence of evolutionary learning equilibriums by the functional ontology of θ-values according to Brouwer and Kakutani's Fixed Point Theorems (Nikaido, 1989).

By an extension of these Fixed Point Theorems to evolutionary continuous and compact subsets of the described topology, the following general result will also yield equilibriums. The results occur in evolutionary open sets, $T[\theta=f(\{x(\theta)\})] \Rightarrow I.h$ $(\theta)=f(\{x(\theta)\})$, and the functional compounding. (See Choudhury, 2006, on evolutionary equilibriums caused by the episteme of unity of knowledge.)

The differentiated nature of "de-knowledge" characterizes the existing scope of science in its submission to the heteronomy of relations between morality and materiality. The potentiality of the holistic science resting on the monotheistic episteme of unity of knowledge and the world-system is governed by the analytics that conform to it. Thus the opposing methodologies of Truth and Falsehood need to be formalized respectively. The "de-knowledge" methodology will be summarized at the end of this chapter.

Generalizing the epistemological formalism to "everything"

The methodology of "everything" is consistent with and applicable to the broadest category of socio-scientific problems overarching the organically unified domains of relationships. Thus the precepts of universality and uniqueness in their analytical sense can study the problems of differentiated domains as falsehood, meaning a false depiction of reality by differentiation. In addition, they can study the organically unified and interrelated learning domains of pervasive complementarities—that is participation also meaning complementarities by way of unifying linkages and the appropriate rules attain this primal property of unification in T. The latter case forms the domain of Truth, meaning a systemic understanding of unity of knowledge across systems. Contrarily, the method of differentiation, methodological individualism, and functional independence between sub-systems and their entities cannot explain the overarching theme of organic unity in the socio-scientific world.

The EP framework in social economic and financial thought: Islamic economics as an example

In Islamic economics and finance, which is today a global practice and academic activity, the primal ontology of (Ω,S) is premised on the moral text of the *Qur'an* and the Prophetic (Muhammad) guidance called the *sunnah*. *Sunnah*, as the mapping "S," explicates the guidance and rules from the *Qur'an* for practical applications. Thus S serves as the primal ontological mapping that carries the ultimate originary (Howard, 1985) premise of the supercardinal topology (Rucker, 1983) of Ω to the world-systems for use as guidance, rules, and functional instruments.

Once the primal ontology of (Ω,S) is invoked to construct theory and application in respect of "everything" in the world-system taken in particular, the guidance and rules so invoked from (Ω,S) are discoursed for reasoned understanding among experts who deal with the problems under examination. It is at this level that the derived knowledge-flows, $\{\theta\}$ (hence also "de-knowledge"-flows, $\{\theta\sim\}$) appear in the functional ontological formalism (Gruber, 1993) of any particular problem under study, while using the learning formalism as a systemic approach premised on the epistemology of unity of knowledge. Along with these ontological and epistemological relations, the derivation of knowledge-flows invokes the guidance, rules, and instruments derived from moral law, which are understood by discourse in the midst of interaction, consensus (integration), and co-evolution over learning processes.

We use the term "integration" for encompassing scientific phenomena for analytical discourse leading to consensus. This full scope of specification is characterized by the learning vector $\{\theta,x(\theta);\ \theta \in (\Omega,S)\}$. Following this determination of the learning vector at any given stage of knowledge-flow to be continuously evolved into subsequent processes of learning, there comes about the post-evaluation of the choice-vector comprising knowledge-induced preferences and menus (say, represented by $\zeta(\theta)$). The prevailing (positivistic) socio-scientific results and their normative reconstruction along lines of guidance and rules are derived from (Ω,S).

In such positivistic-to-normative directional simulations of empirical results, a system of relations that simulates the social wellbeing function $W(\theta,x(\theta))$ is derived to represent the given process of circular causation. Such circular causation relations between $(\theta,x(\theta))$ represent the pervasively complementary—that is, the unifying nature of participatory relations within and between the sets of multivariates $(\theta,x(\theta))$. Circular causation means that every variable is inter-causally dependent on the rest of the variables to explain the degree of existing complementarities between the variables that are selected in the light of the purpose and objective of the Islamic law, referred to as *maqasid as-shari'ah*. Pervasive inter-variable complementarities yield the empirical meaning of unity of knowledge as the episteme, as it is exhibited by the inter-causal set of multivariable participatory system.

Ordinal values of the θ-variable appear as assigned rankings by observing the degrees of perceived and discoursed association between the $x(\theta)$-values. The θ-values may be actual ones in the state of the problem situation "as it is" (positivistic) or normatively revised, expanded, truncated, etc., in several ways in relation to the problem situation "as it ought to be." Such normative meaning of simulation conveys the reconstruction of the knowledge-flow that is now premised on the higher state of realizing unity of knowledge as imminent in the heightened cognition of the monotheistic origin of the primal ontology.

In Figure 2.1, this entire learning process (Process 1) to be carried over in continuum by subsequent learning processes is depicted by a chain of relations. We refer to this chain relation that is ontologically premised in the primal ontology of the monotheistic law as the *Tawhidi* String Relation (TSR). *Tawhid* (thus "of *Tawhid*" as *Tawhidi*) means monotheism in respect of God as being and the unity precept of the monotheistic law. The entire expression (2.1) explains the episteme, the methodological worldview commencing from the primal ontology underlying unity of *a* (specified to the problems and issues under investigation):

$$Y = K^a.L^b.H^c, \text{ with } a + b + c = 1 \tag{2.1}$$

$a,b,c > 0.$

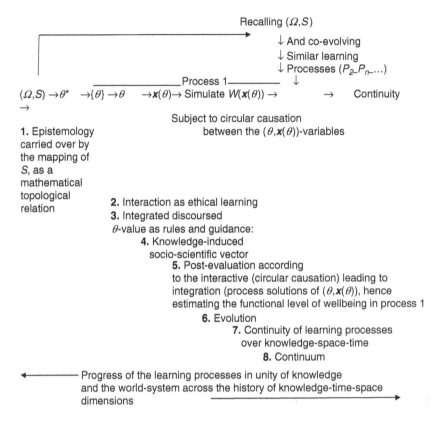

Figure 2.1 The computational learning process methodology of unity of knowledge

A financial problem of the real economy

In the epistemic study of ethico-economics, the dynamics explained by expression (2.1) remains intact. Into it we now insert the knowledge-induced vector[4] of variables.[5] In the specific case of the Islamic financial system, such a financial vector is denoted by $x(\theta)=(\theta, r(\theta), i(\theta), Q(\theta), M(\theta), P(\theta))$. Here, θ denotes levels of discoursed understanding of unity of knowledge as extensively complementary and participatory process of inter-variable and inter-system learning. Thus "$r(\theta)$" denotes the rate of return on financial assets held in the real economy; "$i(\theta)$" denotes interest rates left over during the imperfect state of a unified money–finance–real economy circular causal relationship; and $Q(\theta)$ denotes real output. $M(\theta)$ denotes the quantity of money in circulation (but may be in the *M2* and *M3* forms in the imperfect system). $P(\theta)$ denotes a bundle of policies, guidance, strategies, and instruments.

A brief explanation of the symbol θ^* is needed here: θ^* denotes the initial body of guidance given by the learned in the monotheistic law and derived from the primal ontology of the *Qur'an* and *sunnah*. The set of knowledge-flows is denoted by $\{\theta\}$. Thus $\{\theta\}$ converges into an interactively generated consensus denoted by $\{\theta\} \rightarrow \theta$. Thereafter, the discursively derived body of knowledge-flows arises and continues inter-process. The knowledge-inducing experience of Process 1 is repeated and continued in subsequent processes of similar character. Every emanating process commences by repeatedly recalling the primal ontology for invoking heightened and closer understanding of the monotheistic ontological foundation. This model of learning in evolutionary topological spaces implicates a study of the generalized methodology, first by establishing the general-system worldview. Then, the generalized model is applied to particular sub-systems constructed in the light of the monotheistic worldview in every minute detail. The imminent evolutionary learning experience applies to diverse problems occurring in the continuity of knowledge, space, and time.

An example is the world-system as a generalized discipline studied by the methodology of the monotheistic unity of knowledge in Figure 2.1. This formalistic symbolism explaining the monotheistic law of unity of knowledge is called the *Tawhidi* String Relation (TSR). An example of the study of a sub-system of the generalized world-system is political economy and various economic issues that are induced by moral and ethical values comprising a study of ethico-economics. Yet another example is the generalized mathematical theory of the Fixed Point Theorem that establishes equilibrium not only in compact spaces, but also across unbounded and open spaces characterized by evolutionary learning (Georgescu-Roegen, 1981; Choudhury and Zaman, 2006). Thereby, as in economics and finance, the theory of evolutionary learning equilibriums is a particular element in the general system. The particular is thus studied by the monotheistic dynamics of the generalized theory of TSR, conveyed by Figure 2.1.

A quantitative exploration of the knowledge-induced processes in economic theory

The differences between the mathematical economic way of solving the optimization problem and a simulation problem in the light of the evolutionary learning model shown in expression (2.1) present an example that can be highlighted by working through the following problem in the two cases—of optimization and process—that are distinct from each other.

Consider the constant returns-to-scale, Cobb-Douglas production function (Mankiw, 2003) in three input variables. These are, namely, capital (K), labor (L), and human resource development (HRD) expenditure (H). Y is the economic output in the growth model:

$$Y = K^{1/3}.L^{1/3}.H^{1/3} \qquad (2.2)$$

How is the change in output related with that of the input variables?

The neoclassical optimization method

By taking logarithmic transformation on either sides of expression (2.2), we can write $\partial Y/\partial K=(Y/K)$. By multiplying by price level P, we convert the two sides of money values and write, according to economic theory,

Value of marginal product of capital=Value of output per unit of capital

This is also the value of the productivity of capital.
  Therefore:

Payment to capital=Value of productivity of capital=Value of marginal productivity of capital

Likewise:

Payments to labor=Value of productivity of labor=Value of marginal productivity of labor

Payment of human resource input H=Value of productivity of H=Value of marginal productivity of H

Relative payments to these factors=Respective input ratios

In this case,

$$dY/Y = (1/3).[(dK/K + dL/L + dH/H],$$

in terms of rates of change,

$$g(Y) = (1/3)[g(K) + g(L) + g(H)] \tag{2.3}$$

Owing to the permanence of substitution and competition between inputs in maximizing Y by the rates of change, there will always be substitution between the inputs. The result, then, is a marginalist push-and-pull between the rates of change of inputs as shown, while the growth of output stabilizes. The rate of change of H also plays an independent (exogenous) role played out in such neoclassical economic models (Solow, 1980).

The method of simulation by circular causation in the θ-induced case

We re-write expression (2.2) as:

$$Y = (K.H_1)^a.(LH_2)^b$$

This expression is re-written as:

$$Y^* = K^{*a}.L^{*b} \tag{2.4}$$

where

$$K^* = (K.H_1); L^* = (LH_2)$$

"*a*" and "*b*" are elasticity coefficients of Y^* in respect of K^* and L^*, respectively.

In expression (2.4), K^* is augmented by the HRD-index H_1 and L^* is augmented by HRD-index H_2. Such input augmentations of Y are realized through the common induction by a complementing factor, θ (implied). Contrarily, in the absence of θ, as in expression (2.2), the effect of H remains independently exogenous in relationship with the other input variables.

With the endogenous (inter-causal) effects of θ in all the input variables, the income-shares are worked out in the following ways:

$$dY^*/d\theta = a.(Y^*/K^*).(dK^*/d\theta) + b.(Y^*/L^*).(dL^*/d\theta) \qquad (2.5)$$

Owing to circular causation with inter-causal effects between all the variables, each in terms of the rest of the variables by interrelations, the following expressions are obtained:

$$dK^*/d\theta = (\partial K^*/\partial L^*).(dL^*/d\theta) + (\partial K^*/\partial Y^*).(dY^*/d\theta) \qquad (2.6)$$

$$dL^*/d\theta = (\partial L^*/\partial K^*).(dK^*/d\theta) + (\partial L^*/\partial Y^*).(dY^*/d\theta) \qquad (2.7)$$

By substituting expressions (2.6) and (2.7) in expression (2.5) and organizing the result, we obtain:

$$\begin{aligned} dY^*/d\theta &= a.(Y^*/K^*).(\partial K^*/\partial L^*).(dL^*/d\theta) \\ &\quad + b.[(Y^*/L^*).((\partial L^*/\partial K^*).(dK^*/d\theta) \end{aligned} \qquad (2.8)$$

$$\begin{aligned} (dY^*/d\theta).[1{-}a.(\partial K^*/\partial Y^*)] &-b.(\partial L^*/\partial Y^*)] = \\ a.(Y^*/K^*).(\partial K^*/\partial L^*).(dL^*/d\theta) &+ b.(Y^*/L^*).(\partial L^*/\partial K^*).(dK^*/d\theta) \end{aligned} \qquad (2.9)$$

$$\begin{aligned} dY^*/d\theta &= a.(Y^*/K^*)^+.(\partial K^*/\partial L^*)^+.(dL^*/d\theta)^+ + b.(Y^*/L^*)^+.(\partial K^*/\partial L^*)^+ \\ &\quad .(dK^*/d\theta)^+]/[1 -\{a.(\partial K^*/\partial Y^*)^+ + b.(\partial L^*/\partial Y^*)^+\}] \end{aligned} \qquad (2.10)$$

In expression (2.10), the impact of the learning parameter θ on the pervasively complementary nature of circular causation relations between the variables would yield the signs as indicated in expression (2.10). The implication is that expression (2.10) will be higher in value than expression (2.3) owing to inter-variable complementarities and the multiplier effect of the denominator, $1/[1 - \{a.((\partial K^*/\partial Y^*)^+ + b.(\partial L^*/\partial Y^*)^+)\}]$. Yet this result on the enhanced increase in output Y^* is solely owing to the θ-effect of endogeneity between the inter-causal variables of circular causation relations, with $a+b>1$. These results on process-oriented approach to economic modeling are quite contrary to the neoclassical approach in optimal science.

The contrast in the workings of the two economic models examined here high-lights that neoclassical economic methodology is annulled. Yet, on the other hand, the TSR methodology is capable of studying the neoclassical model in terms of the evolutionary learning model and methodology of the process-oriented type. An example of this type of evolutionary model in neoclassical vintage is given by Nelson and Winter (1982).

For instance, the presence of the key learning variable denoted by θ induces the vector $x(\theta)=(Y,K,L,H)(\theta)$ and causes pervasive complementarities, as explained by the simulated version of the circular causation interrelations between the variables of this vector. Circular causation is the mathematical way of signifying the underlying episteme of unity of knowledge in quantitative manifestation.

A further extension can be obtained here. The wellbeing objective denoted by $W(Y,K,L,H)[\theta]$ can be represented by its monotonic positive function in the form of measured rankings of θ-variable with respect to the socioeconomic data. We can write, therefore,

$$\theta = W(Y,K,L,H)[\theta] \tag{2.11}$$

say,

$$\theta = Y.K.L.H \tag{2.12}$$

or

$$\ln\theta = \ln Y + \ln K + \ln L + \ln H,$$

thereby

$$d\theta/\theta = (1/Y).(dY/d\theta) + (1/K).(dK/d\theta)$$
$$+(1/L).(dL/d\theta) + (1/H).(dH/d\theta) \tag{2.13}$$

The expressions (2.6)–(2.8) would be inserted into expression (2.13). The result and interpretation would be similar to expression (2.10), with economies of scope and increasing returns to scale in the evolutionary learning model of process. Such a process model is absent in neoclassical economics because of the independence among the variables and the consequential properties of the neoclassical linear model of time rates of change in the separate variables that ensue.

In addition, the θ-variable has continuity properties, intra-systems, and inter-systems across continuums. Therefore, the results of wellbeing and inter-variable causality in the evolutionary learning models derived from the theoretical sub-stance of this chapter, and as depicted in Figure 2.1, remain the most general properties of all systems. The same model can be used to show degeneration into the neoclassical model. But, owing to the continuity of the nature of independence, marginalism, and economic rationality postulates of neoclassical economics, this field of economics cannot be made to explain the evolutionary learning model of unity of knowledge. The evolutionary learning model of unity of knowledge is represented by complementarities and participation in reference to consciousness of learning arising from the primal ontology of the monotheistic law in the process-oriented worldview.

A computer-generated configuration of the interactive, integrative, and evolutionary (IIE) learning model in the domains of Truth (T) and Falsehood (F)

This section further extends the field of visual application of the generalized phenomenological model of unity of knowledge of expression (2.1) into the sociological field with economic embedding. In this way, the generalized model is exemplified by its particular application to yet another specific problem. This is the problem of unity of knowledge between religion and socio-scientific thought, contrary to the present state of demarcation between these domains.

To study this problem, we use the spatial domain analysis (SDA) method of the geographical information system (GIS). SDA is a specialized sub-project of GIS. It is applied here to socio-scientific relationships involving economics and religion. Both of these domains are governed by the epistemology of unity of knowledge. In actual practice, the SDA forms a pervasive field of numbers that occur as all possible estimated and simulated values of coefficients representing inter-causal relations between selected variables and the inter-systemic wellbeing function. The wellbeing function relates to the study of integration between economics and religion as two interdisciplinary systems. The pervasive field of numbers next allows simulation choices of improved and revised numerical values of the "estimated" coefficients in order to build on the principle of complementarities between the inter-causal variables of the wellbeing function. The underlying method in such integration arising out of interaction, and thereby growing outwards into evolutionary learning processes, is that of circular causation. Although numbers are invoked in actual estimation and simulation by the SDA method, in our case the representation remains non-parametric and hence illustrative.

The origins of economics and religion denote those of initially disjoint systems. Improvizing the epistemology of unity of knowledge causes the disjoint systems to become knowledge-induced and the circular causation method works, resulting in progress towards greater integration by the interactive, integrative, and evolutionary learning (IIE) processes.

The epistemic principle of unity of knowledge over the universal field of "everything" causes the regions extensively denoted by, say, TU and VS to move toward their complementary integration in the region, say, around a point A. The evolutionary SDA waves that arise signify the progressing IIE learning processes, wherein estimated values of inter-variable relational coefficients represent non-parametric simulations. These parametric evaluations build on the deepening of unity of systemic knowledge as its foundational epistemology. The method underlying the imminent dynamics of the inter-causal relations between the selected variable is the circular causation method. Myrdal (1958a, 1958b) referred to a similar sociological method in his study of the social phenomena from economic and sociological viewpoints as cumulative causation.

Conclusion

This chapter laid the groundwork for the possibility of extension of the scientific project to the ontological foundation of the monotheistic law of unity of knowledge and its construction of the unified world-system in generality and detail. This introduction to the significant project of scientific possibility was applied both in the generalized sense of heteronomy in Kant and more broadly. A scheme of scientific argumentation was laid down to engender our subsequent characterization of the economic epistemological inquiry into heterodox economic theory. Thus examples of the heterodox treatment of the nature of endogenous relations in economics as a particular case in the study of Islamic economics were pointed out.

This chapter targeted its introductory inquiry on the theme of the unified perspective of meta-science resting on the episteme of unity of knowledge and its applications. Such a study takes the form of a grand study in systems and cybernetics. In the existing systemic sense of process-oriented inter-variables and inter-system relationships, socio-scientific modeling is not well served by the optimal models of resource allocation and steady-state equilibriums. In the case of socio-scientific modeling with the contrary approach of process orientation, evolutionary learning becomes the true alternative.

In this chapter, we have modeled the generalized nature of the evolutionary learning model in respect of the episteme of unity of knowledge, while oppositely explaining the dichotomous nature of Kantian heteronomy in socio-scientific reasoning. Within this explanation of generality, we have exemplified the contrasting modeling results for the particular case of economics. The formalism of this latter kind of model in its generality and specificity to economic, financial, and social issues has proved the need for pervasive complementarities between the good things of life and the concomitant choices. Such choices imply an interdisciplinary holistic understanding of embedded world-systems.

This approach is contrary to premising mainstream and Islamic economics ideas on the postulate of economic rationality. This involves the axioms of scarcity of resources, self-interest, methodological individualism, full information, static preferences, marginal substitutions, and competition models of mainstream economic theory in particular and in scientific reasoning in general, as exemplified by the Kantian principle of heteronomy (Kant, 1949).

On the other hand, the repetitive continuity in epistemic evolution across processes of learning in terms of unity of knowledge of the monotheistic ontological foundation establishes that meta-scientific reasoning. It upholds circular continuity between deductive and inductive reasoning as the unified reality. It integrates the normative and positive epistemological methodologies, and bridges between *noumenon* and phenomenon in comprehensive phenomenological thought. The emergence of the episteme of unity of knowledge and its relationship with the details of the world-system establish higher levels of ethical values and economic efficiency of the process-oriented models of unity of knowledge in the evolutionary learning field across continuums.

The process of ethics and economics forming ethico-economics as a significant field of heterodox economic reasoning arising from the epistemic foundations of organic unity of knowledge will now be carried forward.

Notes

1 Also compound functions defined on $U \cap (T,F) \subset (\Omega,S)$ comply with the stated property here. Such compound functions are monotonic transformations of given functional relations. Together, they represent simulacra of simulated forms.

2 $I.\theta = f(x(\theta))$ is written in detail as follows. I denotes the identity matrix. Bold symbols are corresponding vectors and matrices.

$$1 \; 0...0 \; \theta_1 = \theta_1 = f_1(x(\theta_1)) \text{ and all monotonic functional evolutions, such as}$$
$$\theta = \{\theta_1, \theta_2, \theta_3, ...\theta_n\}$$
$$0 \; 1...0 \; * \; \theta_2 = \theta_2 = f_2(x(\theta_2)) \quad x(\theta_1) = \{x_{11}, x_{12}, x_{13}, ..., x_{1n1}\}(\theta_1)$$
$$........ \quad . \quad ....$$
$$0 \; .... \; 1\theta_n = \theta_n = f_n(x(\theta_n))x(\theta_n = \{x_{n1,1}, x_{n,12}, x_{n1,3}, ..., x_{n1,n1}\}(\theta_n)$$
$$(f \bullet g \bullet h \bullet ....)(x(\theta))$$

3 *Qur'an* (36:36): "Exalted is He who created all pairs – from what the earth grows and from themselves and from that which they do not know."

4 The use of the "knowledge-induced vector" results from the ethical integration of the monetary, financial, and real-economy sectors that comes about by the continuous mobilization of financial resources to link up the monetary and real economy in the good things of life. In this matrix of circular causal interrelations, the interest rate is a deterrent to resource mobilization; trade in the good things of life is the catalyst.

5 Note however, that the θ-variable is not a vector in this vector of $x(\theta)$-variables. That is because average ordinal values of the θ-variable apply for each column of data values for the $x(\theta)$-vector. Such sequences of $x(\theta)$-vector values could, over time, be regions, projects, etc. The column-wise θ-values generated as ranks assigned as importance of the values of the variables are averaged by row to obtain the final values of the θ-variables corresponding to the variables. These θ-values can then be further studied to obtain institutional and collegial acceptance and revisions of the calculated θ-values. Such final column θ-values are used in the wellbeing evaluation exercise.

References

Barrow, J.D. (1990). "Laws," in *Theories of Everything: The Quest for Ultimate Explanation*, Oxford: Oxford University Press, pp. 12–30.

Bhaskar, R. (2002). *Reflections on Meta-reality, Transcendence, Emancipation and Everyday Life*, New Delhi: Sage Foundation, p. 146.

Carnap, R. (1966). "Kant's synthetic a priori," in Gardner, M. (ed.), *Philosophical Foundations of Physics*, New York: Basic Books.

Choudhury, M.A. (2006). "Evolutionary equilibrium in learning spaces of unity of knowledge," *Middle East Business and Economic Review*, 18, 2.

Choudhury, M.A. (2013). "Complexity and endogeneity in economic methodology," *Kybernetes: International Journal of Cybernetics, Systems, and Management Science*, 42, 2: 226–240.

Choudhury, M.A. and Zaman, S.I. (2006). "Learning sets and topologies," *Kybernetes: International Journal of Systems and Cybernetics*, 35, 7.

Edel, A. (1970, reprint). "Science and the structure of ethics," in Neurath, O., Carnap, R., and Morris, C. (eds.), *Foundations of the Unity of Science: Vol. II*, Chicago, IL: University of Chicago Press, pp. 1–9, 273–378.

Einstein, A. (1960). "The laws of science and the laws of ethics," in *Lectures in Physics*, New York: Philosophical Library.

Georgescu-Roegen, N. (1981). *The Entropy Law and the Economic Process*, Cambridge, MA: Harvard University Press.

Gruber, T.R. (1993). "A translation approach to portable ontologies," *Knowledge Acquisition*, 5, 2: 199–200.

Howard, D. (1985). "From transcendental to originary philosophy," in *From Marx to Kant*, Albany, NY: State University of New York Press.

Husserl, E. (1965). *The Crisis of European Sciences and Transcendental Phenomenology: An Introduction to Phenomenological Philosophy*, trans. Carr, D., Boston, MA: Northwestern University Press.

Kant, I. (1949). *The Philosophy of Kant*, Friedrich, C.J., (ed.), New York: Modern Library.

Kant, I. (1963). "Natural religion: Prayer," in *Kant's Lectures on Ethics*, trans. Infeld, I., Indianapolis, IN: Hackett.

Maddox, I.J. (1970). *Elements of Functional Analysis*, Cambridge: Cambridge University Press.

Mankiw, G. (2003). *Macroeconomics*, New York: Worth.

Myrdal, G. (1958a). "The logical crux of all science," in Streeten, P. (ed.), *Value in Social Theory: A Selection of Essays on Methodology by Gunnar Myrdal*, New York: Harper & Brothers, pp. 231–236.

Myrdal, G. (1958b). "The principle of cumulation," in Streeten, P. (ed.), *Value in Social Theory: A Selection of Essays on Methodology by Gunnar Myrdal*, New York: Harper & Brothers, pp. 198–205.

Nelson, R.R. and Winter, S.G. (1982). *An Evolutionary Theory of Economic Change*, Cambridge, MA: Belknap Press of the Harvard University Press.

Nikaido, H. (1989). "Fixed Point Theorems," in Eatwell, J., Milgate, M. and Newman. P. (eds.), *New Palgrave: General Equilibrium*, New York: W.W. Norton, pp. 139–144.

Popper, K. (2004). *The Logic of Scientific Discovery*, London: Routledge.

Rucker, R. (1983). "The one and the many," in *Infinity and the Mind: The Science and Philosophy of the Infinite*, New York: Bantam Books.

Solow, R. (1980). *Growth Theory: An Exposition*. Oxford: Oxford University Press.

Appendix

Event, Continuity, and Continuum

The continuous processes of interaction, integration, and evolutionary learning (IIE) in respect of the monotheistic law of unity of knowledge establish three factors simultaneously. The first is the occurrence of what we will now define as *Event* in the knowledge, space, and time dimensions. The occurrence of events happens in *continuity res cogitans* and *res extensa* across the organically complemented domains of systems. This is the meaning of *Continuums* and the function of

Continuity across continuums. Consequently, the processes of historicism as evolutionary learning in respect of the monotheistic law of unity of knowledge reflect the interrelations between Event, Continuity, and Continuums.

We define an Event occurring in knowledge, space, and time dimensions by the symbol $E(\theta\in(\Omega,S), x(\theta), t(\theta))$ and its transformations. One notes that the sole cause of all causations in the phenomenology of the cognized and observed world is knowledge, which induces observed occurrences in space—that is, the occurrence of $\{x(\theta)\}$. The nature of $\{x(\theta)\}$ is of a mathematical kind. Thus $\{x(\theta)\}$ can be vectors, matrices, tensors, and higher transforms of such mathematical categories. It is also noted that the primacy of knowledge arising from the monotheistic law of unity of knowledge, there not being any other ontological source for unity of knowledge that annuls heteronomy in reasoning, causes time to be a moment of recording events. Yet an event is caused primarily by the induction of knowledge arising from the primal ontology of the monotheistic law of unity of knowledge. Thereby, time is induced by knowledge, such as $t(\theta)$. This kind of functional relationship between the primacy of knowledge and the occurrence of a spatial entity at a moment of time also implies that, in the sense of continuity over the domain of continuum, the components of knowledge, space, and time occur simultaneously, once each of these entities is induced by the monotheistic law of unity of knowledge (Choudhury, 2013).

Einstein (1960) referred to light as the primal cause of events in his principle of simultaneity. We argue instead that the universe fails to have an anthropic consciousness in the absence of its reasoned comprehension. Otherwise, in the absence of the primacy of knowledge, our observations would deflect themselves into twisted observations. The multiverse would be subjected continuously to ad hoc errors in observations. The consequence would be failure to know and interpret the universe. The universe would then be uncharted and confused at every point of its trajectory of history. The bewildering consequence is, then, to toss the multiverse into a murky space–time structure of confusion and speculation. Light itself, treated as Einstein's primal ontology, becomes one such phenomenological cosmic confusion. The universe loses its exactness of meaning in space–time to speculation—although the probabilistic nature of the universe abides.

The *Qur'an* (2:30–34) declares that knowledge was firstly bestowed on Adam to make him recognize the meanings and names of existences. This experience then carried on in the history of knowledge-induced events thereafter:

> And [mention, O Muhammad], when your Lord said to the angels, "Indeed, I will make upon the earth a successive authority." They said, "Will You place upon it one who causes corruption therein and sheds blood, while we declare Your praise and sanctify You?" Allah said, "Indeed, I know that which you do not know." And He taught Adam the names – all of them. Then He showed them to the angels and said, "Inform Me of the names of these, if you are truthful." They said, "Exalted are You; we have no knowledge except what You have taught us. Indeed, it is You who is the Knowing, the Wise." He said, "O Adam, inform them of their names." And when he had informed them of their names,

He said, "Did I not tell you that I know the unseen [aspects] of the heavens and the earth? And I know what you reveal and what you have concealed."

With regard to the finality of the knowledge, space, and time dimensions, the *Qur'an* (65:12) declares that God has created as many dimensions under the earth as above the earth:

> God is He Who created seven Firmaments and of the earth a similar number. Through the midst of them (all) descends His Command; that ye may know that God has power over all things and that God comprehends all things in (His) Knowledge.

Perhaps it was the confusion caused by the parallax of events in space–time in the absence of the primacy of the monotheistic unity of knowledge that left behind the great divide between relativity physics and quantum physics; between the large-scale universe and the small-scale universe—causing thereby the *problematique* of divergence to know unity of the entire world-system in its generality and particulars by a single theory of universal reality. Such an emergent *problematique* of science is equivalent to interpreting the multiverse from two divergent viewpoints of physics. Until today, such a divergence has not unified and converged (Hawking, 1980). In the end, as it stands today, we see dichotomies in the scientific understanding of reality caused by the dualism of reasoning and observation in the socio-scientific universe.

In the Islamic world, too, the same *problematique* has been assumed in the misunderstanding of Islamic law in terms of its purpose and objective, referred to as *maqasid as-shari'ah*. The error of the scholars in their ignorance of the methodology of the monotheistic law of unity of knowledge has survived in the Islamic tradition. The functional methodology of the divine law as the *sui generis* of all events *res cogitans* and *res extensa* did not dawn on contemporary Islamic scholars. Yet it is the divine law of oneness that overarches all events between the heavens and the earth. The divine law alone explains this diversity of being and becoming by the sole evidence of unity of knowledge. This is the ultimate sign of God in the order and scheme of "everything." Instead, Islamic scholars annulled the treatment of the cosmological and related laws out of *maqasid as-shari'ah*. They endowed it simply with the law of worldly affairs (*muamalat*). This is definitely not the implication of the meta-scientific, methodological worldview of the monotheistic law.

An example would suggest how vastly different is the understanding of the phenomenological reality of the multiverse between the nature of simultaneity of occurrence of events and cause with and without the primal ontology of the monotheistic law. Abandonment of the monotheistic origin of knowledge in the knowledge, space, and time multiverse, or its oblivion, continues to cause heteronomy in the reasoning and understanding of the unity of the multiverse. This conveys the meaning of organic unity across the nexus of systems. The Islamic world, along with its traditional way of intellection and its subjection by various enforcing institutions governing the conduct of intellection, failed in its drowned parallax of reasoning and novelty. Equally, Muslim intellection today could not offer anything original either to itself or to the world of learning. It could not save the heteronomous ways of thinking, reasoning, cognizing, and observing by the primal ontology of monotheistic law of unity of knowledge and its induction of "everything." This would have marked the rise of meta-science.

Chittick (1989) notes the words of Ibn al-Arabi in this regard:

> The first way is by way of unveiling. It is an incontrovertible knowledge which is actualized through unveiling and which man finds in himself. He receives no obfuscation along with it and is not able to repel it. . . . The second way is the way of reflection and reasoning (*istidlal*) through rational demonstration (*burhan 'aqli*). This way is lower than the first way, since he who bases his consideration upon proof can be visited by obfuscations which detract from his proof, and only with difficulty can he remove them.

Meta-scientific formalism

Finally, we now embody the multiverse of meta-science in the knowledge, space, and time dimensions according to the principle of simultaneity between these elements. The result is the unified and perfectly anthropic meaning of events and history *res cogitans* and *res extensa*. Hawking and Mlodinow (2010: 80) write in this regard:

> Feynman showed that, for a general system, the probability of any observation is constructed from all the possible histories that could have led to that observation. Because of that his method is called the "sum over histories" or "alternative histories" formulation of quantum physics.

The principle of simultaneity between Event, Continuity, and Continuum can now be formalized. Continuity is usually defined as $[E(z) - E(z^*)] \leq \delta$, such that $(z-z^*) \leq \varepsilon$. (δ,ε) are indefinitely small, arbitrary positive numbers.

According to our definition of *Continuity* in terms of evolutionary learning without steady-state equilibrium points and optimum, $\delta_1 < [E(z) - E(z^*)] < \delta_2$, such that $\varepsilon_1 < (z-z^*) < \varepsilon_2$, with δ_1, δ_2, ε_1, ε_2 as positive, but not indefinitely small.

Continuum is defined in our case as $\delta_1(\theta) < [E(z) - E(z^*)] < \delta_2(\theta)$, such that $\varepsilon_1(\theta) < (z-z^*) < \varepsilon_2(\theta)$ over all $\{x(i),t(\theta)\}$ in space–time induced by unity of knowledge.

Because of limiting points existing only around neighborhoods of events along the trajectory of history, there are definable transformations of such points in the same neighborhoods, denoted by $f(.)$. It can then be written as $(d/d\theta)f(E(\theta,x(\theta),t(\theta)) > 0$, for every $\theta \in (\Omega,S)$ and every $\{x(\theta),t(\theta)\}$. This is the property of the historical trajectory wherein event and continuity over continuums occur simultaneously.

The words *continuity across continuums* imply that the entire space–time structure of the multiverse, including cognition and spatiality, is spanned by the primal ontology (Ω,S), such that $\theta \in (\Omega,S)$. The limiting point not being in steady-state, it will not have a supremum in the upper limit (Debreu, 1959).

With the above definitions in place, the design of the world-system via the nexus of IIE learning between the diversity of sub-systems can be encapsulated as follows:

$$\text{System nexus} = \int_{\theta} (\cup_i \cap_j)_s (f_s(E(.))) d\theta,$$

with $(d/d\theta)f(E(\theta,x(\theta),t(\theta)) > 0$ signifying evolutionary learning for every $\theta \in (\Omega, S)$ and for every $\{x(\theta),t(\theta)\}$, where

  i denotes number of interaction

  j denotes number of integration

  f_s are transforms on various systems, such as wellbeing functions.

The embedding of θ in the components of the variables is a conceptual matter as of now. Its actual measured and empirically functional nature will be explained later on in the empirical part of this book.

References

Chittick, W.C. (1989). *Sufi Path of Knowledge*, Albany, NY: State University of New York Press.

Choudhury, M.A. (2013). "The *qur'anic* universe in knowledge, time and space with a reference to matrix game in Islamic behavioural financial decision-making," *Philosophical Papers and Reviews*, 4, 2.

Debreu, G. (1959). *Theory of Value: An Axiomatic Analysis of Economic Equilibrium*, New York: John Wiley.

Einstein, A. (1960). *Relativity: The Special and the General Theory*, London: Methuen.

Hawking, S.W. (1980). *Is the End in Sight for Theoretical Physics?* Cambridge: Cambridge University Press.

Hawking, S.W. and Mlodinow, L. (2010). "Alternative histories," in *The Grand Design*, London: Transworld, pp. 80–82.

3 Filters of heterodox economic thought

Encompassing socio-scientific heterodoxy: the monotheistic methodology of consilience

Chapter 2 introduced the theme of the possible extension of science into the domain of monotheistic analytical law. In this theory, we include the study of economics as a science like any other intellectual enterprise in the wider field of interactive, integrative, and evolutionary (IIE) learning. The resulting society then could be seen as the conglomeration of the global accord across science and society through the path of moral and ethical law (Choucri and North, 1995; Choudhury, 2007)—the monotheistic law of unity of knowledge. Yet this is a new approach. This perspective on religion, science, and economics has not been understood in the history of economic thought or science. This is repeated despite the confusion around the current experiment in Islamic economics, the Bishops' Encycle concerning the state of the North American economy, the renaissance of social thought in Weber (Mommsen, 1989), and, earlier still, among the physiocratic and schoolmen's thinking on the role of the divine law in the social world (Schumpeter, 1968). All such trends of thought have now almost disappeared, leaving behind only the remnant of a disinherited way of social thinking.

What happened at this threshold of intellectual history was the severance of religion by way of heteronomy in the scientific *problematique*, and the failure to construct the methodology of meta-science in the monotheistic analytical and applied worldview. In our work, the field of heterodox economics finds its due place in the field of socio-scientific investigation. Within this intellection, the point is raised that the multidimensional methodology embracing the interaction between science, society, economics, and religion in a unique and universal way is the pressing need of the new worldview. The methodological nature of such a new worldview is the realm of intellectual heterodoxy.

The field of heterodox economic thought takes its meaning within socio-scientific theory and applications encompassed by the emerging worldview of heterodoxy, which is premised on the worldview of monotheistic meta-science. Within this critical investigation, both mainstream economic thought and the existing study of Islamic economics are critically evaluated.

By "heterodox economic thought" we do not mean the restructuring of various economic doctrines that were presented in the history of economic thought.

The heterodox methodology presented here is not oppositional. It is wholly epistemological in substance, and is premised on the methodologically established universal and unique nature of the socio-scientific heterodox worldview. The emergent intellection along the socio-scientific path is left open to argumentation and practicality. Yet this is not a halfway meeting point for the sake of apologetic appeasement between the mainstream and the heterodox. It is, as King (2013: 4) writes: "The task of building a comprehensive and totally self-contained heterodox economics, which is not defined in negative, oppositional terms or as a dual to mainstream economics but as a positive alternative to it."

Pointing out the scope of heterodox economic theory, Lee and Lavoie (2013: 106) continue, noting that:

> Heterodox economics is a specific term, like classical political economy or neoclassical economics, that refers to a particular group of contemporary theories aimed at explaining the social provisioning process, the economic policy recommendations predicted on the theories, and to a community of economists engaged in this theoretical and applied scientific activity.

Post-Keynesianism as heterodox economic thought

Post-Keysianism is thought to be a study of economic uncertainty, using Keynes's theory of subjective probability. Yet many of the neoclassical themes, such as that of rational economic behavior, have been retained. This approach has marked Keynesian aggregate analysis. In this theory, Keynes extended aggregate preference-making behavior to rational choice, to replace the subjective probability of the occurrence of economic events. Keynes always thought that the economic universe would otherwise remain incommensurate in the presence of its multitude of unknowns (O'Donnell, 1989). Also, Keynes applied the neoclassical economic theory of production function to economic growth. He continued by depending on constant returns to scale production, the neoclassical characterization of optimal economic growth, and the nature of equilibrium markets, revenue, and cost identity. Keynes was indeed a thinker in the marginalist tradition (Dasgupta, 1987). Keynes's economic contribution comprised the field of aggregate analysis by a nonlinear methodical approach that was independent of any reliance upon microeconomic preferences. In post-Keynesianism, we continue to see the rift between monetarism and Keynesianism concerning the integration of monetary and fiscal policies. In this regard, Blaug (1993: 29) wrote: "The great debate between Keynesians and monetarists over the respective potency of spending and monetary policies has divided the economic profession, accumulating what is by now a simply enormous literature."

Economic heterodoxy is the area comprising the emergence of non-neoclassical economic and mainstream economic ideas. Neoclassicism is orthodoxy as the science of rational choice. Mainstream economics is the sociology of economics. It embraces the study of multifarious problems involving an admixture of economic thought (Dequech, 2012). Heterodox economics, by and large, is a critique of economic thought and the emergence of economic reasoning based on fresh epistemology and critical realism (*Erasmus Journal for Philosophy and Economics*, 2009). Yet heterodox economics has not been able to establish its distinctive theory and applications.

The argument we carry forward from the predicted nature of socio-scientific meta-science explained in earlier chapters and throughout this book concerns the missing place of the foundational ontological premise that can extend the domain of unity of knowledge. This work will characterize the massive change in the framework of consilience towards the monotheistic law and its induction and applications in socio-scientific thought.

On the philosophical front, Lawson's (*Erasmus Journal*, 2009) agreement with, or critique of, Bhaskar's meta-reality idea remains a speculative ontology. There is no substantive methodological functionalism arising from such foundations to formalize and apply to socio-economic reasoning. An example of this error is seen in the continuation of the a priori and a posteriori heteronomy of the Kantian genre that was discussed in the previous chapters. Thereby, the *problematique* of heteronomy vis-à-vis dualism and antinomy in prevalent scientific reasoning fails to integrate the deductive reasoning with the inductive reasoning in their continuous rounds of inter-causality. Consequently, a critique of neoclassical axioms such as marginalist substitution, opportunity cost, optimization as functional criterion, and the establishment of an endogenous unitary methodology embedding ethics, religion, society, and economics could not be engendered into a science of consilience.

The question, then, is: What can such an ontological search be other than the substantively explanatory premise of the systemic unity of knowledge, which is to be found in the methodological proof of the universality and uniqueness of the primal ontology of monotheistic law? Like the one-dimensional man, so also the replicated one-dimensional socio-scientific order with economics as particularity could not be grounded on any specific theory that would remain devoid of the cost of capital—and in ethico-economics could explain morality and ethics as endogenous phenomenon.

Yet invoking the monotheistic law of unity of knowledge and the induced world-system does not present a study in dogmatism. Contrarily, the dogmatism of God is thoroughly annulled by the establishment of the meta-science of the extended domain of explanation, formalism, and application (Choudhury, 2014). Therein lies the unification of reason between a priori and a posteriori, and between deductive and inductive, *noumenon* and phenomenon. The emergent nature of rigorous explanation by means of the mathematical topology of a relational, yet open and unbounded, supercardinal universe and the primal ontology of the monotheistic unity of knowledge invokes some of the most subtle analytical areas.[1] The mathematical theories of self-referencing (Smullyan, 1992) and Fixed Point Theorems are examined in the closed, yet unbounded, universe of endogenous actions and responses. Besides, this is yet another way of understanding reflexivity in economics, finance, and history (Soros, 1998).

The analytics of evolutionary epistemology inherent in such learning universes that include the study of economics and process, order and entropy provide ideas of subjective probability, convergence, and continuity. Yet the approaches and consequences differ from Keynesian and post-Keynesian conceptions. Keynesian theory has a hidden institutional and policy-theoretic process orientation. However, the articulation of the process as the aggregation of interactive preferences arriving at combined preferences was not used. Later on, public choice theory and rational expectation theory tried to formulate a preference-based microeconomic foundation for macroeconomics (Nordhaus, 1975), but the approach was neoclassical in nature, and based on rational choice theory. This caused the approach to fall into one of those steady-state equilibrium and optimization studies of economic problems. It became benign of behavior as an explained social process (Heilbroner and Milberg, 1995). Post-Keynesianism is critical of neoclassical methodology, yet it could not establish the framework required by a non-neoclassical form of institutional economics. In the epistemological literature, the works on global society by Nitzan and Bichler (2000), and Ruggie (2003), voice their criticism, but have no methodological orientation, which is vital for neoclassical rational choice theory and for which the latter school— despite its vehement criticism—progressed in the academy (Lawson, 2012).

What is therefore required, beyond neoclassical and mainstream economics, is an absolutely new and viable epistemic foundation for studying heterodox economics in the following directions. The new theory would focus on events along the path of process orientation. It would be predictive, while examining continuous trends towards the convergence of objectivity with emergent evolutionary equilibriums. These properties remain continuously complex in nature. They defy the possibility of optimization owing to endogenous, inter-causal relations between the diverse variables of the formal generalized model and its particular applications. Such formal models would lend themselves to empirical and institutional socio-scientific applications. Contrary to current heterodox economists' criticism of the mathematical approach (Lawson, 2013), the new heterodox socio-scientific methodology would be both epistemic and analytical in nature.

Yet this emergent formalism could be mathematical or not. Such a methodological approach may be referred to as the "epistemic analytic (mathematics)" of the methodological worldview of unity of knowledge. This methodological worldview can at once explain the generality of the socio-scientific world-system and its particular sub-systems. Examples are found in economics, science, and society. The mathematics included in the "epistemic analytic (mathematical)" approach would be of the topological and logical type, barring the unnecessary use of calculus to measure and design rational choice behavior, steady-state equilibrium, and optimization.

The outlook of the methodological worldview, beyond the current theory of heterodox economics, would be analytical and formal, if not overly mathematical. It would explain the ontological basis of consilience in the scheme and order of all things (Wilson, 1998). Its complex, non-linear, and endogenous nature of multi-causal formalism between variables would be determined by the episteme of the monotheistic unity of knowledge through a discursive pattern. On the realization of such a methodological worldview devoid of religiosity, the *Qur'an* (27:64) says: "Or, Who originates creation, then repeats it, and who gives you sustenance from heaven and earth? (Can there be another) god besides *Allah*? Say, 'Bring forth your argument, if ye are telling the truth!' " Wilson (1998: 266) writes: "Science pushed too far is science arrogant. Let it keep its proper place, as the God-given gifts to understand His physical domain."

Heterodox academic thought premised on meta-science

Within the above-mentioned extended domain of socio-scientific inquiry, the epistemic path of events continuously evolves and accompanies the history of evolution by learning in unity of knowledge. Such a nexus of multi-causal relations between events and their variables is manifested as continuous occurrences in the knowledge, space, and time dimensions. Knowledge as consilience is derived from the primal ontology of the monotheistic law. Space is determined by the variables that characterize the formal order of the problems under scrutiny. Time is the recorder of occurrences of such elements governing the concept of event. It does not exist as the most essential element of being of anything as primordial. Knowledge, being primal, induces all other categories of entities. Within the context of the new design of post-heterodoxy, this book surmises the nature of evolutionary learning and the process-oriented, non-linear, and complex paths of endogenous evolution of socio-scientific forms. These attributes are derived as properties being premised on the monotheistic epistemic law of unity of knowledge.

Figures 3.1a, 3.1b, and 3.1c explain the nature of the evolutionary learning history (HH) of events $\{(E(\theta,x(\theta),t(\theta))\} \equiv \{E(\theta,x,t)[\theta]\}$ in the knowledge $\{\theta\}$, space $\{x(\theta)\}$, and time $\{t(\theta)\}$ dimensions of knowledge-induced events premised in unity of knowledge derived from the monotheistic primal ontology, which is denoted by $(\Omega \rightarrow {}_S)$.

In Figures 3.1a, 3.1b, and 3.1c, convergence towards the center of intra-systemic domains occurrs with a degree of subjective probability, as was envisaged by Keynes and carried over into post-Keynesian study. In the new post-heterodox paradigm of economics, such a convergence is subjected to evolutionary learning. Events in *HH* across evolutionary learning are caused by, and in turn affect, the subsequent evolutionary events as defined by inter-variable and inter-system, multi-causal relations. The emerging *HH* paths characterizing events of institutional and real economic change make it impossible for any event to avoid subjective probability. The permanent existence of subjective probability along all *HH* paths is the cause and effect of imperfect and evolutionary knowledge arising ontologically from the perfect and primal source, $(\Omega \rightarrow {}_S) \equiv (\Omega,S)$.

The evolutionary trajectories *HH* are multi-causal paths that define history by the continuous reflexivity of cause and effect. While they determine future events along *HH*, they also learn from their past. Each of the events is a bundle of economy–institution perturbation points caused by the embedding of knowledge-flows $\{\theta\}$ in the endogenously interrelated variables. Such perturbations are the result of the circularly generated cause-and-effect of evolutionary learning processes and the absence of optimality and steady-state equilibriums along the *HH* path. An example of such a complex mix of knowledge-induced points will be explained later on in this work by the use of the idea of phenomenology of formalizing and learning by means of the knowledge-induced variables and entities.

We will use the *HH* path of Figure 3.1a to explain its similarity to Sraffa's (1960) resource allocation path of producing commodities by means of commodities.

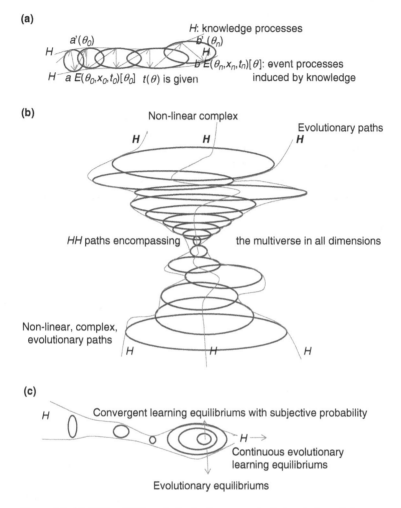

Figure 3.1 (a) $\{E(\theta,x,t)[\theta]\}$ evolution by inter-causal relations in knowledge, space, and time dimensions; (b) non-linear, complex, and endogenous evolutionary learning paths *HH* in multiverse; (c) cross-sectional view of evolutionary learning equilibriums with subjective probability

We will further extend Sraffa's methodology by the substantive nature of knowledge-induced relations determined by the primal ontology of the monotheistic unity of knowledge. The result is a formalism of the socio-scientific case of epistemic analysis. The endnotes explain this mathematical formalism.

Unlike the failure of post-Keynesianism to formalize a robust theory of organizational behavior and of institutional policy-making processes, the non-linear complex *HH* paths explain how such processes are actively used to explain the effects of multi-causal interrelations between the variables and entities concerned.

Furthermore, evolutionary learning, despite being premised on the foundational monotheistic primal ontology of unity of knowledge, is not guaranteed to be a continuously smooth evolutionary path. Consequently, *HH* historical paths of the lifecycle of evolutionary learning and their effects on simultaneously induced variables and their relations are non-linear in form.

Figures 3.1a, 3.1b, and 3.1c are the principle illustrations to be used throughout this work to critically examine the selected theories of mainstream and orthodox economics. Islamic economics are included in this span of ideas and the heterodox economics of recent developments are examined. These figures, along with subsidiary ones, will be used to explain the nature of socio-scientific analysis in general and economics in particular in relation to selected economic issues. The emergent nature of heterodox economic theory will be treated within the context of meta-science, which can be studied by the "epistemic analytic (mathematics)" of the monotheistic unity of knowledge and its induction in the unified world-system.

On the topic of post-Keynesian economics and the use of the methodology introduced here and used throughout this work, the points to note are the following:

1   The emergent methodology is premised on the primal ontology of the monotheistic unity of knowledge and the epistemic derivation therefrom of the unity of the knowledge-induced world-system. The monotheistic unity of knowledge as episteme is the sole axiom of the entire socio-scientific construction. There is no other axiom, except sparing assumptions pertaining to the particular problems under study.
2   The resulting formalism arising from (1) is referred to as "epistemic analytic (mathematics)." The nature of this approach applies to complex, non-linear, and evolutionary learning processes in the absence of steady-state equilibrium and optimization.
3   Evolutionary learning equilibriums exist in the framework of the pervasive history of knowledge-induced events. The theorems arising from this enunciation will be proved.
4   According to the "epistemic analytic (mathematics)" nature of formalism that emerges, the resulting methodology constructs the scientific domain of "everything" everywhere (Barrow, 1991).

Subjective probability Keynesianism and post-Keynesianism

The specific problem to study here with respect to post-Keynesianism is to investigate the subjective probability of the convergent, yet evolutionary, learning nature of the generality and particulars of the world-system addressed by the epistemic methodology, the monotheistic unity of knowledge.

Subjective probability of the occurrence of an event is connected to the perception of the observer, not to the measured probability of the event called risk. An example is the formation of preference in choices of events. Mainstream and orthodox economics consider preferences to be assigned by rational choices, and hence remaining datum to be assigned by particular choices. Consequently, a preference is well determined. It thereby gives rise to a deterministic event situation. Subjective probability, on the other hand, argues that preferences are not datum. They vary according to the perceptions of the choice-maker regarding the nature, information, and positioning of the event. For instance, how close is the attainment of the full-employment level of real output in the Keynesian general equilibrium model? The value for this indicator may be assigned, as Keynes did, to a 3 percent unemployment rate. Yet it cannot be fully determined: In the long run of expectations that change preferences continuously, we are all dead. The question of the decision-maker's perception, information, and expectations concerning uncertainty is yet another set of problems upon which subjective probability rules.

Subjective probability is thereby a deeply epistemological problem concerning uncertainty, information asymmetry, and expectations applying to the determination of events. Yet Keynes (1973), Ramsey (1928), and Hicks (1979) launched a systemic study of this problem of subjective probability. At the end, in order to make economic problems solvable, these sages had to assign the assumption of rationality to the choice-maker's predictive behavior. This was despite the fact that the substantive part of the economic and social universe, and, it can be argued, of the multiverse, by its complexity, remains unknown. Subjective probability cannot therefore be measured, estimated, and assigned. Subjective probability denotes the chance of the occurrence of an event based on the epistemologically assumed relationship between observers and observed events relating to the problem under study. Subjective probability is conditional and based on the degree of belief in and information about the occurrence of an event, given the occurrence of other contingent events, with lags.

The theme of subjective probability remains inherent in post-Keynesian methodology. For instance, the investment decision endowed institutionally would be bedevilled by the missing information on expectations of the future and by reactions to such various expectations at the present time of decision-making. The subjective probability associated with such information gaps regarding future expectations would defy the exact attainment of the full-employment equilibrium. Consequently, the position of the general economic equilibrium will forever be denied. Expectations and measured probability are simply based on a predicted epistemological notion of rationality in the perceiver and his or her matching of this with the state of the perceived event in all states of nature.

The entire economic epistemology is affected by the lack of measurement of subjective probability and the impossibility of accurately explaining the economic and social universe in the presence of subjective probability. Post-Keynesianism recognizes such problems that are associated with the measurement and valuation of events by its inclusion of the studies of new institutionalism theory and evolutionary economic episteme. The problem of failing to read and predict the state of future economic trends has caused continuing uncertainty in the face of financial crisis. This now shows no signs of abating without immense financial rescue packages provided by the International Monetary Fund (as seen with the Greek debt in 2015).

Addressing the problem of subjective probability by the monotheistic methodology of unity of knowledge

The evolutionary learning *HH* path is characterized by the following properties: the continuity of the inter-causal relationship of unity of knowledge, also referred to as participation and complementarities; non-linearity, complexity, pervasive inter-variable endogenous relationships in the formal model; and convergence, yet tangential evolution, around temporary evolutionary equilibrium points. Evolutionary dynamics never allow equilibrium points to arrive at steady-state points. These properties are analytically derived from the sole, primal ontological axiom of the monotheistic unity of knowledge acting on the world-system in its generality and, within this, in particular sub-systems.

The analytical deduction concerning evolutionary equilibrium points is that either within or across processes over knowledge, space, and time dimensions, there are no steady-state equilibria and optimal states of resource allocation. Consequently, the subjective probability of attaining an event at the core equilibrium point continues to exist permanently along the HH paths. Subjective probability exists permanently, and it is rational foolishness to try to measure and model the valuation of events with such a vague subjective probability measure. The conclusion from these properties of evolutionary learning equilibriums is that the evaluation of objective criterion functions can be simulated at convergent, but evolutionary, equilibrium points with only a degree of certainty. The uncertainty denoted by subjective probability will exist permanently, yet it can be narrowed down to the degree of intensity gained in knowledge and information. This occurs through increasing degrees of complementarity between multi-causal variables in the "epistemic analytic (mathematical)" models pertaining to the problems under study.

The assumption of rational choice is eliminated. The generalized and particular evolutionary equilibrium models are calculated within the limits of an unavoidable degree of uncertainty, which is governed by the corresponding subjective probability of events of uncertainty. Yet the inherent expectation connected with the event under subjective probability is positively subjected to the intensity of evolutionary learning in and across systemic processes. The imminent systemic nature of learning processes is set in motion by the properties of pervasive inter-variable complementarities, which are derived in accordance with the episteme of the monotheistic unity of knowledge that causes the properties of interaction, integration, and evolutionary learning all along the trajectory of history HH path. The primal ontology exists as the supercardinal topological representation of the monotheistic law. It is topologically mapped in bits by the well-defined mapping denoted by "S" onto the epistemic and explanatory world-system of unity of knowledge and unity of being and becoming (Sztompka, 1991).

The post-Keynesian quandary—with its elements of uncertainty, subjective probability, processes and policies in institutionalism, incomplete information, and the datum of preferences in forming expectations—is resolved by the methodological approach of the monotheistic episteme. The multiverse remains an incomplete picture short of the complete one. The latter is unattainable, yet it represents the bedrock of relational epistemology and multi-causality generated by knowledge-flows as these arise intensively from the primal ontology of the monotheistic unity of knowledge in relation to the entire world-system. In this regard, the *Qur'an* (72:26) declares: "He (alone) knows the Unseen, nor does He make any one acquainted with His Mysteries."

Formalism regarding the evolutionary learning space of the monotheistic unity of knowledge

The underlying the monotheistic formalism of unity of knowledge and the unified world-system is represented in expression (3.1). There are many details involved that will be covered as we proceed.

$$(\Omega \to s) \to \{\theta\} \to \{E(\theta, x, t)[\theta]\} \to \text{Continuity in knowledge,} \\ \text{space, and time dimensions} \tag{3.1}$$

Evaluate $W(x(\theta))$ subject to the formal interrelations between variables in the structural relations.

Explanation

$(\Omega \to s)$ denotes the primal ontology, with Ω denoting the monotheistic super-cardinal law of unity of knowledge; "S" denotes the process of mapping to derive knowledge from Ω in bits continuously.

Thus $\{\theta\}$ denotes the worldly knowledge derived from the primal ontology in terms of comprehending and applying it to the construction of diversity of things in the framework of unity of knowledge.

Moreover, $\{E(\theta,x,t)[\theta]\}$ denotes the diversity of events; each is characterized by formal relations between $\{(\theta,x,t)[\theta]\}$, leading to the evaluation of the objective function—say, of wellbeing—that represents the evaluated degrees of complementarity between the variables.

An evaluation of the wellbeing function, comprising estimation followed by simulation in relation to inter-variable complementarities, involves a series of non-linear, but complex, functions with changeable coefficients as they are required, explainable, and institutionally discoursed for acceptability. This exercise is done for each process and across evolutionary learning processes.

Evolutionary learning processes continue by referring to the primal ontology every time, at the beginning of each process.

The evolutionary learning processes of unity of knowledge thereby continue repetitively.

The string expression (3.1) summarizes the "epistemic analytic (mathematics)" overview of the model of unity of knowledge, which will be analyzed.

Post-Keynesian implications of the monotheistic methodology of unity of know-ledge and the world-system in general and in particular are immense. Issues of uncertainty, expectation, information, the subjective probability of events, and the valuation of assets are addressed in substantive details at the event points. So also are issues of institutionalism and a new way of aggregation of preferences across evolutionary learning processes. A new form of model for asset valuation—called the overlapping generation model with polity–market interaction and knowledge-induced endogenous inter-variable relations—is made possible. Some of these details will be taken up through the course of this book.

Post-Keynesian issues regarding valuation of the investment function

The problems of Keynesian and post-Keynesian economics associated with uncertainty, expectation, aggregation, information, and the general economic equilibrium are reflected in the macroeconomic specification of the investment function (Lawson and Peseran, 2009). Uncertainty and expectation are related to the issue of subjective probability, which, although unavoidable epistemologically, is forced into measurement by assuming rational expectation behavior. The logical result is the absence of value per se associated with imprecision in valuation and information. This lack of information in the face of uncertainty, expectation, and datum of preference function under the assumption of rational expectation theory causes learning equilibriums to evolve continuously. This, though, is not formalized in Keynesianism and post-Keynesianism. The missing characteristics cause errors when reading the full-employment level of equilibrium output and factor employment. The result, then, is the non-predictive and imprecise nature of the entire theory of general economic equilibrium in contrast to an essentially evolutionary system equilibrium that ought to be developed as methodology for application (Hunt, 1979). Such a possibility, on the other hand, is granted by the monotheistic methodology of unity of knowledge explained by means of the imminent evolutionary model, which allows for subjective probability in the pervasively probabilistic world-system that emerges, causing deflected convergences around learning equilibriums.

While resulting in the probabilistic and assumption problems of the general economic equilibrium model, the effects of such imprecision are spread out over all sectors of the economy. Thus the monetary and spending sectors do not yield the expected theoretical general equilibriums of the Keynesian type. Blaug (1993) has long marked such discrepancies in economic arguments between monetarism and Keynesianism. We surmise that the same is true of post-Keynesianism because of its missing methodology and formulation of an evolutionary general economic equilibrium model that would integrate opposing arguments and cast light on a more precise and predictable model.

The failed predictability property of a desired post-Keynesian model, with its evolutionary learning consequences of deflected convergences of equilibrium points and the allowance of subjective probability in the emergent valuation, has an effect on the macroeconomic investment function. For instance, in the simplified form of the investment function, let the included variables be output, interest rate, profit rate, inflation rate, and expectations on these. We will treat preferences differently in the two cases: First, we treat preferences as datum, as in rational expectations theory; second, we treat dynamic preferences as evolutionary learning equilibriums. In the case of evolutionary economics with deflected convergences around evolutionary equilibriums, the preferences are aggregated over interactions, leading to integration or consensus. Thereafter, interactions and integration lead into dynamic convergences in every variable around their individual evolutionary equilibrium neighborhoods. The convergence coefficients—like Koych coefficients—become knowledge-induced. The aggregation of dynamic preferences includes dynamic preferences of investors formed in response to interactive influences of markets, institutions, and other agents. Consequently, rational expectations theory cannot be used to generate preferences as datum over time. Neither variations in knowledge nor knowledge-induced variables depend upon time; only knowledge remains the primal determiner of events. Time follows as recorder, without having any means to generate causality. Aggregate preferences on investment decisions are reflected by the interaction between investors, markets, other agents, institutions, and polities, involving a broader domain of cultural and social considerations. In such ways, the conscious investment decision is made in the respective choices induced by knowledge. Such choices were denoted by the knowledge-induced vector $\{x_s(\theta), t(\theta); \wp(\theta)=(U_j \cap_k)_s \wp_{jk}^s)(\theta)\}$.[2] These form conscious choices and the interactive domain, including markets, forms the conscious institution leading to the integration of preferences. An example of such a case is the investment in environmental ecology, and human and social ecology, with the variables $\{x_s(\theta), t(\theta); \wp(\theta)=(U_j \cap_k)_s \wp_{jk}^s)(\theta)\}$ bearing the attributes of social capital (Hawley, 1986). Thus, "*j*" denotes the number of interactions; *k* denotes integration; *s* denotes the systems over which interaction and integration proceed, such as investors, markets, polities, and institutions.

In conjunction with the Keynesian and post-Keynesian problem of uncertainty of determination of the investment function, post-monetarist implications can also be invoked. Now, the evolutionary learning possibility of the general economic equilibriums in its various sectors can be passed on to the unsteady nature of the intersection between aggregate supply and aggregate demand curves, and thereby between the *IS* and *LM* curves. The consequence, finally, is a fully uncertain and unpredictable framework of general economic equilibrium involving all sectors.

The implications are serious, for such a state of economic theory subjects the project of economic theory to the question of lack of predictability and sound decision-making. McCloskey (1985) presented his views along similar lines of questioning. With the monotheistic methodological approach to unity of knowledge, the implications are that only specific socio-scientific states need to be studied, without the need for prediction and the nicety of analytics. The "epistemic analytic (mathematics)" does not allow for any permanence of prediction except through its methodology of studying the monotheistic reality of the organic unity of knowledge of the evolutionary learning world-system in general and in particular. The "epistemic analytic (mathematics)" of the monotheistic unity of knowledge offers a vastly developed formalism for conceptualization in respect of socio-scientific processes and their application (Choudhury, 2014).

The uncertainty of prediction and the logical explanation of economics, finance, and society by means of existing theoretical approaches opens a wide gap in the attempt to stabilize the unsettled conditions of the global economic crisis. This is because once every socio-scientific sector and activity is adversely influenced by methodological uncertainty, the global management picture becomes uncharted, fuzzy, and misleading. Likewise, policy, strategy, and institutional governance are affected accordingly. The future remains unguided, except for a scientific relishing of theoretical categories. Science is pursued without human realism. This is something that the neoclassical economic school has bequeathed to the world.

Now, the same outlook is being pursued by heterodox economic theory under the variant guises of post-Keynesianism, monetarism, and their offspring. The extent of the uncertain and unpredictable path of intellection with no original epistemological idea placed at the head of a revolutionary new socio-scientific theory by a deconstruction of the general economic equilibrium theory affects all micro-activities. In the final analysis, the valuation of investment decisions, assets, financial markets, markets for goods and services in closed and open economies, and the understanding of preference aggregation are all affected by unresolvable uncertainty, while the socio-economics of consciousness and its dynamics remain unknown and distanced.

This is an epistemological failure, and it requires revolutionary, reconstructive steps to move forward for the generality of global wellbeing. It is also necessary for the emergent generalized worldview to be universal and unique, thus enabling all socio-scientific issues to be discussed with consensus and awareness (Commission on Global Governance, 1995). The epistemic beginnings of the new methodological worldview must lead the way, otherwise science would remain muddled (Bohr, 1985). The constructive basis of the epistemic worldview must be structured within its "epistemic analytical (mathematical)" formalism.[3] The explanatory basis of the emergent worldview must be discursive and factual in nature.

Heterodox economics in Piero Sraffa's tradition

The outstanding theory of the production of commodities by means of commodities of Piero Sraffa (1960) focused on the determination of value of production in terms of commodity prices, profit rates, and wages. The study involved different single industries producing different kinds of goods independently. Sraffa's simple model is outlined in note 4. In light of the intricate functions of the complex and highly interrelated nature of the economic and social world that we have inherited in recent times, it becomes evident that Sraffa's model cannot be a candidate of such interdependencies. Sraffa's model is based on the assumption that independent industries act in their own interests, as per the classical economic idea. The model does not have any explicit process, technology, and (thereby) reality for the study of the newly emerging phenomena of a conscious way of looking at economic, social, and politico-economic interrelated events. Even when Sraffa discusses systems towards the end of his book, he deconstructs the economic system into smaller sub-systems, each of which preserves the property of independence. The book is silent with regard to technology. As a classical economic adaptation of ideas, Sraffa's model is based on labor as the only explicit input of production. Consequently, the topic of joint production function, with interdependent outputs producing the final output, cannot be formalized and applied.

In the case of joint production, several outputs are produced in each process of production. Yet the equations that arise are unable to explain any degree of inter-relation between the quantities of various commodities.[4] Consequently, whether by systems of production or joint production by processes, Sraffa's equations cannot explain the much-needed complexity and endogeneity of inter-causal relations concerning various outputs and productive factors of joint production.

In the realm of heterodox economics, with new epistemic and formal practices, post-Sraffian economics ought to be reformulated in the midst of complexity and non-linearity, the inter-variable circularity of relations, and the conscious realization of ethicality in markets and institutional relations for the common good. Without such a holistic understanding of economics and social sciences, the place of these disciplines in the holistic concept of wellbeing remains null and void. Science fails encompass human meaning. Yet, in the new socio-scientific paradigm and the central role of morality and ethics within it, the monotheistic scientific place of unity of knowledge as consciousness is of ineluctable importance.

Sraffa's model can be reformulated along lines of ethical relevance (since Sraffa wanted to rejuvenate classical economic theory), to which Adam Smith contributed his ethical views of *The Theory of Moral Sentiments*. On a basic level, let the vector of quantities of commodities $(a, b, \ldots, k)$ be denoted by $(A_a, B_b, \ldots K_k)$. Let the vector of productive factors for producing the commodities be denoted by (x_1, x_2) as labor and capital inputs, respectively. Let the prices of commodities and productive factors be denoted by $(p_a, p_b, \ldots p_k, w, r)$. The quantity vectors are then converted into values as $(A_a p_a, B_b p_b, \ldots, K_k p_k, x_1 w, x_2 r)$. We consider a joint production function in the commodities and productive factors. Considering the details of organic unity of knowledge between the variables in their value form denoting the participatory and complementary nature between them, the full vector of values of commodities and productive factors is denoted by the θ-effect as $y(\theta) = (A_a p_a, B_b p_b, \ldots, K_k p_k, x_1 w, x_2 r)[\theta]$. Let the wellbeing function, $W(y(\theta))$, replace Sraffa's production function in its market context. The complete "epistemic analytical (mathematical)" model of computational general equilibrium is now written as expression (3.2). This model system is applicable via estimation and simulation of the wellbeing function. The circular causation equations as interrelations between the variables are expressions of interrelated joint production function outputs and productive factors, each in terms of the rest of the elements of the value-vector.

We write the full ethically induced computational general equilibrium model as follows:

$$\text{Evaluate } W(y(\theta)); \; y(\theta) = (A_a p_a, B_a p_a \ldots, K_k p_k, x_1 w, x_2 r)[\theta] \qquad (3.2)$$

To "Evaluate" means "estimation" followed by "simulation", which is achieved by changing the estimated coefficients as required for improving the complementary relations between the variables.

The following non-linear relations, explained further by the complexity of variable coefficients, are the constraints of the evaluation exercise of the wellbeing function:

$$A_a p_a = f_1(B_a p_a \ldots, K_k p_k, x_1 w, x_2 r, \theta) \tag{3.3}$$

$$B_a p_a = f_2(A_a p_a \ldots, K_k p_k, x_1 w, x_2 r, \theta) \tag{3.4}$$

$$K_k p_k = f_k(A_a p_a, B_b p_b \ldots, x_1 w, x_2 r, \theta) \tag{3.5}$$

$$\theta = F(A_a p_a, B_b p_b \ldots, K_k p_k, x_1 w, x_2 r) \tag{3.6}$$

Note that expression (3.6) is the "measured" form of the similar wellbeing function in expression (3.2), which is the conceptual explanation of the underlying idea of wellbeing.

The circular causation model of evaluating the social wellbeing function and Sraffa's model are distinct categories, although both are different forms of the computational general equilibrium system of relations. The circular causation relations are for the system of interrelated endogenous variables that are tested and improved for their complementarities. Inter-variable complementarities explain degrees of organic unity of knowledge attained in the system, as signified by the simulation of the estimated coefficients. Thus policy and strategic implications of estimation and simulation can be made. The objective of the circular causation model is wellbeing. It includes the joint production outputs as a representation of the organic complementarities between the variables. The same property applies to the statistical relations for productive factors. Sraffa's model is neither built upon, nor it is capable of addressing, the market process in the light of induced ethical values, as signified by consciousness (θ-value $\epsilon\ (\Omega,S)$) as the epistemic origin of unity of knowledge.

In the end, we find that, in the present times, much of the perspective, outlook, demand for complexity, and the sociology of multiple factors have together dwarfed the nature of economic theory of old. What is required now is a multidimensional, methodological approach to study complex phenomenon within the social and economic domains. Such socio-scientific investigation need not be an unnecessarily mathematical burden, as would be the case if we were using calculus as a means of quantitative intellection. Yet we cannot exclude the important place of "epistemic analytic (mathematics)" in all of this formalism, which would lead to real-world applications. The central theme of wellbeing will remain the objective criterion for the multidimensional world-system problems under investigation. Thus the rise of ethical consciousness by the monotheistic methodology of unity of knowledge becomes the permanent and indelible mark of meta-science in post-orthodoxy and the idea of heterodoxy presently held in the disciplines.

Neo-Marxism and dialectics as a mark of heterodoxy

The question looms whether post-Marxist and post-Hegelian thought is still alive in the dialectical approach to socio-scientific study in this age of heterodoxy. The return to the dialectical approach in studying evolutionary epistemology and the corresponding epistemic world-system is a fact (Campbell, 1988). Yet neither can the dialectical conception that leaves permanently open the evolutionary world-system and prescribes no other than the inductive human mind as the *sui generis* of creation yield a methodology that can ascribe objective abstraction nor can such an endless evolutionary world-system of mind and matter lead to the resolution of unsolved socio-scientific problems.

The underlying *problematique* of such rudderless charting of any issue and problem was explained in earlier chapters to be heteronomous between the a priori and a posteriori domains of reasoning, between deductive and inductive reasoning, and between *noumenon* and phenomenon. Thereby, morality and ethics remain divorced from materiality in the pursuit of socio-scientific facts: As Sztompka (1991) says, faith and fate have no place in the study of human rationalism concerning multidimensional system study. This is exactly the point that is deeply contested by the monotheistic methodological worldview of unity of knowledge and the unified world-system of morality, consciousness, mind, and matter.

According to Popper (2004), whose epistemology is dialectical, the monotheistic law of consilience would be immersed in pseudo-science. Yet we note that there is no well-defined premise of convergence of ideas for an abstraction that cannot establish a certain objective criterion. Thus history would evolve rudderless between and across diverse ideas, social systems, and socio-scientific cultures. These are all dialectical in nature, yet there is nothing more certain of predictability in them than the unsettled nature of creativity, capitalist prognosis, and historicism without bringing out any definitive purpose.[5] Consequently, the monotheistic methodology of unity of knowledge that extends the formal, explanatory, and applied vista of socio-scientific inquiry concerning abstraction, and mind and matter problems, supersedes pseudo-science. It broadens the scope of meta-scientific possibilities. Unity of knowledge is upheld. Heteronomy is eschewed.

The dialectical processes of open universe conjecture of Popper (2004), and the dialectical materialism in Marx's explanation of the historical process, open up the problem of over-determination of epistemologies of variant and contesting theories (Resnick and Wolff, 1987). The imminent Marxist model of social becoming stands upon a continuous evolution of conflict between the old and the dialectical new—the idea of antithesis and synthesis, followed by recurrence of de-synthesis. Consequently, the problem of the lack of well-defined abstraction and convergence into any predictability by ontological form is impossible for Marx. Predictability is simply imposed, such as the rise of the proletariat state from the destruction of capitalism by its inner contradictory forces. Yet such a historical scenario never happened. Marxism and socialism disappeared because of their inability to explain anything that is certain, predictable, and attainable. Note 5, at the end of this chapter, explains this fact for all such dialectical evolutionary processes that rest upon methodological individualism, atomism, or conflict, yet without any definite historical convergence to an evolved state of being. Sullivan (1989) remarks on such a failed state of neo-liberalism. Marx too, when he raised his finger against religion, considered only the European case. There is no sign in his writing that he considered the study of Islam, revolutionary thought, and historicism (Berman, 1989).

The conclusion for the heterodox age of socio-scientific thought post-Marx and post-Hegel lies in their inability to explain historical processes in alternative ways that can encompass ethical issues based on a compendium of cultural factors that over-extend the narrow space of economics and a contested society. Post-Marxism, by pursuing the Marxist tradition, is bound to sweep the historical process away from a world-system that unifies across cultures rather than dissociating it by sustained conflict.

The meta-scientific base of socio-scientific thought

The opportunity for meta-science to explain the monotheistic methodology of unity of knowledge in the age of socio-scientific heterodoxy is necessary for any prospect of unification across the sciences. Included in this idea will be the study of a heterodox theory of economics as "epistemic analytic." Ethics is again at the centerpiece of the revolutionary reconstruction of socio-scientific thought, so that that there can be a universal and unique theory of the monotheistic genre that will lay down the worldview and "epistemic analytic" of the generality of the underlying methodology. The particular case studies and applications follow the same generalized principle, apart from differences in the problems under review.

The foundation of a single method and the formalism between theoretical physics and economics as a historic scientific pursuit can be understood in the words of Hawking and Mlodinow (2010: 80). They conclude about learning (probabilistic general system) histories:

> [F]or a general system, the probability of any observation is constructed from all the possible histories that could have led to that observation. Because of that (t)his method is called the 'sum over histories' or 'alternative histories' formulation of quantum physics.

In Marxist economic methodology, we note the centerpiece given to dialectical materialism as the historical method of change towards a contra-capitalist disequilibrium theory of political economy. Marx wanted to collect all such diverse historical developments and establish a single universal theory of economics of the proletariat for world history. Yet he failed, owing to a lack of sensitivity to ethical and cultural dynamics beyond simply that economic dynamic to which he adhered.

In post-Marxist era, the question for the search and discovery of a universal and unique theory of "everything" remains vividly alive. The "epistemic analytic" pursuit in this academic venture is not futile when one can find the beginning and end of the intellectual pursuit in the unique historicism of being and becoming on the basis of the monotheistic construct of unity of knowledge.

The methodological convergence of the monotheistic genre in the fold of consilience in meta-science is found in the "epistemic analytic" formalism in its generality. This formalism is a mathematical reality in the garb of the sure reality of the multiverse. It can be applied to the generalized worldview and to its particulars, with the unification of their methods converging into the generality. The theme of morality and ethics, which is central to all vintages of the heterodox era of socio-scientific thought to address the critical realism of our age and beyond, is not to be found either in previous heterodox economic doctrines or in the present era of post-orthodoxy.

An example of this is the reality of the circular causation model of pervasively endogenous cases. These are to be found in theoretical physics, as in the case of the model of the monotheistic unity of knowledge. Hawking and Mlodinow (2010: 72) explain such compound (extensive) probability distributions of endogenous variables: "According to quantum physics, no matter how much information we obtain or how powerful our computing abilities, the outcomes of physical processes cannot be predicted with certainty because they are not *determined* with certainty." Likewise, for the case of the evolutionary learning model of historicism in consilience histories, we have extended the underlying principle of uncertainty to the knowledge-induced multiverse. These histories forever learn from the beginning to the end.

Conclusion

A brief review of the ideas comprising the history of heterodox economics up to present times showed that there is great need to re-orient socio-scientific thought in general and economics in particular by an altogether new and revolutionary worldview. The old paradigms have failed to provide the meaningful meeting ground of wellbeing and materiality as self-asserting forces that bring common good to all. Within the discipline of ethico-economics, with the endogenous role of ethics meaning consciousness by the multi-causal organic unity of knowledge, there is a pressing need for future intellectual activity and application for the benefit of the global community.

Where can such a revolutionary methodological worldview be found in order to set in motion the project of moral reformation of the world-system and the human understanding of it? The option is left open, although the critical review of socio-scientific thought presently received and existing in post-orthodoxy annuls rationalism and its offshoots as candidates. The other worldview—when developed in methodological ways and bestowed by its own "epistemic analytic"—is found to be premised on the monotheistic law of unity of knowledge and its induction of the unified world-system in general and in particular. The project would take up a rigorously elaborate exercise because of its vast socio-scientific nature of episteme, formalism, and applications.

The project of the monotheistic worldview of unity of knowledge has not attained its due socio-scientific place because of its long history of metaphysical and speculative thought. This is true both of Occidental and Islamic thought. Islamic intellectual thought has intensified in its dormant state in present days. Its state of intellectual slumber has overshadowed the Muslim mind because of its inability to derive monotheistic socio-scientific thought from the *Qur'an* and bestow it in the best form to the world of learning, old and new.

Throughout this book, the search for and discovery of the monotheistic methodological worldview as the bedrock of the most universal and unique worldview of unity of knowledge in the generality and particulars of "everything" is of primary importance. The project is a rigorous one. It involves critical examination of the entire domain of rationalism. Rationalism is the partitioned, as opposed to the unified, understanding of reality. The monotheistic methodology of unity of knowledge is the worldview premised on unity of the divine law, the ontology of being, and the episteme of continuous becoming emanating from and belonging to the nature of the monotheistic law. In addition, the project launched is rigorous and premised on the "epistemic analytic," with its applications of the elaborate model of monotheistic unity of knowledge and the world-system that emanates as unitary in the good things of life, thus rejecting the bad and the ugly.

Notes

1 A non-mathematical definition of supercardinal topology of primal ontology is this: Topology is the set of all possible subsets of relations and mappings that can be contained within it, including the null set and the universal set. Supercardinal topology is the largest possible set of the highest denumerable category that can be considered only as the universal set of creative relations of all cognitive and material worlds. Yet, by itself, this supercardinal topology cannot be caused by the latter categories. The supercardinal topology remains primal and final by the act of the creator. Thus it acquires the meaning of the primal ontology in the beginning and the end by the divine monotheistic law ordained by God to give meaning and explanation to world-systems in general and in particular. Such world-systems learn by the induction of unity of knowledge of the monotheistic law between the terminal points of the beginning and the end. The *Qur'an* (57:3) declares, regarding the terminal ontological points of being and the passage between them of becoming in unity of knowledge, in the following verses: "He is the First and the Last, the Evident and the Immanent: and He has full knowledge of all things." Because of the terminal being of existence and source of the ontological form, the end points are described as primal ontology. The nature of evolutionary learning world-systems is one of organic pairing, conveying relational epistemic via multi-causal relations conveying participation and complementarities as relational pairing of organic forms and their worldly character of mathematical transformation, which we refer to as functional ontology, making the distinction with primal ontology.

The supercardinal relationship with epistemology and functional ontologies is written as follows:

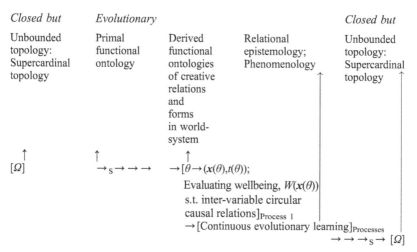

Closed but	*Evolutionary*			*Closed but*
Unbounded topology: Supercardinal topology	Primal functional ontology	Derived functional ontologies of creative relations and forms in world-system	Relational epistemology; Phenomenology $\uparrow$	Unbounded topology: Supercardinal topology $\uparrow$
$\uparrow$ [Ω]	$\uparrow$ $\to$ s $\to$ $\to$ $\to$	$\uparrow$ $\to$ [$\theta \to (x(\theta),t(\theta))$; Evaluating wellbeing, $W(x(\theta))$ s.t. inter-variable circular causal relations]Process 1 $\to$ [Continuous evolutionary learning]Processes $\to$ $\to$ $\to$ s $\to$ [Ω]		

Summarized as: $[\Omega] \to s \to$ World-system$(\theta,x(\theta),t(\theta)) \to s [\Omega]$

2 Let the investment function be denoted by

$$I(x_s(\theta),t(\theta); \wp(\theta) = \cap_s \wp_{jk^s})(\theta)) = A(\theta,t(\theta)) + \sum_s (\alpha_s x_s)[\theta,t(\theta)] + (\beta \wp)[\theta,t(\theta)]$$

where $x(\theta,t(\theta))=\{x_s(\theta,t(\theta))\}=(Y,i,r,p)[\theta,t(\theta)]$ with "Y" as output; "I" as interest rate; "r" as profit rate; and "p" as inflation rate, all induced by $(\theta,t(\theta))$. Thus (j,k) denote interactions leading to consensus (integration) in agential preferences $\{\wp_{jk^s})(\theta)\}$ aggregating to the overall dynamic preference $\wp(\theta)$, all being based on the induction of knowledge as consciousness, θ.

None of these variables can be governed by the convergent Koych coefficient owing to the influence of θ-value. Consequently, the probability limit, $plim[\theta,t(\theta)]$ $\{I(x_s(\theta),t(\theta);$ $\wp(\theta)=\cap_s \wp_{jk^s})(\theta))\}$ is indeterminate except at specific processes denoting events, $E(x_s(\theta),t(\theta); \wp(\theta)=\cap_s \wp_{jk^s})(\theta))$.

3 A theoretical, although not numerical, representation of the entire systemic nexus of organic interrelations between variables in knowledge, space, and time dimensions is this:

$$\int_{convoluted\ by\ systems} \Pi_s W_s(x_s(\theta))dx_s(\theta)=\text{Systemic nexus for each set } \{\theta, x(\theta), W_s(x(\theta))\}$$

These functions are compounded together.

4 Piero Sraffa's initial set of equations combining commodities, labor, and profit rates with market-determined prices, as in the case of classical economic theory, are as follows:

There are commodities $a, b, c, \ldots k$ produced independently by industries $A, B, \ldots, K$ in quantities $A_a, B_a, \ldots K_a$ for industry A; $A_b, B_b, \ldots K_b$ for industry B; and so on to $A_k, B_k, \ldots K_k$. The total quantities produced by the industries are denoted by $A, B, \ldots, K$, respectively. Market-determined prices of the classical vintage for the quantities $a, b, \ldots, k$ are $p_a, p_b, \ldots p_k$, respectively. The wage rate is w for quantity of labor L. The rate of profit is denoted by "*r*." Thus *p* denotes the market price of each commodity *a, b, . . . ,k*. The equations of production and exchange are given as:

$$(A_a p_a + B_a p_b + \ldots K_a p_k)(1 + r) + L_a w = A p_a$$
$$(A_b p_a + B_b p_b + \ldots K_b p_k)(1 + r) + L_b w = A p_b$$
$$- - - - - - - - - - - - - - - - - -$$
$$(A_k p_a + B_k p_b + \ldots K_k p_k)(1 + r) + L_k w = A p_k$$

The surpluses of the various industries of produced quantities are denoted by:

$$A_a + A_b + \ldots A_k \leq A; B_a + B_b + \ldots B_k \leq B; \ldots; K_a + K_b + \ldots K_k \leq K$$

The joint production relations that still display independence of relations between the joint production of commodities are given by the following linear equations, which cannot show interdependencies:

$$(A_1 p_a + B_1 p_b + \ldots + K_1 p_k)(1 + r) + L_1 w = A_{(1)} p_a + B_{(1)} p_b + \ldots + K_{(1)} p_k$$
$$(A_2 p_a + B_2 p_b + \ldots + K_2 p_k)(1 + r) + L_2 w = A_{(2)} p_a + B_{(2)} p_b + \ldots + K_{(2)} p_k$$
$$- -$$
$$(A_k p_a + B_k p_b + \ldots + K_k p_k)(1 + r) + L_k w = A_{(k)} p_a + B_{(k)} p_b + \ldots + K_{(k)} p_k$$

Thus $A_i, B_i, \ldots ,K_i$ denote quantities of commodities *a, b, . . . ,k*, respectively as means of production produced by *i*th. Processes $i = 1,2, \ldots ,k; A_{(i)}, B_{(i)}, \ldots ,K_{(i)}$ denote quantities of commodities *a, b, . . . ,k*, respectively as products by processes $i = 1,2, \ldots ,k$.

5 Denote an event by $E_h(\phi_h, x_h(\phi_h),t)$, with ϕ_h as dialectical knowledge for a particular differentiated ontology along the historical dialectical process. Thus $x_h(\phi_h)$ denotes a particular representation of the problem under investigation in vector form corresponding to the differentiated ontological reference to ϕ_h. Therefore, "*t*" denotes time along history and ontological evolutions (h, ϕ_h) that remain independently distributed owing to differentiation of evolutionary epochs. Therebye, $lim_h[\,U^i \cap^j]_h\,[\phi_h] = \phi^{ij}*$, for a particular ontology of *H* in its intra-historical evolution. Symbols (i,j) denote interaction (*i*) followed by integration (*j*). Thereby, $U^i \cap^j \phi^{ij}_{H}* = \Phi$, nullity.

Next consider an objective function, $W_h(E(.))$. It has the same properties with $U^i \cap^j W_h(E(.))_{H}* = \Phi$, nullity.

Hence the entire historicism of rationalist dialectics is marked by disjoint *h*-episodes. In it, no identifiable convergence to objectives and knowledge exists. This is resultant of the rationalist world characterized by conflict, dualism, and lack of convergence to any settled objectivity.

References

Barrow, J.D. (1991). "Laws," in *Theories of Everything: The Quest for Ultimate Explanation*, Oxford: Oxford University Press, pp. 12–30.

Berman, H.J. (1989). "Beyond Marx, beyond Weber," in McCullough, H.B. (ed.), *Political Ideologies and Political Philosophies*, Toronto, ON: Wall & Thompson. Extracted from H.J. Berman, (1983). *Law and Revolution*, Cambridge, MA: Harvard University Press, pp. 144–147.

Blaug, M. (1993). *The Methodology of Economics*, Cambridge: Cambridge University Press, p. 29.

Bohr, N. (1985). "Discussions with Einstein on epistemological issues," in H. Folse (ed.), *The Philosophy of Niels Bohr: The Framework of Complementarity*, Amsterdam: North Holland Physics.

Campbell, D.T. (1988). "Evolutionary epistemology," in Radnitzky, G. and Bartley, W.W. III (eds.), *Evolutionary Epistemology, Rationality, and the Sociology of Knowledge*, La Salle, IL: Open Court, pp. 47–89.

Choucri, N. and North, R.C. (1995). "Global accord: Imperatives for the twenty-first century," in Choucri, N. (ed.), *Global Accord*, Cambridge, MA: MIT Press, pp. 477–508.

Choudhury, M.A. (2007). *The Universal Paradigm and the Islamic World-System: Economics, Ethics, Science and Society*, Singapore: World Scientific.

Choudhury, M.A. (2014). *Tawhidi Epistemology and its Applications: Economic, Finance, Science, and Society*, Cambridge: Cambridge Scholars.

Commission on Global Governance (1995). "Global civic ethic," in *Our Global Neighbourhood: A Report of the Commission on Global Governance*, New York: Oxford University Press.

Dasgupta, A.K. (1987). "Marginalist challenge," in *Epochs of Economic Theory*, Oxford: Basil Blackwell, pp. 74–98.

Dequech, D. (2012). "Post-Keynesianism, heterodoxy and mainstream," *Review of Political Economy*, 24, 2: 353–368.

Erasmus Journal for Philosophy and Economics (2009). "Cambridge social ontology: An interview with Tony Lawson," 2, 1: 100–122.

Hawking, S.W. and Mlodinow, L. (2010). *The Grand Design*, New York: Bantam Books, p. 72.

Hawley, A.H. (1986). *Human Ecology*, Chicago, IL: University of Chicago Press.

Heilbroner, R. and Milberg, W. (1995). "The crisis of vision," in *The Crisis of Vision in Modern Economic Thought*, Cambridge: Cambridge University Press.

Hicks, J. (1979). *Causality in Economics*, Oxford: Basil Blackwell.

Hunt, W.H. (1979). *The Keynesian Episode: A Reassessment*, Indianapolis, IN: Liberty Fund.

Keynes, J.M., (1973 [1936]), *The General Theory of Employment, Interest and Money*, London: Macmillan, for the Royal Economic Society.

King, J.E. (2013). "Post-Keynesian and others," in Lee, F.S. and Lavoie, M. (eds.), *In Defense of Post-Keynesian and Heterodox Economics*, Abingdon: Routledge, p. 4.

Lawson, T. (2012). "Mathematical modeling and ideology in the economics academy: Competing explanation of the failings of the modern discipline?," *Economic Thought*, 1, 3: 22.

Lawson, T. (2013). "What is this 'school' called neoclassical economics?," *Cambridge Journal of Economics*, 37, 5: 947–983.

Lawson, T. and Peseran, H. (2009). *Keynes' Economics: Methodological Issues*, London: Routledge.

Lee, F.S. and Lavoie, M. (eds.) (2013). *In Defense of Post-Keynesian and Heterodox Economics*, Abingdon: Routledge.

McCloskey, D.N. (1985). *The Rhetoric of Economics*, Wisconsin, MN: University of Wisconsin Press, pp. 36–61.

Mommsen, W.J. (1989). "Politics and scholarship: The two icons of Max Weber's life," in *The Political and Social Theory of Max Weber*, Chicago, IL: University of Chicago Press, pp. 3–23.

Nitzan, J. and Bichler, S. (2000). "Capital accumulation: Breaking the dualism of 'economics' and 'politics'," in Palan, R. (ed.), *Global Political Economy: Contemporary Issues*, London; Routledge, pp. 67–88.

Nordhaus, W.D. (1975). "The political business cycle," *Review of Economic Studies*, 2, 42: 169–190.

O'Donnell, R.M. (1989). "Some philosophical background," in *Keynes: Philosophy, Economics & Politics*, London: Macmillan, pp. 11–28.

Popper, K. (2004). *The Logic of Scientific Discovery*, London: Routledge.

Ramsey, F.P. (1928). "A mathematical theory of savings," *Economic Journal*, 38, 152: 543–550.

Resnick, S.A. and Wolff, R.D. (1987). *Knowledge and Class: A Marxian Critique of Political Economy*, Chicago, IL: University of Chicago Press.

Ruggie, J.G. (2003). "Introduction: What makes the world hang together? Neo-utilitarianism and the social constructivist challenge," in *Constructing the World Polity*, London: Routledge, pp. 1–40.

Schumpeter, J.S. (1968). "The scholastic doctors and the philosophers of natural law," in *History of Economic Analysis*, New York: Oxford University Press.

Smullyan, R.M. (1992). *Godel's Incompleteness Theorems*, New York: Oxford University Press.

Soros, G. (1998). "Fallibility and reflexivity," in *The Crisis of Global Capitalism*, New York: Public Affairs, pp. 3–45.

Sraffa, P. (1960). *Production of Commodities by Means of Commodities*, Cambridge: Cambridge University Press.

Sullivan, W.M. (1989). "The contemporary crisis of liberal society," in McCullough, H.B. (ed.), *Political Ideologies and Political Philosophies*, Toronto, ON: Wall & Thomson.

Sztompka, P. (1991). *Society in Action: The Theory of Social Becoming*, Chicago, IL: University of Chicago Press.

Wilson, E.O. (1998). *Consilience: The Unity of Knowledge*, New York: Vantage Press.

4 The epistemic methodology of heterodox Islamic financial economics and its consequences[1]

Objective of this chapter

The role of epistemology is central in the construction of socio-scientific thought (Infeld, 1951). In the socio-scientific field, the study of Islamic economics and finance has not invoked epistemological inquiry into its theoretical foundation and application in any significant way. Nonetheless, if the proponents of this field of scholarly investigation want to claim it as a revolutionary structure of scientific thinking, as one that can contribute new epistemological depth, then a return to foundational Islamic issues is necessary. Thus there comes about the prospect of discovering a new vista of socio-scientific thinking. There is a need to address the question of how, in this field of inquiry, ethical reasoning as a form of consciousness is construed for socio-scientific inquiry as a pertinent field of the Islamic methodological worldview.

The Islamic scholarly and practitioner world in current times has failed to invoke serious epistemological inquiry into the socio-scientific field arising from the *Qur'an* and the *sunnah*. Therefore, in the world of Islamic economics and finance, the epistemological pursuit and the consequential nature of socio-scientific thought have not yet dawned. The field of Islamic economics and finance has continued to remain subservient to the questionable and existing axiomatic premises of mainstream economics in its varied perspectives. Consequently, the field of Islamic financial economics has failed to progress as a revolutionary worldview. Instead, it continues to rely on the commercialized outlook of acquisition of wealth in the *shari'ah*-compliant context. Accepted Islamic methodology thus continues to target the objective of maximization of shareholders' wealth. The inherent prosaic conception in the absence of embedding morality and ethics as endogenous dynamics in intellectual inquiry misleads by its objective criteria of maximization of economic and financial rewards.

This chapter aims to place the legitimate role of epistemological inquiry within the intellection of the new theory of Islamic financial economics and to treat the emergent theory as a methodology with logical formalism. We referred to this methodology arising from the monotheistic law of unity of knowledge as the "epistemic analytic (mathematical)" approach. Thus the ontological, epistemological, and applied contexts of the holistic episteme of unity of knowledge are brought into the framework of the study as a rigorous methodological worldview (Nasr, 2003). The epistemic theory imminent in the foundational study of Islamic financial economics is thus found to give rise to a revolutionary field of socio-scientific study. From such an investigative search arises a deeply epistemological, Islamic socio-scientific methodology that is distinctly different from the mainstream one.

Introduction

This chapter begins by explaining certain key terms in relation to the socio-scientific methodology that will be used to bring out the epistemological and functional nature of the concept and application of any emergent theory. The discovery of such a new and revolutionary theory is compared with other theories to establish its importance in respect of its maturity and application to the widest field of socio-scientific investigation (Bohr, 1985). In Islamic socio-scientific intellection, based on its methodological worldview, we would further include the superiority of such a worldview to the embedded nature of morality and ethics epistemologically derived elsewhere (Edel, 1970). Other terms will be explained during the course of the chapter to identify and construct the underlying theory arising from the methodology. The chapter will then carry this theory onwards into applications. In our case, the derivation of the emergent epistemological methodology, its underlying theory formulation, and its application will be in relation to the generalized field of financial economics and a specific application within this field.

Selected definitions

Epistemology is the study of the theory of knowledge. In it, the derivation of knowledge belongs to the axiomatic origin of a comprehensive law and text from which a certain assumed totality of logical formalism and consistent mode of theoretical and applied implications can be drawn up. When the original axiomatic basis of the epistemology belongs to the foundational domain of the primordial law and text, then such an axiomatic origin is termed by us the *primal* ontology.

From the primal ontology, as the foundational theory of the existence of critical thinking and through the derivation of the logical formalism offered by the derived epistemology, there flows a diversity of formalisms that explain the various details of the primal ontology. The primal ontology and its epistemic derivation can be carried through into pertinent applications.

Figure 4.1 shows the integral role that is played out interactively between ontology, epistemology, and the applications of the derived theory and logical formalism to specific problems. Such a systemic realization is further continued over processes of similar types, thus marking the sustainability of the derived formal methodology. This comprehensive meaning of sustainability takes up the meaning of *episteme* (Foucault, 1972).

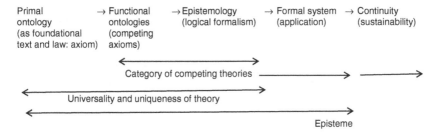

Figure 4.1 Epistemic formation of socio-scientific theory, application, and continuity of formalism

The meaning of *episteme* in Figure 4.1 conveys the idea offered by Foucault (ibid.: 191):

> By *episteme* we mean . . . the total set of relations that unite, at a given period, the discursive practices that give rise to epistemological figures, sciences, and possibly formalized systems. . . . The episteme is not a form of knowledge (*connaissance*) or type of rationality which, crossing the boundaries of the most varied sciences, manifests the sovereign unity of a subject, a spirit, or a period; it is the totality of relations that can be discovered, for a given period, between the sciences when one analyses them at the level of discursive regularities.

The distinctly different nature of epistemic methodology between Islam and other worldviews

The *universality and uniqueness of theory*—although not of theory construction by the formal method—is established by the fact that the primal ontology denotes the most reduced form of ontology as the domain of the law and text that gives rise to a theory of knowledge. The universality of a theory is proved by a comparative search and its ultimate formalism. The emergent theory then characterizes the following analytical problem.

Let $O_i\, i = 1, 2, \ldots n$ denote various *functional* ontologies (Gruber, 1993), with the assumption of mathematical continuity on the set $U(\cap_i O_i\} \subset O^*$. Now, O^* denotes the primal ontology. If $O^* \supset O_1 \supset O_2 \supset \ldots \supset O_n$ and it is implied from this that $O_n \supset O_{n+1}$, for all n number of *functional ontologies*, then such functional ontologies are characteristic functions of O^*—that is, carrying the same law and text as O^* by their commonness of unity of knowledge, signified by $U(\cap_i O_i) \subset O^*$.

Thus O^* is unique if its property of universality cannot be found in the nature of any other episteme other than the epistemology of the world-system that is constructed on the basis of O^*. The further issue is that, logically, there cannot be any other O^{**}, such that $O^{**} \supset O^*$ followed by other functional ontologies that are of a relative type. This is evident from the fact that, if it were true that $O^{**} \supset O^*$, then O^* is not unique. In this case, O^* is one of the relations in the series of functional ontologies in the class of $\{O^*, O_1, O_2, \ldots, O_n, ..\}$. The property of universality of O^* is contradicted.

Science does not claim universality of its theories, since it is an open-ended system of analytical investigation that does not fix its argument in any given set of abiding axioms for all situations. This very characteristic of scientific inquiry is in turn caused by the permanent *problematique* of heteronomy or dualism between a priori and a posteriori reasoning (Bhaskar, 1978; Carnap, 1966). Therefore, in such a rationalistic concept of relativism, the absence of a unified way of reasoning that can otherwise integrate the a priori and the a posteriori parts of reasoning cannot be found in the closed limits of a beginning and an end in evolutionary learning and its induced world-system. Such a characteristic of open-ended conjectural reasoning causes all ontologies to be relative in nature (Nozick, 2001; Popper, 1998).

Contrarily, with the *Closure*—that is, the containment of the knowledge-induced world-system between the beginning and the end of evolutionary learning—there would be the following relations:

$$O^* \to \{\theta, x(\theta), t(\theta)\} \to O^{***} \tag{4.1}$$

where $\{\theta, x(\theta), t(\theta)\}$ denotes epistemologically derived knowledge-flows $\{\theta\}$ that are combined with the space–time occurrence of knowledge-induced events that continuously occur in knowledge, space, and time dimensions. An event here is denoted by $\{\theta, x(\theta), t(\theta)\}$ and its continuity occurs by transformation of the same category of relations.

Now, it must be true that $O^{***} = O^*$. If the contrary were the case, then O^{***} would be a functional ontology. The upper limit of the sequence of processes in Figure 4.1 becomes unbounded. Now, during this evolutionary learning process, by means of induction by $\{\theta\}$, there will be an instance whereby $O^{***} \supset O^*$. Consequently, the closure is defined by $(O^* \supset O^{***}) \cap (O^{***} \supset O^*)$. This implies that $O^* = O^{***}$, and that $\{\theta, x(\theta), t(\theta)\}$ and its positive functional transforms are attainable. Such transforms are continuous and bounded in the limiting evolutionary learning processes.

The universality and uniqueness of the evolutionary learning system,

$$O^* \to W(\theta, x(\theta), t(\theta)) \to \ldots \to O^* \tag{4.2}$$

defines the *Closure*. This means that there cannot be any other primal and closure ontologies of such a system in spite of allowing for the diversity of multi-systems to exist. Contrarily, if this were possible, then either O^* would turn into a functional ontology or the multi-system of learning processes would remain independent between the processes. This is the case of the *problematique* of heteronomy between the a priori and a posteriori differentiation in reasoning. A unified perspective of an integrated domain of reasoning and knowledge is lost. The resulting knowledge-induced world-system cannot arise.

The conclusion from the above formalism is this: Knowledge and its induced events, as the conscious choices made possible by invoking the purpose and objective of the Islamic law (*shari'ah*, referred to as *maqasid as-shari'ah*), are attainable in the sense of evolutionary learning. Therefore the epistemological inferences become well defined along the evolutionary learning string of finite closures within the largest scale of *Closure*. Contrarily, in the absence of the closure in knowledge, space, and time dimensions, as defined above, the ultimate reality of the knowledge-induced world-system, like that of financial economy as a particular, remains unexplained. Socio-scientific reasoning remains differentiated and incomplete. Epistemic knowledge, as derived from primal ontological foundations, remains random and unattainable.

Logical formalism in the Islamic epistemic model contra mainstream reasoning

The evolutionary learning model of *Closure*—namely, $O^* \to W(\theta, x(\theta), t(\theta))$ $\to \ldots \to O^*$—has its internally consistent properties. These together convey the nature of both the Islamic and, by contrast, other formal models of knowledge and their embedding in the generalization and specifics of the unified world-system. We offer a symbolic explanation of such properties and use them to construct the logical formalism of the entire episteme. The episteme comprises the totality Ontology $\to$ Epistemology $\to$ Phenomenology and the continuous circularity between these. We define "phenomenology" as the study of consciousness explaining the integration of knowledge and its induced forms in mind and matter multiverses.

Properties of Islamic ontological and epistemological foundations

These are as follows.

1   The cardinal attribute of the ontological, epistemological, and embedded nature of knowledge in the entities of the world-system is the monotheistic unity of knowledge and the unified nature of the world-system induced by the episteme of unity of knowledge. The *Qur'an* and the *sunnah* point out two distinct realities: truth and falsehood. The third category of undetermined knowledge (*mutashabihat*) is temporary, as it becomes determined finally between truth and falsehood with the advance of *qur'anic* knowledge. Yet between these two attributes of reality it is only truth that is manifest in O^*. The *Qur'an* (10:32) declares: "Such is *Allah* your real cherisher and sustainer. Apart from truth what remains but error? How then are you deluded away from the truth?" This fact can be explained in mathematical terms.[2]

2   Let O^* denote the text of the totality of laws. The totality of laws denotes the completeness of knowledge. Such a totality can therefore be treated as the mathematical topology signifying extraordinary completeness. Completeness cannot logically rely on partnership in the ownership and functioning of the totality of laws. Such non-partnered completeness of the knowledge domain that is embodied in O^* causes the law that emanates from it to be universal and unique across the widest expanse of systems of embedded relations.

3   Since knowledge, by its nature, is defined as creatively evolved understanding towards perfection, as is the case with evolutionary knowledge enabling learning,

the totality of knowledge and laws in $O*$ comprises the good things of life. Where the bad things exist as a contrary reality, it is to explain the truth (good) by negating the false (bad) in intellection and experience. This marks the attributes of evolutionary learning in good choices while rejecting bad choices.

4   The completeness and absoluteness of $O*$ cannot be comprehended all at once; $O*$ can be learned only incrementally by means of the knowledge that $O*$ generates along the evolutionary learning string of the *Closure*. Such a continuous derivation of knowledge-flows in evolutionary learning, and thereby in the identification of knowledge-induced variables and events in knowledge, space, and time dimensions, is enabled by a well-defined mapping denoted by "S" (*sunnah*).

5   Finally, the *Closure* property establishes the inference that truth is showered over the generalization and specifics of the world-system by the process of repetitive evolutionary learning in reference to $O*$ and the mapping S, and thereby through functional ontologies across multi-systems.

We formalize all of these properties together, symbolically, in a string of unity of knowledge as illustrated in Figure 4.2.

The ontological and epistemological premises of the Islamic methodological worldview being the *Qur'an* and the *sunnah* together—followed by the discursive

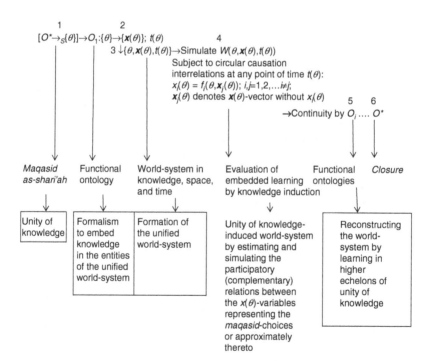

Figure 4.2 The *Tawhidi* String Relation (TSR) in the knowledge, space, and time dimensions

practices of the *qur'anic* text of the monotheistic laws, the permanent nature of the law, text, and the knowledge-induced evolutionary world-system—are characterized by the structure of organic unity in the good things of life, while rejecting the bad and ugly ones. The phenomenology, as the inner structure of mind and matter to explain the consciousness of the ontological and epistemological truth, is governed and fully explained by logical formalism in reference to the law of unity of knowledge. The supercardinal attribute of the monotheistic law in unity of knowledge is referred to as *Tawhid* in the *Qur'an. Tawhid* is the primal attribute of God as One in respect of His non-partnership and absolute knowledge in the act of creation and ownership of the multiverse (*a'lameen*). For this reason, we refer to the episteme connected with Figure 4.2 as the "*Tawhidi* String Model" (Choudhury, 2014a).

Thus, in the broadest context, the nature of Oneness of God is taken up in terms of the oneness of the monotheistic law. Both of these implications of the monotheistic law are equivalently taken up as the precept of unity of knowledge.

It is impossible to cognitively know the monotheistic meaning of Oneness of God. Besides, such a monotheistic precept of Oneness of God cannot be usable. It refers to the corporeal worldly representation. Therefore, the way in which to represent the law of monotheistic oneness is by means of the totality of monotheistic knowledge as a meta-mathematical entity: the supercardinal topological manifold (Rucker, 1983; Dewitt, 1992). Such an approach yields the ontological formalism and the analytical evaluation of the world-system in terms of unity of knowledge and the construction of the unified world-system along the continuity of knowledge, space, and time dimensions.

The model of "de-knowledge" (rationalism) by the *Tawhidi* (monotheistic) String Model

Yet another critical property of O^* is that of falsehood ("de-knowledge"), which is contrary to truth. We will refer to the nature of falsehood and its induction of the false world-system in general and in particular in respect of the negation of any or all of the five attributes presented earlier. Let such negation be referred to as "de-knowledge." Two of the ninety-nine attributes of *Allah*, as the powerful (*matin*) and the sublime (*mutakabbir*), explain a part of the ultimate nature of O^* in all of reality between the heavens and the earth in their generality and details of organic unity of knowledge in and between the diversity of entities and their systems. Such attributes of *Allah*, along with all others, signify the ultimate meta-reality of the multiverse, which, by the very significance of these attributes, conveys the functional existence of organic monotheistic unity. The episteme of *Tawhidi* unity of knowledge is thus the primal and ultimate ontology of being and becoming (Mullah Sadra).[3]

Contrary to the *Tawhidi* methodological worldview, there is the domain of knowledge, which has its own independent consequences. Yet, as explained regarding the omnificence of this methodology studied in its ontological, epistemological, and structural sense of organic unity of knowledge, the same Figure 4.2 can be applied to study the nature of "de-knowledge" and its socio-scientific structure and relations.

In this case, the starting point of differentiation in reasoning is the dualism of the a priori and a posteriori dichotomy. Likewise, the problem of heteronomy causes differentiations between deductive and inductive reasoning, between *noumenon* and phenomenon, and between pure reason and practical reason (Kant, 1964; Hume, 1988). The ontological and epistemological implications, and thereby the phenomenological structure of consciousness in knowledge, space, and time, devolve into the functioning of the a posteriori alone, while leaving out the a priori domain of morality, ethics, God, and the divine laws. These attributes of the a priori domain remain dysfunctional as endogenously embedded reality in the inter-causal organic unity between the a priori and the a posteriori, and so on. God, in the a priori domain, although felt, remains exogenous in the sphere of consciously invoking God in the affairs of the multiverse. The multiverse, in the framework of unity of knowledge induced in it as being continuously conscious along evolutionary paths of learning, frames the system and cybernetic nature of the formal methodological worldview (Choudhury, 2014b).

Figure 4.3 explains the permanent *problematique* of heteronomy found in all of socio-scientific reasoning in a methodological framework. This figure brings out the contrast between *Tawhidi* and contrary methodological worldviews. It also conveys the contrariety between the pervasively unified worldview, with its five attributes mentioned earlier, and the differentiated dialectical worldview caused by socio-scientific heteronomy. The accent (') in the symbols in Figure 4.3 denotes entities induced by rationalism *qua* heteronomy and the exclusiveness of the solely a posteriori domain of actions and responses by induction of the rationalist "de-knowledge" flow, $\{\theta'\}$.

The epistemic roots of new modernisms

The epochs marked by functional ontologies O_i, $i=1,2,\ldots$, being diverse and non-integrated, and not belonging to any universal and unique genre of primal ontology, give rise to diverse and differentiated epistemologies and social structures, like socio-scientific Darwinism (Hull, 1988). Premised on rationalism thereby are also the random emergences of a vast number of classifications of differentiated thinking. These carry with them transnational interpretations of cultures, religion, geopolitics, economic, and social dialectics by conflict. Integration is seldom the result of convergence between such differentiated O_i's. Such epochs of new modernisms at junctures of O_i's being driven by the dialectics of contrasts rather than convergence to universality in a unique primal ontology and the emergent epistemologies that follow, generate examples of a plethora of heteronomy. The result is differentiated classes of worldviews and world-systems (Smart, 2000).

In the field of financial economics, examples of these emergent new modernisms are the new epistemic ways of configuring the nature of economic theory out of tensions and conflicts. Heterodox economic thinking is an example of such a new modernism. Its domain of axioms and perception of economic reality congruous with social reality forms the unsettled questioning of the modernist prescription of neoclassical economic schools in all of economic theory. The divergences between

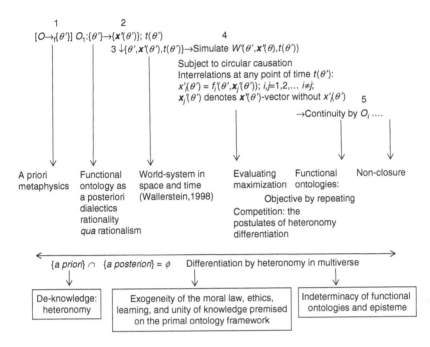

1   2
$[O \rightarrow_f\{\theta'\}] \; O_1:\{\theta'\} \rightarrow \{x'(\theta')\}; \; t(\theta')$ 4
      3 $\downarrow\{\theta', x'(\theta'), t(\theta')\} \rightarrow$ Simulate $W'(\theta', x'(\theta), t(\theta'))$

Subject to circular causation
Interrelations at any point of time $t(\theta')$:
$x'_i(\theta') = f_i'(\theta', x_j'(\theta')); \; i,j=1,2,\dots \; i \neq j;$
$x_j'(\theta')$ denotes $x'(\theta')$-vector without $x'_i(\theta')$ 5

$\rightarrow$ Continuity by O_i ....

A priori metaphysics	Functional ontology as a posteriori dialectics rationality *qua* rationalism	World-system in space and time (Wallerstein, 1998)	Evaluating maximization	Functional ontologies: Objective by repeating Competition: the postulates of heteronomy differentiation	Non-closure

$\longleftarrow$ $\longrightarrow$

$\{a \; priori\} \cap \{a \; posteriori\} = \phi$ Differentiation by heteronomy in multiverse

De-knowledge: heteronomy	Exogeneity of the moral law, ethics, learning, and unity of knowledge premised on the primal ontology framework	Indeterminacy of functional ontologies and episteme

Figure 4.3 The heteronomous nature of the non-*Tawhidi* methodological worldview

new modernisms, despite the hegemony of neoclassicism, are reflected in the new interpretations of neoclassical economic theory: neo-Keynesianism and neo-Marxism (Lawson, 1997). They are also born out of conflicts between heterodox and other economic theories.

The postulate of heteronomy in economic reasoning follows (Choudhury, 2010). This problem is reflected in the methodical independence of ethical, moral, and social issues in economic theory. Phelps (1989) points out that the issues of social justice cannot be resolved in neoclassical economic theory. Likewise, the endogenous nature of ethical and conscious behavior cannot be explained by neo-classical economic theory (Sen, 1977). The core problem of economic theory is the scarcity of resources of all kinds. Through this axiom, the subsequent consequences, as of maximization of "objective" functions, steady-state equilibrium, preference ordering, and competition for scarce resources, all together follow the axiom of economic rationality.

Despite this foundational axiom of rational choice in economic theory, there have been significant shifts. Examples are of stochastic preferences, bounded rationality, and complexity (Simon, 1957). Consequently, there have been significant shifts in the nature of the neoclassical economic theory of rational choice. Each of the new modernisms in the emergent nature of economic theory has marked the functional ontologies of such new paradigms. Examples are Piero Sraffa's (1960) critique of neoclassical economic theory, Paul Romer's (1986) new growth theory, Gunnar Myrdal's (1957) sociological economic theory, Joseph Schumpeter's (Gaffard, 2009) dialectical growth model, John Rawls's (1971) critique of neoclassical economics in a theory of justice, Herbert Simon's (1957) bounded rationality and dialectics, heterodox economic theory, and a long list of economic schools with divergences from neoclassical economic theory in the history of economic thought (Dasgupta, 1987).

The differentiated nature of O_i's with paradigm shifts in the normal science of economic theory as new modernisms of financial economics is shown in Figure 4.4.

The episteme of the unified worldview in Islamic economics: consequences

New modernisms in the form of paradigm shifts rather than scientific revolution, and with heteronomous functional ontologies yielding a differentiated episteme, cannot result in the *Tawhidi* String Model of Figure 4.2. Yet, as has been shown, the *Tawhidi* String Model can explain the contrary methodological worldview that centers on rationalism oppositely to the primal ontology of unity of knowledge. This was also the ground upon which the theorem of the universality and uniqueness of the monotheistic methodology of unity of knowledge was established. The monotheistic premise inheres in and overarches across all things between the heavens and the earth.

Such a phenomenological structure of the multiverse world-system is referred to in the *Qur'an* as *tasbih*. The discursive nature of deriving knowledge (epistemology) from the primal ontology of *Tawhid* is permanently taken up in the light of interaction between the inherent phenomenology and the consultation (discourse) dynamics in deriving rules from the primal ontology (*Qur'an*) through the mapping of the *sunnah*. Thus the dynamics of *tasbih* (phenomenology) and *shura* (consultation and discourse) exist all along the evolutionary learning path of unity of knowledge.[4] The *Tawhidi* methodological worldview is thus contrary to rationalism in respect of events

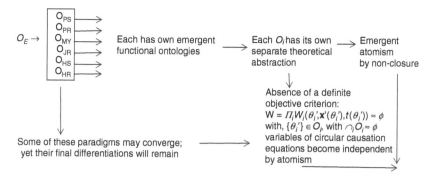

Figure 4.4 The ultimate differentiation between new modernisms in economic thought

regarding "everything" and everywhere.[5] This domain of actions and responses comprises the multiverse existing in knowledge, space, and time dimensions.

The *Tawhidi* methodological worldview thus presents itself as the revolutionary structure of socio-scientific knowledge. This worldview is beyond the paradigm shift that we explained in terms of new modernisms in economic reasoning. The worldview is foundational. Yet it is not well understood in the realm of socio-scientific inquiry. On this point, Kuhn (1970: 154) writes, regarding the nature of scientific revolution, "scientific revolutions are here taken to be those *non-cumulative* developmental episodes in which an older paradigm is replaced in whole or in part by an *incompatible* new one."

The definition given by Kuhn befits the scientific revolution that can ensue from *Tawhid* and its inter-causal relationship with the unified world-system of evolutionary learning from, by, and towards *Tawhid*. This claim is concluded from the emergence of mind and matter throughout history. The place of the Islamic worldview in respect of *Tawhid* across history can be depicted by Figure 4.5.

The consequence of the *Tawhidi* episteme in the heterodox Islamic theory of financial economics

In this section, an application of the *Tawhid* methodology will be made to explain the participatory (complementary) interaction leading to integration between money, spending, and real economy ($MFRE(\theta)$) according to the principle of pervasive complementarities. This principle presents the methodology of the embedded unity of knowledge as the consciously interactive (I) and integrative (I) organic relations between these variables. The "II" properties lead to evolutionary learning in continuity and continuums (E). Thus IIE-learning processes represent the dynamics of inter-causality of organic unity between the *maqasid as-shari'ah* choices. The $MFRE(\theta)$-model of unity of organic relations is thus sustained and further evolved.

The MFRE model as example of evaluating wellbeing in unity of knowledge

By taking stock of the above-mentioned arguments, we can formulate the complete $MFRE(\theta)$ model as follows:

Simulate wellbeing function, $W = W(M, TRADE, IN, \theta)$ (4.3)

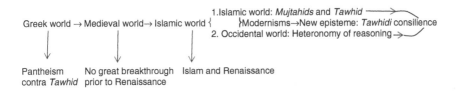

Figure 4.5 Islam, Occident, and possibility of *Tawhidi* consilience episteme

subject to the circular causation (inter-causal) relations in respect of estimation followed by simulated levels of complementary relations between $\{M, TRADE, IN, \theta\}$, the following variables are defined, where:

M denotes quantity of money in circulation
IN denotes investment (as spending)
TRADE is as is
θ denotes knowledge computed as parametric values by averaging the level of the *maqasid as-shari'ah* associated with the choices of the observed variables

The circular causation equations used to evaluate the degree of complementarities between the variables and simulating the estimated coefficients therefrom are as follows:

$$M = F_1(IN, TRADE, \theta) \text{ in log-linear form} \tag{4.4}$$

$$TRADE = F_2(M, IN, \theta) \text{ in log-linear form} \tag{4.5}$$

$$IN = F_3(M, TRADE, \theta) \text{ in log-linear form} \tag{4.6}$$

$$\theta = F(M, TRADE, IN) \text{ in log-linear form} \tag{4.7}$$

Estimation and simulation of circular causation relations in money and real-economy relations: the case of Malaysia

The following results point out how the estimation and simulation of wellbeing, subject to circular causation relations, is carried out and the results obtained therefrom in order to analyze the inter-variable complementarities for evaluating wellbeing (see Tables 4.1 and 4.2, and Figures 4.6–4.9).

Estimated equations[6]

$$\ln\theta = -0.514 + 0.792 \ln M - 0.244 \ln IN + 0.123 \ln TRADE \tag{4.8}$$

$$\ln TRADE = 6.53 - 1.63 \ln M - 0.022 \ln IN + 1.57 \ln\theta \tag{4.9}$$

$$\ln M = 1.20 + 0.244 \ln IN - 0.176 \ln TRADE + 1.09 \ln\theta \tag{4.10}$$

$$\ln IN = 1.32 + 2.27 \ln M - 0.022 \ln TRADE - 3.11 \ln\theta \tag{4.11}$$

Table 4.1 Estimated values of the natural logarithm variables and the wellbeing index $\ln\theta$

Year	lnM	lnIN	lnTrade	lnTheta
1990	3.028729	2.281141	4.474355	1.89087
1991	3.016001	2.271952	4.493234	1.838109
1992	2.934276	2.435738	4.436823	1.77571
1993	3.04094	2.249392	4.480648	1.903995
1994	3.034887	1.741766	4.756527	2.047363
1995	2.937106	1.93596	4.695302	1.927509
1996	2.952987	1.958982	4.698482	1.84772
1997	2.769532	2.219091	4.626825	1.735273
1998	2.657149	2.162338	4.742497	1.577921
1999	2.902974	1.17243	5.151269	2.01929
2000	2.785608	1.304155	5.083616	2.103191
2001	2.809719	1.332004	5.067209	2.085399
2002	2.892835	1.137896	5.149293	2.123856
2003	2.987651	0.967619	5.214237	2.159127
2004	2.949029	0.951494	5.223702	2.184113
2005	2.959712	0.895367	5.249401	2.198976
2006	2.928511	1.111181	5.130819	2.168849
2007	3.000422	1.10347	5.097477	2.222949
2008	2.921725	1.169502	5.081687	2.218552

Table 4.2 Simulated (predictor) values of the natural logarithm variables and the wellbeing index θ

Year	lnM	lnIN	lnTrade	lnTheta
1990	3.033362	0.460517	5.122838	1.8785
1991	3.008144	0.474554	5.133444	1.872984
1992	2.915919	0.671824	5.065107	1.761356
1993	3.046929	0.420285	5.132153	1.896692
1994	3.132733	−0.076	5.403994	2.049692
1995	3.007119	0.172046	5.323586	1.917336
1996	2.993872	0.217396	5.318813	1.924687
1997	2.803798	0.553654	5.220033	1.70711
1998	2.683936	0.60593	5.29687	1.646178
1999	3.082529	−0.5183	5.753487	2.132689
2000	3.008451	−0.39361	5.68834	1.999273
2001	3.019396	−0.36925	5.673175	2.009555
2002	3.10907	−0.58386	5.762562	2.132842
2003	3.204128	−0.78043	5.83687	2.257472
2004	3.182752	−0.79333	5.845187	2.231982
2005	3.199642	−0.85268	5.872034	2.257299
2006	3.14622	−0.64327	5.755731	2.165343
2007	3.214216	−0.69688	5.738739	2.220077
2008	3.149172	−0.60986	5.715475	2.139696

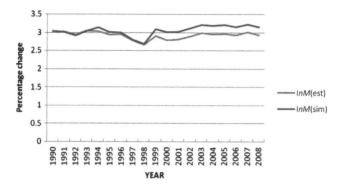

Figure 4.6 Percentage change of estimated ln*M* and simulated ln*M* over the period 1990–2008

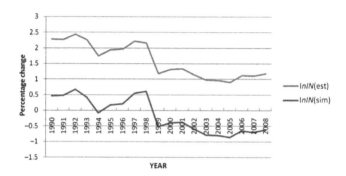

Figure 4.7 Percentage change of estimated ln*IN* and simulated ln*IN* over the period 1990–2008

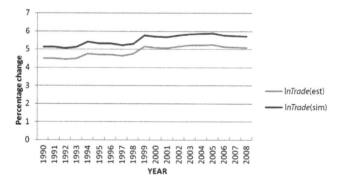

Figure 4.8 Percentage change of estimated ln*Trade* and simulated ln*Trade* over the period 1990–2008

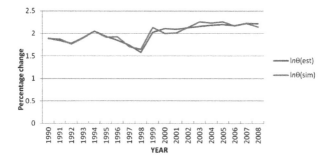

Figure 4.9 Percentage change of estimated lnθ and simulated lnθ over the period 1990–2008

Simulated equations (using the SDA numerical choices for selected coefficients)

$$\ln TRADE = 6.53 - 1.417 \ln M - 0.022 \ln IN + 1.57 \ln\theta \qquad (4.12)$$

$$\ln M = 1.20 + 0.103 \ln IN - 0.103 \ln TRADE + 1.09 \ln\theta \qquad (4.13)$$

$$\ln IN = 1.32 + 1.672 \ln M - 0.022 \ln TRADE - 3.11 \ln\theta \qquad (4.14)$$

$$\ln\theta = -0.514 + 0.792 \ln M - 0.244 \ln IN + 0.123 \ln TRADE \qquad (4.15)$$

Regression analysis

Regression analysis: ln$M$*100, lnIN%, ln$TRADE$*100, lnθ

1   *Regression analysis*: ln$M$ versus lnIN, ln$TRADE$, lnθ
The regression equation is:

$$\ln M = 1.20 + 0.244 \ln IN - 0.176 \ln TRADE + 1.09 \ln\theta \qquad (4.16)$$

Predictor	Coef	SE Coef	T	P
Constant	1.2043	0.5362	2.25	0.040
lnIN	0.2444	0.0564	4.33	0.001
ln$TRADE$	−0.1763	0.0715	−2.46	0.026
lnθ	1.0860	0.1129	9.62	0.000

$S = 0.0408542$ R-Sq = 88.1%   R-Sq(adj) = 85.8%
Durbin-Watson statistic = 1.57629

2   *Regression analysis*: ln*IN* versus ln*M*, ln*TRADE*, lnθ

The regression equation is:

$$\ln IN = 1.32 + 2.27 \ln M - 0.022 \ln TRADE - 3.11 \ln\theta \tag{4.17}$$

Predictor	Coef	SE Coef	T	P
Constant	1.317	1.859	0.71	0.490
ln*M*	2.272	0.525	4.33	0.001
ln*TRADE*	−0.022	0.259	−0.08	0.935
lnθ	−3.106	0.454	−6.84	0.000

$S = 0.124582$ R-Sq = 96.0%   R-Sq(adj) = 95.1%
Durbin-Watson statistic = 1.45823

3   *Regression analysis*: ln*TRADE* versus ln*M*, ln*IN*, lnθ

The regression equation is:

$$\ln TRADE = 6.53 - 1.63 \ln M - 0.022 \ln IN + 1.57 \ln\theta \tag{4.18}$$

Predictor	Coef	SE	T	P
Constant	6.532	0.8467	7.71	0.000
ln*M*	−1.635	0.6632	−2.46	0.026
ln*IN*	−0.022	0.2577	−0.08	0.935
lnθ	1.568	0.8266	1.90	0.077

$S = 0.124388$ R-Sq = 87.1%   R-Sq(adj) = 84.5%
Durbin-Watson statistic = 0.887537

4   *Regression analysis*: lnθ versus ln*M*, ln*IN*, ln*TRADE*

The regression equation is:

$$\ln\theta = - 0.514 + 0.792 \ln M - 0.244 \ln IN + 0.123 \ln TRADE \tag{4.19}$$

Predictor	Coef	SE	T	P
Constant	−0.5142	0.5125	−1.00	0.332
ln*M*	0.7923	0.0824	9.62	0.000
ln*IN*	−0.2437	0.0357	−6.84	0.000
ln*TRADE*	0.1234	0.0651	1.90	0.077

$S = 0.0348958$ R-Sq = 97.2%   R-Sq(adj) = 96.6%
Durbin-Watson statistic = 1.87454

Other questions regarding Islamic financing as it stands today: the epistemic problem

The problematic nature of financing in general, as reflected in the national economy and exemplified by the case of the Malaysian economy, which boasts

21 percent of its total banking asset share at USD135 billion, is found to be highly concentrated around secondary financing instruments. Table 4.3 shows the distribution of Islamic financing by the highly concentrated secondary Islamic financing instruments and the slim and declining percentage by primary Islamic financing instruments.

The high percentage of concentration around secondary Islamic financing instruments prevails around the deferred payments arrangements of *bai bithaman ajil* and *murabaha*. Both of these instruments are questionable ones according to the following perspectives of the *shari'ah*:

1   Fixed pricing of an intertemporal good and service spread over time and at the point of establishing a contract is tantamount to pricing in the presence of full information of a sale that is really intertemporal otherwise.
2   This type of pricing, as a mark-up, can be interpreted as a shadow interest rate and is like the time value of money.
3   Deferred payments net of present down payments are problematic in terms of *shari'ah* interpretation and thus Islamic legitimacy. The setting of the mark-up on present down-payments (5–10 percent over the market value) and on the deferred payments accruing over time is not market reality.
4   The underlying risk and profit components of the mark-up remain undetermined.
5   Consequently, the meaning of trade as exchange and the pricing of a real good in exchange becomes null and void.

In the midst of such indeterminacy, the social and ethical valuation of assets in the presence of mark-up (*murabaha*) and deferred pricing on present sale (*ijara* and *bithaman ajil*) and future cash-flows for the seller go against the meaning of fairness and determination of the real value of assets.

In spite of such *shari'ah*-related problems, Table 4.3 shows that almost all of Islamic financing has centered on the secondary financing instruments of *bithaman ajil*, *murabaha*, and *ijara* (and *ijara thumma*). On the other hand, the primary Islamic financing instruments of *musharakah* and *mudarabah* have remained subdued and have declining in a dismal way. Portfolio diversification and risk diversification is thus reduced. The real economy response that would enhance participatory development and appropriate technological change—and resource development and ownership in ethical and social directions—is reduced. Capital market and joint venture networking via *musharakah* financing as a required strong form of participation between Islamic banks remains weak.

This is the epistemic problem of existing Islamic financing that relies extensively on secondary modes of financing to raise the up-front profitability of the financiers. The conclusion is that Islamic financing, in both its understanding and application, is an experiment in the partitioned view of profit motivation, but in the absence of a sustainable future of participatory social objectives and integration between the financing instruments. Such a participatory development future is indeed the

Table 4.3 Islamic financing by modes of financing, millions of Malaysian ringgit, and percentages, December 2006–2014 and February 2015

Bihaman Ajil	Ijara	Ijara Thumma	Istisna	M1: Murabaha	M2: Musharakah	M3: Mudarabah	Other	Total
				M1	M2	M3		
2006								
29845	762.9	21470.4	509.4	5300.9	156.8	147.9	15174.9	73368.1
40.68	1.04	29.26	0.69	7.23	0.20	0.20	20.68	100
2007								
31630.3	1153.5	25806.1	804.1	9681.7	374.4	109.8	15818.8	85388.6
37.04	1.35	30.22	0.94	11.34	0.40	0.12	18.53	100
2008								
35278.3	2809.5	32275.8	1410.4	19556.6	854.0	326.3	12646.1	108157.1
32.62	2.60	29.89	1.30	18.08	0.79	0.30	11.69	100
2009								
42913.6	4033.0	38953.3	1406.5	23022.3	2360.3	373.6	20354.4	133406.8
32.16	3.02	29.20	1.05	17.26	1.76	0.28	15.25	100
2010								
53697.4	3940.2	43497.4	1621.0	23296.9	3958.3	276.8	28924.1	159211.0
33.73	2.47	27.32	1.02	14.63	2.49	0.17	18.17	100
2011								
63211.2	4121.6	50981.9	1466.2	30384.9	7307.6	251.6	39181.1	196995.1
32.09	2.40	25.88	0.75	15.42	3.71	0.13	19.89	100
2012								
74280.6	4635.7	54574.7	989.3	40018.4	11832.2	142.2	40324.7	232797.8
31.91	1.99	23.44	0.42	17.19	5.08	0.06	17.32	100
2013								
83139.5	6373.2	62370.3	696.2	57026.9	16354.2	146.0	54799.6	280905.8
29.60	2.27	22.20	0.25	20.30	5.82	0.05	19.31	100
2014								
79783.2	7677.8	67253.2	1016.7	83842.7	23113.1	77.3	71417.9	334181.9
23.88	2.30	20.12	0.30	25.09	6.92	0.02	21.37	100
2015 (February)								
79135.7	7863.1	68116.5	1056.4	93395.8	23938.9	78.4	73553.6	347138.5
22.80	2.27	19.62	0.30	26.90	6.90	0.02	21.88	100

Source: Internet webpage on Islamic financing by concepts.

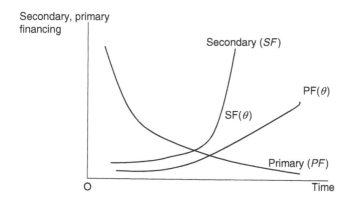

Figure 4.10 Present state of Islamic bank financing and its epistemic participatory reconstruction

epistemic worldview of unity of knowledge in the strict Islamic epistemological context.

Alternative ways of reforming the present understanding and Islamic epistemic reconstruction of the secondary and primary modes of Islamic participatory financing can be formulated. Such approaches and the epistemic foundation of Islamic financing and participatory development have not been examined.

Figure 4.10 explains the relationships between primary and secondary Islamic financing instruments in the actual (estimated) and participatory (simulated) case of the epistemic meaning. In the first case, there is no role of knowledge to create a scenario of participatory financing. In the second case, the participatory case is to be reconstructed by the choice of modes of financing, strategies, and epistemic understanding of *maqasid as-shari'ah* relating to unity of knowledge inducing the variables $PF(\theta)$ and $SF(\theta)$. The resulting economy of scope and economy of scale of financing would be explained by $\alpha+\beta > 1$. In the actual case, the absence of the endogenous effect of θ would be shown by $\alpha+\beta \leq 1$:

$$SF^{\alpha}*PF^{\beta} = \theta \approx \text{Constant in the case of marginalism with } \alpha+\beta \leq 1; \uparrow \text{ with } \alpha+\beta > 1 \text{ in the case of the participatory reconstruction of evolutionary learning}$$

By the interrelationship of circular causation, we note $SF(\theta) = f_1(\theta,PF(\theta))$; $PF(\theta) = f_2(\theta,SF(\theta))$; $dSF(\theta)/d\theta = (\partial f_1/\partial \theta) + (\partial f_1/\partial PF(\theta)).(dPF(\theta)) > 0$ identically. Likewise it is the case with $dPF(\theta)/d\theta > 0$.

The wellbeing function is $\theta = W(PF(\theta),SF(\theta))$ or a monotonic positive function of θ. Thereby, $d\theta = (\partial W/\partial PF)dPF(\theta) + (\partial W/\partial SF)dSF(\theta) > 0$ by the monotonic positive function of θ on $PF(\theta)$ and $SF(\theta)$.

Hence, as inter-variable knowledge by their participatory relations, $\theta\uparrow \Rightarrow PF(\theta)$ and $SF(\theta)$—that is, $\{PF(\theta)\} \cap \{SF(\theta)\}\uparrow$. This is explained by Figure 4.10.

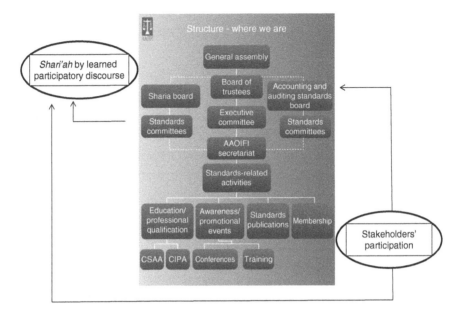

Figure 4.11 AAOIFI decision-making structure as is and in the epistemic participatory sense

Source: AAOIFI www.islamicbanker.com/education/aaoifi-standards

Problem of participatory decision-making in the AAOIFI structure and its epistemic reconstruction

The continuation of the prevalent state of misinterpretation of a participatory (unity of knowledge) methodological worldview and its application in Islamic financing is also to be found in the institutional views of the Accounting and Auditing Organization of Islamic Financial Institutions (AAOIFI). The participatory investigation of *shari'ah* potentiality in the participatory stakeholder model is left out in the AAOIFI institutional model. The participatory understanding of the broader principle, potentiality, and application of the discoursed *shari'ah* rules are necessary in order to show the epistemologically premised change of institutional participation as the sign of unity of knowledge according to the greater understanding of *maqasid as-shari'ah* in a discursive environment.

The collective view of Islamic financing and its major decision-making structure shows that the organic participatory nature of interactive, integrative, and evolutionary relations is grossly lacking. This creates a major gap in promoting the total wellbeing aspect of Islamic financing beyond simply the commercially viable aspect and in the shareholding model as opposed to the social stakeholding model, which is much desired. Such is the conclusion received from the financing data and the AAOIFI standards setting framework.

The epistemic nature of extensively participatory decision-making in the presence of inter-causality between critical modes of financing and in the AAOIFI decision-making structure is the extensively wellbeing-oriented framework of organic dynamics. Such a comprehensive wellbeing objective should replace the overly commercialized nature of Islamic financing found to prevail today. Our thesis of the epistemic basis of unity of knowledge brings out the epistemic reconstruction of the prevalent narrow perspective of Islamic financing. We have shown these extensions by the interactive and circular causation role of the relationship that ought to exist between stakeholders and institutional decision-makers, and between learned participatory agents and institutions in the dynamic development of the *shari'ah* in the light of *maqasid as-shari'ah* (see Figure 4.11).

Conclusion

This chapter ends as it began: Full understanding of the epistemic foundation is necessary for the birth of any type of scientific doctrine. Yet such a realization has not been noted by Islamic groups and institutions in the narrow field of mainstream Islamic economics and the like of present times. Epistemological thought arising from the primal ontological roots of the episteme of unity of knowledge was shelved in the scholastic Islamic period of the great thinkers and never invoked in contemporary times. When modernism entered the mind and matter of the Muslim world, it did not spark any kind of revolutionary contribution. The Islamic socio-scientific world of today is like it was in earlier times. During the Islamic scholastic period, philosophical pursuits overshadowed material applications that could otherwise be used to construct a world-system based on the epistemic groundwork. Likewise, in the present era, there is no interest in rediscovering the world of revolutionary contribution by means of erudition in the epistemic premise of the Islamic methodological worldview.

Yet there always remained the potential of Islamic contribution to the field of epistemic reconstruction of scientific horizons in the direction of what modern socio-scientific thought is trying to discover by consilience (Wilson, 1998). Such is the pursuit for the epistemology and applications of unity of knowledge and its endogenous induction of the unified world-system. This chapter has argued that the epistemology based on intrinsic heteronomy cannot offer the possibility for consilience either in Occidental or Islamic scholarship. Thus the episteme of *Tawhid* as the consilience by unity of knowledge is uniquely placed for deeper investigation.

In the field of financial economics, the *Tawhidi* construction of the world-system and its applications is possible because of the need to steer away from the turmoil that exists in the domain of financial economics. What creates stability by thought and application in the field of financial economics is the extension of commercial objectives to the realm of wellbeing with its ethical and economic embedding. Such ethical embedding conveys the idea of the endogenous nature of preference formation, choices, technology, and wellbeing by way of organic unity of being and becoming of the new world of unity of knowledge. The heterodox Islamic epistemic worldview offers this possibility. Yet, paradoxically, it is shunned by Islamic academics, practitioners, and institutions that enforce their will in closed circuits of groups and syndicates. Scholarship is eschewed. The current Islamic world of scholarship and its originality for the world of learning has been disabled.

The result has been an unhappy failure in the field of Islamic economics and finance as a learned discipline with applications. This is because although the financial state of Islamic banking remains commercially robust in terms of concentrated financing instruments, its application to actualize wellbeing by means of the balance of social justice, alleviation of poverty, and moral elements has not dawned. Likewise, on the financial and economic fronts, the Islamic financial portfolio is not well diversified in terms of risk and production and investment menus. The academic community ought to establish synergy with practitioners and institutions through socio-scientific complementarities concerning the monotheistic methodology and the mind–matter engagement.

It is therefore high time to enter the epistemic area of academe and to establish the synergy between academic intellection, practitioners, and institutions of the Islamic world—and with the rest as well. This direction of substantive change should start by the reformulation of educational disciplines, practical training, and foundational understanding, along with active participation by academia, training, practitioners, and institutions (Choudhury, 2015).

Notes

1 This chapter is based on a lecture given at the Department of Finance, University of Salford, Manchester, UK, May 9, 2015.
2 The common domain of Falsehood (F) has the property $F_1 \cap F_2 \subset F; F_1 \subset F, F_2 \subset F$. The Truth function being T, then $T \cup F = T$, implying $T \cup (F_1 \cap F_2) = (T \cup F_1) \cap (T \cup F_2) = T \cap T = T$. Thus, between T and F, T is the ultimate functional reality. Thus, while $T \cap F = \phi$, it is true that $T \cup F \neq \phi$. The monotheistic law being the truth of reality in the context of unity of knowledge between the good things of life, it governs all functions to prove itself in truth.
3 Nasr and Leaman (1996) write on Mullah Sadra thought: "Being is like light in that it processes degrees of intensity while being a simple reality. The universe in its vast multiplicity is therefore not only unified but is also thoroughly hierarchical."
4 Combine the verses on *shura*, *tasbih*, and *siratal mustaqim* for gaining exegesis.
5 *Qur'an* (48:23): permanence of the divine law.
6 This section is adapted from Choudhury et al. (2013).

References

Bhaskar, R. (1978). "The logic of scientific discovery," in *A Realist Theory of Science*, New York: Harvester Wheatsheaf.

Bohr, N. (1985). "Discussion with Einstein on epistemological issues," in Folse, H. (ed.), *The Philosophy of Neils Bohr: The Framework of Complementarity*, Amsterdam: North Holland Physics.

Carnap, R. (1966). "Kant's synthetic *a priori*," in Gardner, M. (ed.), *Philosophical Foundations of Physics: An Introduction to the Philosophy of Science*, New York: Basic Books.

Choudhury, M.A. (2010). "Unity of knowledge versus Kant's heteronomy with a reference to the problem of money, finance and real economy relations in a new global financial architecture," *International Journal of Social Economics*, 37, 10: 764–778.

Choudhury, M.A. (2014a). *Tawhidi Epistemology and its Applications, Economics, Finance, Science, and Society*, Cambridge: Cambridge Scholarly.

Choudhury, M.A. (2014b). *Socio-cybernetic Study of God and the World-System*, Philadelphia, PA: IGI Inc.

Choudhury, M.A. (2015). *The Islamic Epistemological Worldview and Empirical Study of Socioeconomic Integration in the Ummah*, Kuala Lumpur: International Islamic University of Malaysia Press.

Choudhury, M.A., Halid, N., Ahmed, M.S. and Hossain, M.S. (2013). "Fiscalism as spending and monetary integration," *International Journal of Management Studies*, 20, 1: 1–39.

Dasgupta, A.K. (1987). *Epochs of Economic Theory*, Oxford: Basil Blackwell.

Dewitt, B. (1992). *Supermanifolds*, Cambridge: Cambridge University Press.

Edel, A. (1970). "Science and the structure of ethics," in Neurath, O., Carnap, R. and Morris, C. (eds.), *Foundations of the Unity of Science*, Chicago, IL: University of Chicago Press.

Foucault, M. (1972). *The Archeology of Knowledge and the Discourse on Language*, trans. Sheridan, A.M., New York: Harper Torchbooks.

Gaffard, J. (2009). "Innovation, competition, and growth: Schumpeterian ideas within a Hicksian framework," in Cantner, U. Luc Gaffard, J. and Nesta, L. (eds.), *Schumpeterian Perspectives on Innovation, Competition, and Growth*, Springer: New York, pp. 7–24.

Gruber, T.R. (1993). "A translation approach to portable ontologies," *Knowledge Acquisition*, 5, 2: 199–200.

Hull, D.L. (1988). "Science as a selection process," in *Science as a Process*, Chicago, IL: University of Chicago Press, Chapter 12.

Hume, D. (1988). *An Enquiry Concerning Human Understanding*, Buffalo, NY: Prometheus Books.

Infeld, L. (1951). "General relativity and the structure of our universe," in Schilpp, P.A. (ed.), *Albert Einstein: Philosopher-Scientist*, New York, NY: Tudor.

Kant, I. (1964). *Groundwork of the Metaphysics of Morals*, trans. H.J. Paton, New York: Harper & Row.

Kuhn, T.S. (1970). *The Structure of Scientific Revolution*, Chicago, IL: University of Chicago Press.

Lawson, T. (1997). "Towards a richer ontology," in *Economics and Reality*, London: Routledge.

Myrdal, G. (1957). "An unexplained general traits of social reality," in *Rich Lands and Poor: The Road to World Prosperity*, New York: Harper & Row.

Nasr, S.H. (2003). *Science and Civilization in Islam*, Cambridge: Islamic Texts Society.

Nasr, S.H. and Leaman, O. (eds.) (1996). *History of Islamic Philosophy I & II*, London and New York: Routledge.

Nozick, R. (2001). *Invariances: The Structure of the Objective World*, Cambridge, MA: Belknap Press of the Harvard University Press.

Phelps, E.S. (1989). "Distributive justice," in *The New Palgrave: Social Economics*, New York: W.W. Norton.

Popper, K. (1998). *Conjectures and Refutations: The Growth of Scientific Knowledge*, London: Routledge & Kegan Paul.

Rawls, J. (1971). *A Theory of Justice*, Cambridge, MA: Harvard University Press.

Romer, P.M. (1986). in "Increasing returns and long-run growth," *Journal of Political Economy*, 5, 94: 1002–1037.

Rucker, R. (1983). "Large cardinalities," in *Infinity and the Mind: The Science and Philosophy of the Infinite*, New York: Bantam Books.

Sen, A. (1977). "Rational fools: A critique of the behavioural foundations of economic theory," *Philosophy and Public Affairs*, 6, 4: 317–344.

Simon, H. (1957). *Models of Man*, New York: John Wiley & Sons.

Smart, N. (2000). "The nature of morality," in *Worldviews*, Upper Saddle River, NJ: Prentice Hall, pp. 114–116.

Sraffa, P. (1960). *Production of Commodities by Means of Commodities*, Cambridge: Cambridge University Press.

Wallerstein, I. (1998). "Spacetime as the basis of knowledge," in Bordo, O.F. (ed.), *People's Participation: Challenges Ahead*, New York: Apex Press, pp. 43–62.

Wilson, E.O. (1998). *Consilience: Unity of Knowledge*, New York: Vantage Press.

5 Is there a possibility for heterodox Islamic economics?

A post-orthodoxy criticism

Objective

This chapter will critically examine the present state of Islamic economics in respect of its leaning on mainstream economics. Thus the argument is made that, for quite some time now, while the intellectual discipline of economics has been investigating the possibility of a heterodox school, Islamic economics as it stands today has failed to contribute to any such challenging dimension. It has simply remained an insignificant addition within economic orthodoxy. The same failure has thus happened to the associated discipline of so-called Islamic finance and Islamic banking, which merely clamors for stable profits and shareholders' wealth. The greater vision of Islamic intellection in academia and productively philanthropic activities has been drowned by a focus on commercialism that uses Islamic financial instruments and outmoded *shari'ah* rules. This chapter points out that the intellectual gap in Islamic economics has arisen in the absence of any epistemological scholarship that could otherwise develop from a methodological understanding and its application of the principles laid down in the cardinal Islamic worldview of the primal ontology comprising the *Qur'an* and the *sunnah*. This worldview is of the monotheistic law, referred to as *Tawhid*, in which most religions and people believe in one form or another. It is the methodological derivation and imminent methodical formalism arising therefrom, which remains at variance. After taking a critical look at the current state of Islamic economics as a mainstream field searching for its identity, the chapter focuses on the construction of the true monotheistic epistemological worldview, its methodical formal derivation, and selected economic applications resting upon the epistemological foundation. It is argued that, on the basis of such an authentic academic approach, Islamic economics can indeed become a distinctive scientific revolution.

We begin by referring to an important quote from Tony Lawson and Hashem Pesaran (1989) that questions the scholarship of orthodox economic reasoning in the context of economic and social reality. The arguments made join existing disgruntled views of economic orthodoxy. The analysis invokes epistemological and ontological arguments under the guise of critical realism to search for newer grounds for economic and social worldviews. Lawson and Pesaran (ibid.: 1) write:

> When a field of study becomes marked by dissatisfaction and disillusionment, methodological analyses and debates tend to become prominent and often

provide pointers to faithful directions for the subject to move in. Economics is currently undergoing just such a period of crisis.

A central keynote of post-orthodoxy debate and criticism rests on the need for the moral, ethical, and social embedding of economic reasoning. This element in traditional economic reasoning was abandoned as economics focused on analytical specialization without the component of social embedding. Holton (1992), borrowing the social embedding praxis from Polanyi (1957), sees the need for the economic worldview to be a social embedding study. The differentiated perspective of economic reasoning is abandoned as it has been carried out in the name of specialization and a claim for distinction as a science (Blaug, 1968). So the rumbling inside economics, as science claimed for specialization and distinction as a separate discipline, is not new.

The question that remains to be investigated is the new epistemological praxis that heterodox economic reasoning raises. The question is a wide one, for even the inception of economic theory over the ages has not remained independent of the value judgment of the proponents of different schools of economic thought. On this issue, Schumpeter (1968) writes: "Economic analysis has not been shaped at any time by the philosophical opinions that economists happen to have." But this opinion was not sustained in the course of Schumpeter's bible of economic thought. Likewise, the clamor for the moral and social embedding of economics in the present age of globalization raises serious questions. On this issue, the subtle words of Hazel Henderson (1999: 56) note:

> The good news is that this is forcing us to 'go inside ourselves' and ask some pretty basic questions. What do I want to pay attention to? Who am I and what do I want written on my tombstone? Such basic defensive reactions will define the growing sectors of our Attention Economies and their inexorable shift from material goods (measured by traditional GNP/GDP per capita), to services and more tangible factors in living standards, measured by the new Quality of Life scorecards.

The project of heterodox economic reasoning now rests on the epistemological derivation, formalism, and application of a new body of thought that addresses economic issues and problems as moral and social embedding. Sen (1977) refers to such an approach of economics in the wider issues of social valuation as deontological economics. The issues of preferences, choices, and objective criteria of economic theory within its social embedding are now examined accordingly. When such fundamental axioms are raised to oppose the postulates of rational choice, then the very pedestal of economic reasoning is questioned. Such a fundamental reconstruction of the epistemological praxis accumulates into a new foundation of economic choices and human behavior. Now, even the methodology of microeconomics and macroeconomics as two distinct branches of economic theory comes to be questioned. This is happening in the heterodox area of economic theory, as it is found also to shape the new epistemic approaches in theoretical physics between relativity physics and quantum mechanics. The project of unification and harmonization is sought (Lee and Lavoie, 2013: 109; Hawking, 1988).

Thus the question of the possibility of heterodox economics in general and in particular needs to be answered on the basis of epistemological argument, formalism, analytics, and applications, given the heterodox worldview (Laclau, 1996). All of these taken together do not escape the domain of scientific inquiry. Subjectivity must be replaced by the objective criterion, and still without sacrificing the moral and social embedding scope of the new economic science. The earlier chapters have referred to the rigorous methodical formalism of the monotheistic methodological approach as "epistemic analytic (mathematics)." Feiwel (1987) remarked on why mainstream economic theory, despite its many failures in explaining reality from the viewpoint of institutional and policy realism, was still successful, while traditional economic historicism remained unsuccessful. This was because of the success of mainstream economics in premising its worldview on theory and formalism. All other approaches lacked this.

A similar kind of heterodox offshoot was Marxist political economy. It wanted to address the theme of social justice by the process of social collectivization. The procedural part of Marxist theory in explaining an epistemological prognosis of capitalism and asserting the economics of socialism (Marxism) was a fine work that was later on expounded in terms of evolutionary social beliefs (Resnick and Wolff 1987; Sztompka, 1991). Yet, as Hayek points out, it is such ebullient ideas in sociological theory that made it dysfunctional, while denying even alternative constructs replacing rational choice. In the same way, the grandiose moral treatise of Adam Smith in his *Theory of Moral Sentiments* faded away in his *Wealth of Nations* (Coase, 1994).

The emergence of heterodox Islamic economic reasoning: post-orthodoxy heterodox thought

Among heterodox developments in the field of economics, markedly Marxism, post-Keynesianism, deontological economics, and the ontological project of economics by Lawson and his group (*Erasmus Journal for Philosophy and Economics*, 2009), there has arisen the field of Islamic economics. One starts by critically examining this new field of economic reasoning in terms of the question of its possibility. As mentioned above, without the substantive groundwork of establishing the components of possibility, any such heterodox outburst remains an unsustainable exercise. The essential theme of social embedding in its subtle meaning explained in this chapter remains unfitting in explaining realism if this is not properly understood in the claimed heterodox clamor.

First, therefore, we define the scope of Islamic economics as it has endeavored to survive over the last thirty years or more—in fact, over a hundred years now if we are return to the resilient beginnings of Islamic economic thought in the Islamic scholastic past (Ghazanfar, 1991; Islahi, 1988). Islamic economics, conceived as a social science, aims at the broader field of moral valuation that needs to be embedded in economic and social domains. This wider field of valuation comprises the moral domain of the "good" choices found to arise from the verdicts of the *Qur'an* and the *sunnah* (prophetic guidance). A discursive process concerning the rules derived in the context of the generality and particulars of issues and problems employs the rational process of human participated involvement in discoursing the rules derived from the *Qur'an* and the *sunnah* on diverse matters of choices in the "good things of life." The combination of deriving knowledge from the *Qur'an*, the *sunnah*, and discursive practice based on the verdicts of this fundamental premise forms the groundwork of Islamic law, the *shari'ah*. The field of *shari'ah* is thus established by the objective and purpose of moral choices to enhance the wellbeing of all in a codetermined way (*maqasid as-shari'ah*).

The above definition is a broad one by way of the vision of Islamic economics as a body of thought that extends the embedded moral and social inquiry of economic issues and problems in the wider field of the monotheistic law (*Tawhid*). Monotheism derived from the *Qur'an* and the *sunnah* becomes the ontological framework of all intellection and application in Islamic thought. Yet this ontological premise by itself is not fully functional without its transmission via the edicts of discourse, formalism, analytics, and application in the wider context of the law of monotheism, bereft of metaphysical speculation, and aiming towards the morally and socially embedded economic world-system.

While the general vision of Islamic economics is described by the above-mentioned perspectives, it has not taken up any functional form. Thus, as it exists today, the *possibility* as opposed to the *vision* of Islamic economics is known to be only epistemologically premised in, but not formalized by, the explication of the monotheistic ontology.[1] To address the project of the *possibility of Islamic economics* as a field of heterodox economics, we use the schema shown in expression (5.1). We then unpack this schema to bring out the various unified components that can establish Islamic economics in its distinctive form of a truly heterodox domain of socio-scientific reasoning. This will ultimately be followed by a cursory explanation of why the underlying epistemic methodology of Islamic economics as heterodox socio-scientific inquiry forms a universal and unique logical formalism premised on the *functional* ontology[2] of the monotheistic law.

The advent of the Islamic economic project in its contemporary form—about thirty years ago—could not premise its reasoning in the epistemological nature of Step 1 as follows.

Step 1

1	2	3	4
Monotheism→	*Shari'ah*→	Worldly affairs→	Applications→Continuity
(*Qur'an, sunnah*)	(the learned)	(specific issues)	(Islamic finance, Islamic banking)

$$(5.1)$$

As the mainstream Islamic economics orients it:

1	2	3	4
Exogenous premise	No formalism exists between the monotheistic law and the development of a methodo-logical worldview	An exogenous development of mainstream economic approaches independently of any methodological reason-ing arising from the mono-theistic origin	Consequences of the nature of 1–3

The scholarly developments that took place under expression (5.1) can be sensed in its almost random character, to borrow from mainstream or traditional leanings of thought in both Muslim and other schools. Moreover, the writings represent the expressions of individuals on the basis of their own understanding of the themes, without the challenge of relying on the premise of epistemic argumentation and construction of challenging scholarly thought. Popular writings without this epistemological challenge are found in Chapra (1992), Siddiqi (2013), and recent articles published in the *Review of Islamic Economics*. Choudhury's own earlier works, excluding those of the last twenty years, were also of the hardcore neo-classical type (Choudhury, 1986). Yet Choudhury's recent contributions have increasingly expressed dismay with these other approaches. He has focused on the essentially epistemological content, which applies the foundations of Islamic economics, finance, and world-system studies within the socio-scientific argu-mentation (Choudhury, 2013a). Many of these works were critically examined by Mahomedy (2013).

The failure of Islamic economics as a socio-scientific inquiry has been the result of its oblivion of the universal methodological formulation and the discovery of a unique theory arising from the universal roots of functional ontology. We mean to show the possibility of Islamic economics by methodological approach on how the monotheistic law, the cardinal principle of Islamic economics, works in the gen-erality and particulars of the world-system. It is in this light that a most credible foundation for scientific revolution can be laid down. The emergence of the methodological understanding and application of the monotheistic law in the *Qur'an*, known as *Tawhid*, would be of the non-cumulative in nature. Yet it would present a scientific revolution beyond being simply a paradigm. Thomas Kuhn (1970: 154) wrote on this point: "[S]cientific revolutions are here taken to be those non-cumulative development episodes in which an older paradigm is replaced in whole or in part by an incompatible new one." Kuhn (ibid.: 68) continues: "Such changes together with the controversies that almost always accompany them are the defining characteristics of scientific revolution."

The epistemological divide is projected in Step 1 by the discontinuous nature of transmission and recursion between parts 1, 2, and 3. Thereby, the whole of Step 1, in the light of the existing pursuit of Islamic economic thinking, crumbles into pieces of discontinuous reasoning, formalism, analytics, and application. The continuity of the Islamic economic project has proceeded through this kind of dissociative thinking. Consequently, no actualization of Islamic economics took place in the world of learning. Its application to Islamic finance and banking remained a mere expression of the avoidance of interest rates and their replacement with participatory financing instruments. Yet the emanation of the inter-causality between participatory financing instruments, interest rates, and the greater moral, social, and development design was never understood, never formalized, and never applied. Indeed, the opposing relationship between trade in the good things of life that mobilizes resources and interest rate (*riba*) as the abhorring practice that obstructs the mobilization of resources is to be understood in the epistemological sense as an "epistemic analytic (mathematical)" formalism. On the other hand, Islamic economics, finance, and banking take the *riba* law at face value. According to the heterodox and epistemological process of methodological inquiry, the *riba* law is formulated as an analytical model to establish the trade versus *riba* relationship in the wider context of resource mobilization and simulation of well-being with a vast range of complementary factors in the face of a synergistic pairing between the diversity of things. Such is the worldly manifestation of the mono-theistic law in unity of knowledge.

It is a common complaint today that there has not come to be any higher edu-cational institution that adopts a globally recognized field of Islamic economics and socio-scientific study beyond adapting it to the mainstream medium (Faruqi, 1982) as an Islamic palliative, not with originality (Rahman, 1988). The drawing boards of all major Islamic activities today fail to consciously recognize the great monotheistic understanding beyond a simply religious sanctimony. Among such leading plat-forms are the learned conferences—that is, the International Conference in Islamic Economics (ICIE)—the failed development outlook of the Islamic Development Bank (IDB) beyond the mere financing of country projects, and the mainstream economic research of the Islamic Research and Training Center of the IDB. The pedagogy and research programs of institutions of higher learning worldwide have all contributed to a stalemate of progress in Islamic economics as a universal and unique heterodox discipline with revolutionary consequences for the fullest con-tribution to the world of learning beyond religious demarcation. This epistemic challenge—and appropriate understanding, application, and sustainable continuity —was not embraced by the contemporary field of Islamic economics (or some of the traditional fields) once it took to rationalist groundwork to explain its peculiar version of economic reality.

Some examples can be examined here in respect of the failed potential of Islamic economics and socio-scientific inquiry in the world of learning and application. Data giving the time-trend of rates of return (turnover rates) and commercial interest rates and central bank rates (that is, prime rates) point to the absence of inter-causal relations between Islamic participatory rates (trade) and interest rates. Yet the study of inter-causal relations between critical variables is essential for understanding the organic evolutionary learning design of processes of social transformation ripening into an Islamic economic community by the understanding and application of a model of inverse relationship between Islamic participatory financing instruments (trade) and the rate of interest.

Even the global Islamic banking portfolio itself remains poorly diversified and non-complementary. Choudhury has argued that the concentration of Islamic funds has long been in *murabaha* and *musharakah*. There is now a growing increase of risky ventures in Islamic *sukuk* bonds. All of these instruments defy the principle of inter-instrument linkage, which is otherwise needed to establish sustainability from organic unification of inter-causal relations. The implication, then, is of the deepening failure of complementary interaction and integration between the various parts of Step 1, even as Islamic economics has proceeded to date.

Yet it must be understood that Islamic erudition and Islamic finance and banking are highly popular subjects among all people. On this issue, even the Pope has commented (Bloomberg, 2009) that "[t]he ethical principles on which Islamic finance is based may bring banks closer to their clients and to the true spirit which should mark every financial service." This was reported by The Vatican's official newspaper *Osservatore Romano*. The problem arises in the worldview and the mobilization and management of Islamic ways of using finance for the common wellbeing. This is a matter that rests on the proper intellection of the Islamic methodological worldview of the monotheistic law and in explaining its formal and applied functioning in the world-system. Pope Benedict XVI, in a speech on October 7 2008, reflected on crashing financial markets, saying that "money vanishes, it is nothing" and concluding that "the only solid reality is the word of God." Money, the real economy, and wellbeing comprise a theme that must be close to the epistemic community of true Islamic economic thought.

Step 2

Imam Ghazali as microeconomist

Going back to the history of economic thought, we find a terrain of original thinking among Muslims of the scholastic period. Some of this arose from the epistemic roots of the *Qur'an* and the *sunnah*. Other theories arose from the rationalist roots of Greek thought, which incongruently mixed up the *qur'anic* episteme with rationalist thinking (Qadri, 1988).

Ghazali (n.d.) wrote incisively against the Muslim school of rationalist thinking concerning monotheism and the world-system (Ghazali, 1997: 217). Indeed, Islam and rationalism are opposed to each other in the light of the monotheistic methodological worldview. The challenge for Islamic socio-scientific reasoning, with the specific case of Islamic economics, on the one hand, is to formulate a methodological worldview that, denies the rationalist approach to epistemology and formalism. On the other hand, a unique and universal epistemological approach leads to the use of the monotheistic law on morally embedded perspectives of the economy driven by the good things of life. These comprise the goods and services belonging to the domain of the objective and purpose of the *shari'ah*, referred to as *maqasid as-shari'ah*, as mentioned earlier. The contributions of the Islamic scholastic thinkers were deeply epistemological in nature. Imam Ghazali merits special mention in this area of intellection relating to God, the self, and the world-system.[3]

On the matter of money and its productive and just function, Ghazali argued the following: Financial interest was considered to be a form of counterfeiting or defacing of the true value of money. Besides this, the usual meaning of counterfeiting of currency was shown to be a grave sin in Islamic financial arrangements. In respect of these two viewpoints, Ghazali wrote that the first man who uses counterfeit coins gathers the sins of every person who transfers it to others. Counterfeit is seen to be worse than theft of coins, for counterfeit coins circulate over long periods of time, thereby devaluing the true value of currency. Consequently, it is unlawful to exchange even a large quantity of counterfeit coins for a small quantity of pure coins in economic exchange of any kind—consumption, production, investment, and earnings.

Financial transactions based on interest rates were considered by Ghazali to be equivalent to the devaluation of pure currency value. Ghazali followed the Prophet's saying on this matter: "A counterfeit coin is one which has nothing of gold and silver. The coin in which there is something of gold or silver cannot be called counterfeit." This is reported by Ghazali (n.d.). Now, referring to the circulation of pure currencies according to the gold standard, the stable value of the currency and its use in good and productive activities equates to the use of currency in financing good spending and shuns bank savings. Saving (of the type that we will refer to as bank saving) was equivalent to hoarding in Ghazali's time.

On the topic of the social wellbeing function, Ghazali is of the utilitarian type seen in modern mainstream social choice theory. For the lateral aggregation of morally framed preferences by consciousness to form social preferences, Ghazali appealed to personal psychology to establish goodness and moderation in the good things of life as ordained by the *maqasid as-shari'ah*. The institutional nature of moral and ethical preferences was reflected by their lateral aggregation. The implication of such an early version of utilitarian welfare function is Ghazali's wishful dream of a good society formed by the aggregation of conscious preferences of all morally motivated individuals. In modern times, we find a similar implication of welfare function and social choice in Arrow (1951), Harsanyi (1955), and Hammond (1987). The latter-day Islamic scholars did not cast critical examination of social welfare implications as of Ghazali's utilitarian, linearly additive concept of consciousness and a consequentialist good society. This led them to study Ghazali's welfare implications as though they were in tune with the theory of consumer behavior of mainstream economics (Islahi, 1988).

On the above-mentioned topic of the theory of consumer behavior pre-dating utilitarianism, Ghazali has much to say. Three kinds of states of acceptance of goods and services exist. Ghazali (n.d.: 86) quotes the Prophet Muhammad's saying: "Lawful and unlawful things are clear in their own given states." In between these categories are the doubtful ones. Ghazali quoted the Prophet Muhammad as having said that he who saves himself from the doubtful things upholds religious belief.

Ghazali points out four origins of doubtful things that ought to be avoided according to the *shari'ah*.

1   A thing that was determined as unlawful before is now considered to be possibly lawful: Such a thing should be declared as doubtful and hence unlawful.

2   A thing is known to be lawful—but, under a changed situation, its legality becomes questionable: Such a thing should be avoided as being unlawful.
3   A thing is known to be unlawful—but, in a certain situation, the thing becomes lawful, yet the doubt remains on such a matter of legality: Such a thing remains lawful unless proven to be unlawful.
4   A thing is lawful, but later on is declared to be unlawful by an interpretive ruling (*fiqh*). Doubt is created. The prevalence of doubt makes the thing unlawful.

Ghazali pointed out that those lawful and unlawful things, if mixed together, cause doubt as to their lawful and unlawful nature after all and become unlawful. However, if the mixture cannot be proportioned exactly between lawful and unlawful, the whole is considered to be lawful. Thus if unlawfulness of a thing cannot be proven by strong proof and conclusively, that thing remains lawful in the *shari'ah*. Thus, if the lawful and unlawful proportions of mixed goods are known to the owner, he is required to separate the two kinds of goods and he must know the modes of spending in the lawful goods.

Ibn Taimiyyah as macroeconomist

In contrast to Ghazali, who looked into the moral reconstruction of individual preferences to lead into social preferences and choices, Ibn Taimiyyah was a macro-moralist. Ibn Taimiyyah's (1982) theory of the social regulation of market order, called the *hisbah fil-Islam*, laid all duties on public authority to perform such ethical supervision in the light of the *shari'ah*. This was the flip side of moral preference formation for social choice. A criticism of *al-hisbah fil-Islam* can thus be raised from the unwanted hegemony of the state in the name of the moral imposition of the state on a free, but conscious, market-based economy.

Indeed, the social welfare function was not a lateral utilitarian linear aggregation, perfectly formed by ethical individual preference, as was the case with Ghazali's form of moral utilitarianism. Likewise, it was not the case of a state-formed conception of welfare based on the hegemonic conception of a good society regulated by the state. The theme of a discursive society injecting moral consciousness in socially embedded choices was found neither in Ghazali nor in Ibn Taimiyyah.

On the impossibility of such kinds of aggregation, Rousseau (1968) wrote in his *Social Contract*:

> It is said that Japanese mountebanks can cut a child under the eyes of spectators, throw the different parts in the air, and then make the child come down, alive and all of a piece. This is more or less the trick that our political theorists perform – after dismembering the social body with a sleight of the hand worthy of the foreground, they put the pieces together again anyhow.

Contemporary Islamic scholars: the absence of intellectual emergence

Contemporary Islamic scholars have not raised the challenge of critically investigating the theory of welfare and social choice in neoclassical economics and, on the other side, the non-optimal and non-Pareto states of an evolutionary learning Islamic society that can be changed by degrees of consciousness into a good society. Even at the level of semantics, but with substantive difference in meaning and formalism, Islamic scholars have not endeavored to find the true meaning of "wellbeing" (*maslaha*) as opposed to "welfare."

Wellbeing is a deontological objective criterion in the Islamic epistemological context of the integrated functioning of the law of monotheism in the world-system. Welfare is a neoclassical and utilitarian objective criterion—based on the postulates of non-learning and non-evolution—that is optimality based on rational economic behavior, having full information and transitive alternatives. Emanating from these two disparate premises of social contracts are different economic, institutional, and social policy implications for moral transformation. At the level of intellection, these variant approaches lead to abiding differences in the distinct methodologies and methods they use. Meticulous investigations of the episteme and explanation of the methodological inquiry into the social contract of Islamic social political economy have not been made.

Step 3

Step 3 comprises two important undertakings. First, we derive the methodological origin of the Islamic worldview from the *Qur'an* and the *sunnah* in reference to the cardinal postulates of Islamic economics. This is the monotheistic law expressed as the unity of knowledge in the good things of life. It is termed in the *Qur'an* as *Tawhid*. *Tawhid*, as monotheism, is understood in its intellectual explanation as the total functioning of the monotheistic law.

Second, this section applies its cohesive explanation—that is, despite the disparate views between the methodology and the imminent methodical model of the epistemological foundation of unity of knowledge and the non-foundational perspective of Islamic economics and Muslim intellection in this area, there is scope for reforming the rationalist (*kalam*) ideas of the *kalam* school by the methodology of organic unity and relational symbiosis between *maqasid* choices. The idea underlying such an authentic moral and social reconstruction of Islamic intellection was voiced by Imam Ghazali.

We proceed now by first formulating the epistemological methodology of Islamic economics as it applies to all areas of socio-scientific intellection. The epistemological origin of revolutionary thought must be based on foundational axioms that do not change in any socio-scientific pursuit, be this mathematics or economics, social sciences, or pure science. The world-system is then explained thoroughly by this foundational and severely reduced methodological worldview. There are just two premises for this epistemological approach to the study of economic reality. First, there is the school of rationalism upon which the entire Occidental world-system is premised. This is true of the classical and neoclassical non-process orientation of optimal science (Shackle, 1971). It is also true of all of dialectical thought, as in Hegel, Marx, Popper, and Hayek (Spechler, 1990; Adomo, 2007; Resnick and Wolff, 1987; Popper, 2004). There is also the school of bounded rationality of modern exponents, such as Herbert Simon (1957) and Ronald Coase (1994), the evolutionary school of Schumpeter (1968), Boulding (1967), Georgescu-Roegen (1981) and Piero Sraffa (1960), and the Austrian School of Economics (Nelson and Winter, 1982).

A summary perspective of all of the different forms of intellection based on rationalism and economic rationality is offered in Figure 5.1.

Epistemological basis of Occidentalism: rationalism

Agency institutionalism is defined by the utilitarianism of welfare economics, or political economy is defined by conflict and power in the acquisition and distribution of wealth. These factors are included in Figure 5.1.

The most critical basis of rationalism is its Kantian heteronomy: the dichotomy between the a priori and the a posteriori praxes and their agential and institutional consequences based on a disintegrated worldview. The problem of Kantian heteronomy is best explained in Kant's (1949: 25) own words:

> This, then, is a question which at least calls for closer examination, and does not permit any off-hand answer: whether there is any knowledge that is thus independent of experience and even of all impressions of the senses. Such knowledge is entitled *a priori*, and is distinguished from the empirical, which has its sources *a posteriori*, that is, in experience.

The a priori domain of reasoning may be identified in many ways. It can be the domain of the divine law, the deductive premise of reasoning, and the moral imperative formed out of pure rationalism. The a posteriori domain can also be identified in many ways. It can be the domain of the material world, the inductive premise of reasoning, and the corporeal world-system of sensate phenomena. Heteronomy is then defined by the disjoint phenomenon of $\{a\ priori\} \cap \{a\ posteriori\} = \phi$. Such a disjoint relationship being a universal fact in rationalism induces all of Occidentalism. Thus individual and social ethics remain independent of each other. Such a social epiphenomenon is

Classical and neoclassical	Dialectical		Evolutionary	
Orthodoxy	School		School	
Praxis	Liberalism	Neo-liberalism	Rationalism	Rationalism
	Economic rationality		Human ego	
Domain	Ethically benign: exogenous		Ethically benign: exogenous	
of ethics	Endogenous as an economic theory of ethics and values			
Objective	Optimal and steady-state		No precise objective function	
	Equilibrium allocation of resources		and equilibrium state is defined	
	for self-interest and property rights		leading to openness and	
			dialectical randomness of	
			human behavior.	

Figure 5.1 The universal rationalist basis of Occidentalism

further intensified by institutionalism into culture, society, institutions, and the consequential concept of knowledge in science. Therefore the field of mainstream economics remains exogenously independent of morality and ethics.

This methodological independence is particularly questionable when morality and ethics are capable of discovering their roots in the divine law. The meaning of morality and ethics in the latter case takes up an epistemological nature, being derived in formal ways from the monotheistic (*Tawhidi*) methodology. This is subsequently endowed by its methodical formal model as invoked by the *Qur'an* and the *sunnah*, the guidance of the Prophet Muhammad.

However, the invoking of scientific ways of understanding the meaning and ontological functions of morality and ethics is not new in the literature of mainstream thought. Edel (1970) and Albert Einstein (n.d.) wrote on such methodological and functional issues of ethics and science in the sense of their endogenous interrelations.

Yet where did these important concepts of morality, ethics, and scientific thought go wrong? The problem arises from the kind of Kantian heteronomy. As a result, well-defined correspondences (*inter*-relational mappings) of the type of inter-causal circular causation between the moral domain of the a priori and the material domain of the a posteriori do not exist. This dissociation of the otherwise much-needed organic unity of circular causation relations between the two premises is the severest failure of heteronomy in respect of the episteme of unity of knowledge.

The episteme of unity of knowledge that embeds in the unified world-system is, otherwise, the principal characteristic of the divine law. It comprises the law and function of monotheism acting in all of reality and in two perspectives: the unity of knowledge as episteme, and its depiction of the world as it normatively "ought to be" and away from the morally fallen "as it is" world of methodological individualism and absence of moral choices (*maqasid as-shari'ah*). Methodology and its methodical formalism form the *functional* ontology of the endogenously moral and ethical world-system. Such a critical aspect of the monotheistic law and its functional working in the world-system is not to be found in mainstream doctrines and in the mainstream pursuit of Islamic economics in contemporary times.

Taking this characteristic of the episteme of unity of knowledge at the economic level as a particular sub-system of the world-system *res cogitans* and *res extensa*, we note the following fundamental flaw in mainstream and Islamic economic reasoning of the mainstream genre:

> *The axiom of transitivity of choice under full or bounded information is inadmissible in reality.*

Let A, B, and C, etc., be various alternatives, which, in the mainstream axiom of rational choice under full information, yield the transitivity axiom of $(A \ \wp \ B \ \wp \ C \ \wp \ldots)$. Here, $\wp$ means "preferred to." We now prove that this is rational foolishness, as Sen (1977) remarks.

Consider that, instead of the full-information condition, there exists evolutionary knowledge denoted by $\{\theta\}$. This set of knowledge variables is simulated to new levels as experiences, since any one choice continuously changes and moves towards other continuous choices. In this sense, as θ changes continuously, so also the alternative choices change continuously. Such a scenario is found with continuously technologically induced innovative human resource development (HRD) in the growth function (Romer, 1986). We denote this case as a *possibility*:

$$\{A \ \wp \ (\theta_1) \, B \leftrightarrow B \ \wp \ (\theta_2) \, A \leftrightarrow \text{etc.}\} \text{ as } \theta\text{-values remain in}$$
$$\text{evolutionary state} \quad (5.2)$$

Likewise:

$$\{B \ \wp \ (\theta_1) \, C \leftrightarrow C \ \wp \ (\theta_2) \, B \leftrightarrow \text{etc.}\} \quad (5.3)$$

This implies:

$$\{A \ \wp \ (\theta_1) \, B \leftrightarrow B \ \wp \ (\theta_2) \, A \leftrightarrow \text{etc.}\} \leftrightarrow \{B \ \wp \ (\theta_1) \, C \leftrightarrow C \ \wp \ (\theta_2) \, B \leftrightarrow \text{etc.}\}$$
$$(5.4)$$

$$\Rightarrow \text{Convex-type indifference functions } do \ not \text{ exist between } (A, B, C, \dots.)$$
$$(5.5)$$

In other words, we cannot define the axiom of transitivity of choices as of:

$$(A \ \wp \ (\theta^*) \, B \ \wp \ (\theta^*) \, C \ \wp \ (\theta^*) \ \dots.) \text{ as under full information with optimal } \theta^*$$
$$(5.6)$$

Next, expressions (5.2)–(5.4) can be expanded by continuously differentiable mappings (*f*s, and *f*'s) in respect of the continuity and differentiability of evolutionary θ-values, such as:

$$f_1(A) \leftrightarrow f_1{}'(B); f_2(B) \leftrightarrow f_2{}'(C), \text{ etc.} \quad (5.7)$$

$$\Rightarrow f_1(A) \leftrightarrow f_2{}'(C), \text{ etc.} \quad (5.8)$$

Given the choices $(A,B,C\dots)$ over evolutionary learning domain, transitivity axiom, and convex indifference maps, utility functions and the like cannot exist. Consequently, the θ-evolutionary knowledge-induced bundle $(A,B,C,\dots)[\theta]$ forms a non-optimal and non-steady-state of equilibrium fields of continual evolutionary learning. Such evolutionary learning equilibrium points are parameterized around their proximity by the expandable analytic function (Dadkhah, 2007).

These results can be further disaggregated into their components by inner variables. For example, if the vectors $\{x(A), x(B), x(C), \text{ etc.}\}[\theta]$ denote such variable-specific disaggregation (such as work, leisure, work–leisure, etc.), then a greater degree of complexity is generated by the inter-variable organic causality. Examples of such perturbations are product-diversification, changes in preferences, cultural impact, social policies, and ethical induction—as in the case of the choice of Islamic basket of life-fulfillment needs, etc. We can now denote a complex field of evolutionary learning possibilities whose interactions under unity of knowledge are represented by expandable properties of the *f*-functions around evolutionary learning equilibriums, as follows (Choudhury and Korvin, 2002):

$$\{f_1(x(A)) \leftrightarrow f_2(x(B)) \leftrightarrow f_3(x(B)) \leftrightarrow \text{etc.}\}[\theta] \tag{5.9}$$

When the above results of knowledge-induced dynamic effects are injected in preference maps, the mainstream economic theory of consumer behavior ceases to exist. Thereby the entire field comprising utility function, its objective criterion of utility maximization, consumer indifference curves, concepts of opportunity cost, and the consequential entire gamut of demand curves, elasticity coefficients and their related predictions and policy implications all fail to be accepted in the Islamic epistemological context. Now, there is no linear way of aggregating the consumer demand curves to yield straightforward market demand curves of goods and services. The existence of complex evolutionary equilibriums denies the existence of steady-state or sheer time-dynamic states of market equilibrium and Pareto-optimality. The axiom of rational choice in consumer theory is thus fully abandoned. Still, we find that such misleading perceptions are being followed in the outmoded precincts of Islamic economics of the mainstream genre today.

In the methodological explication of the monotheistic law of unity of knowledge in the unified world-system, the existence of evolutionary equilibriums extendable by analytic functions of complex interactive variables gravitates by inter-variable causal relations. The inter-variable causality defines the objective criterion of wellbeing—that is, the wellbeing function is the observed and reconstructed measure of the balance of unification relationships between critical selected variables, subject to the system of complex organic relations under the condition of evolutionary learning impact.

Such a methodological feature of the monotheistic law in its extended *functional* ontology is unique to the Islamic methodological worldview of unity of knowledge. The monotheistic methodological approach, along with its imminent methodical formal model of wellbeing as balance and simulated by circular causation in the complex field of interaction between the critical variables, is of significant import. First, it arises from and endogenously responds to unity of knowledge by the continuity of inter-causal relations. Second, the selected vector of variables is of the good things of life. We have identified such bundles with life-fulfillment goods (*maqasid as-shari'ah*). Third, it establishes sustainability through continuity of evolutionary learning in the above features in every field of social action and response. These are the properties of the methodology of unity of knowledge and its methodical model formalism that make the Islamic monotheistic methodology uniquely universal.

Because of the unique property of the above-mentioned methodological and methodical orientation of heterodox Islamic economics, premised indispensably in the episteme of unity of knowledge, there arise important consequences in economic reasoning. The deductive and the inductive, as for the a priori and the a posteriori, are not disjoint areas of reasoning any more; they complement each other in the continuity and sustainability of the complementary (participative) field of inter-variable causality. This kind of methodological derivation of methodical formalism invokes the formalism of circular causation between complementary variables that explains the simulation of the wellbeing criterion function.

Pricing theory of the firm in contrasting worldviews

In this regard, we investigate the opposing treatment of the pricing theory of the firm in mainstream economics and the Islamic economic approach to this topic that leans on mainstream economics. The same topic is treated differently in the heterodox Islamic epistemological worldview. Islamic economists of the mainstream genre continue with the mainstream objective function of profit maximization. Yet in Step 3 of our reconstruction of economic methodology in the random field of interaction, causality, and evolution with unity of knowledge, we note that the optimal equilibrium points of classical and neoclassical economic methodology are untenable in the evolutionary context. Consequently, no concept of price relative can logically exist. The production possibility surfaces, like the consumer indifference curves, are marked by complex perturbations. As a result, the postulates of marginal factor productivity, the marginal cost of production, factor payments, prices, output, and the economic expansion path are all subject to non-steady and non-optimal fields of evolutionary equilibrium points. Such points are extendable by analytic functions around convergent points that remain evolutionary in character (Choudhury, 2011).

Now, combining the knowledge-induced dynamic forms of the consumer indifference and the production possibility curves, there cannot logically exist any steady-state equilibrium. No optimal value of the objective criterion, such as utility maximization and profit maximization, can exist. The intensity of such non-optimal and non-steady-state equilibrium consequences deepens with the growing endogenous nature of knowledge-induced interaction and evolution in the midst of the unity of inter-causal systems. In such complex fields, the study of economics intersects with those of morality, ethics, institutions, society, and science. Likewise, none of these other sub-systems remains independent of the others. The result is the socially endogenous embedding of systems. Economics now turns into a socio-scientific study of political economy from the combined positivist and normative states of knowledge-induced, embedded world-systems.

The combination of the theory of consumer behavior with the pricing theory of the firm is now translated into the theory of complex perturbations, but temporary convergent points, of evolutionary fields. The section here summarizes the explanation on perturbations and interactive evolution of embedded systems in unity of knowledge caused by the monotheistic law. The three-dimensional space and thereby the n-dimensional space is described by the event point $(\theta, X_1(\theta), X_2(\theta))$. To this can also be included time, to denote the event as the occurrence in knowledge, space, and time dimensions. It is best to define such spaces and their monotonic transformations, as by the f'-functions, as topological spaces generated by the knowledge space. Knowledge parameters are now expressed as ranks, yet they are derived from the monotheistic law of divine Oneness. More on this method of assigning parametric θ-values is done with the empirical works.

The uniqueness of the imminent methodical formalism arising from the methodology of the monotheistic unity of knowledge is further established as the universal theory. To prove this fact, we note the permanence of heteronomy of reality in every field other than the Islamic monotheistic methodological worldview. Consequently, reasoning in the heteronomy system remains divided in all intellection other than Islam. This dichotomy happens between the deductive and inductive reasoning, between a priori and a posteriori domains of reality, and thus between God and the world-system taken in its generality and specifics (Carnap, 1966). The consequence of the imminent knowledge-induced reality is the evolutionary learning, reasoning, and induction of the world-system by dynamic convergences to unity of knowledge. Yet the reality of the opposite kind of any world-system is contrasted with the unified world-system phenomena by the same methodical formalism, which is derived methodologically from the monotheistic unity of knowledge in "everything" (Barrow, 1991).

In the topology of the continuously evolutionary learning world-system and its epistemic intellection, points such as "A" and "A^*" are θ-induced analytic "neighborhoods." These points are expandable by the continuity of θ-values, as with the Taylor series.[4] Likewise, there is the similar resulting effect of continuity and sustainability on the incident world-system. For this reason, the annulment of the postulates of mainstream economics leads to the prevalence of the principle of pervasive complementarities (participation) in the monotheistic orientation of Islamic economics.

We therefore write: In the finite convergence points such as "A" to "A^*", $x_i(\theta) \rightarrow x_i(\theta^*)$, even though $|\theta-\theta^*|$ is not "absolutely" less than an indefinitely small value (say, $\varepsilon > 0$). Thereby, continuity exists, but no optimal state from process to process of evolutionary learning exists.[5] Hence A^* is never attained; it is bypassed into sequential levels of evolutionary learning $\{\theta\}$-values and, thereby, $\{x(\theta)\}$-values. The property of continuity and sustainability of the evolutionary learning topological space is critical in this deduction. Moreover, in the discontinuous case, the attained neighborhoods and their temporary non-evolutionary learning states can be contained in a mathematical set of finite measure. Consequently, the continuity and sustainable nature of the finitely and temporarily non-evolutionary learning points is said to be enclosed in a set of "finite measure." The entire evolutionary learning space is then said to be measurable "almost everywhere" (ae) by dissecting the temporary non-evolutionary learning exceptions "ae" (Halmos, 1974).

Hence the property of evolutionary learning in the organically relational topological space is governed by the positive aspect of unity of knowledge, which remains universal (Maddox, 1970; Rucker, 1982). The principle of pervasive complementarities (participation) in unity of knowledge is universally valid.

Marginal substitutions and the postulates of rational choice and rationalism can form only temporary and finite incidents in the event space of (knowledge, space, and time) dimensions.

The universality of the Islamic monotheistic law influencing the unification of the world-system in reasoning, concrescence, and participatory (complementarities) forms of evolutionary learning across processes also establishes the finiteness of the non-evolutionary learning phenomenon "ae" (the language of mathematical measure theory). The latter is exemplified by mainstream economic postulation and by postulation of the rationalist forms of evolutionary reasoning. This is uniquely universal in respect of the most extended domain of the monotheistic law explaining "everything" (Barrow, 1991). The monotheistic law now overarches the widening evolutionary learning of the intersected God- and universe-embedded domains in terms of the episteme of unity of knowledge. The Oneness of God is now interpreted as the unity of knowledge arising from the monotheistic law and having its constructive impact on the unification of the world-system.

The end result of these argumentations is that, as in the case of Keynes (O'Donnell, 1989) and, more recently, Lawson (1988), who explains why probability theory as we know it cannot help in the estimation of functions within the simulacra of evaluations that ensue around points such as "A" and along its sequential evolutionary convergent points in learning processes, frequency-related probability distribution functions relegate domains into measurable context in order to evaluate such contexts out of simplification. This bounded nature of the probabilistic domains may not reflect reality. The exclusion of the "butterfly" effect (Gleick, 1988) and the appearance of several "black swans" (Taleb, 2007) reduce the space of reality into one of convenience. Yet, within this bravado of thought, extreme forms of randomness, which are rare, are untenable (Choudhury, 2013b). Following upon this argument, the methods of frequency probability, stochastic surface studies, data enveloping, etc. cannot be acceptable methods for studying the simulacra systems of functional relations.

Conclusion

The emergence of a field that can be genuinely called Islamic economics has not occurred to date. It is much needed, but its origin lies in the epistemological foundations of the moral and ethical paradigms of unity of knowledge of the monotheistic law. This project is also deepened by its rigorous "epistemic analytic (mathematics)" and application. There has been complete ambivalence to this gigantic field, which is required for the emergence of the meta-science of the monotheistic law of unity of knowledge. There has been a complete displacement of Islamic economics from the realm of heterodox socio-scientific thought.

It is now time to re-commence our intellectual journey. A broader heterodox scope of the socio-scientific project must be launched for the benefit of the world of learning in this heterodox era. Its application must mark the benefit of wellbeing for all. In the end, the integration between studies on materiality, as of the economic discipline, is fused with the moral and ethical dimensions of the socio-scientific order toward constructing the holistic worldview of wellbeing and the common good. In the same way as Islamic economics faded away and never rose in the absence of the epistemological worldview, so also there is now the knell of a parting reality for Islamic finance and thereby for Islamic financial economics. The use of the caption "Islamic" without the substance of the monotheistic methodology of unity of knowledge does not do rightful service for Islamic socio-scientific erudition.

Notes

1 Alfred North Whitehead (1978) defines ontology in a way that serves our purpose of understanding how Islamic socio-scientific reasoning in general and Islamic economics in particular converge into an organically unified evolutionary learning process theory of unity of knowledge. Whitehead (ibid.: 43) writes:

> The ontological principle asserts the relativity of decision; whereby every decision expresses the relation of the actual thing, for which a decision is made, to an actual thing by *which* that decision is made. But "decision" cannot be construed as a casual adjunct of an actual entity. It constitutes the very meaning of actuality.

2 Gruber (1993) defines *functional* ontology as follows:

> In the context of knowledge sharing, I use the term ontology to mean a *specification of a conceptualization*. That is, ontology is a description (like a formal specification of a program) of the concepts and relationships that can exist for an agent or a community of agents. This definition is consistent with the usage of ontology as a set-of-concept-definitions, but is more general. And it is certainly a different sense of the word than its use in philosophy.

3 "There is no way for cultivating morals except through observing in works the canon of the religious law so that man would not follow his whim, such that 'he makes his caprice his god" (*Qur'an*, 25:45, 45:22).

> Rather, he must imitate the law, advancing on holding back [action] not as he chooses, [but] according to what [the law] directs, his moral dispositions becoming educated thereby. Whoever is deprived of this virtue in both moral disposition and knowledge is the one who perishes. For this reason God, exalted be He, said: "Whoever purifies it has achieved success and whoever corrupts it fails."
>
> (*Qur'an*, 91:9–10).

"Whoever combines both virtues, the epistemological and the practical, is the worshipping 'knower', the absolutely blissful one" (Ghazali, 1997).

4 Taylor series in cubic form approximation to account for inflexions of functions in complex domains:

$$
\begin{aligned}
W(\theta, x(\theta)) = {}& W(\theta^*, x^*(\theta^*)) + [(d/d\theta).(W(\theta^*, x^*(\theta^*)))/1!].(\theta\text{-}\theta^*) \\
& + [(d/dx(\theta)).(W(\theta^*, x^*(\theta^*)))/1!].(x(\theta)\text{-}x^*(\theta^*))] \\
& + [(d^2/d\theta^2).(W(\theta^*, x^*(\theta^*)))/2!].(\theta\text{-}\theta^*)^2 \\
& + [(d^2/dx(\theta)^2).(W(\theta^*, x^*(\theta^*)))/2!].(x(\theta)\text{-}x^*(\theta^*))]^2 \\
& + [(d^3/d\theta^3).(W(\theta^*, x^*(\theta^*)))/3!].(\theta\text{-}\theta^*)^2 \\
& + [(d^3/dx(\theta)^3). \ (W(\theta^*, x^*(\theta^*)))/3!].(x(\theta)\text{-}x^*(\theta^*))]^3 + \text{Higher valued terms}
\end{aligned}
$$

5 On this point, others have prevailed. Hodgson (1989: 18) writes: "Behavioural theorists such as Cyert and March ... reject the very idea that the firm is maximizing at all: it is 'satisficing' instead."

References

Adomo, T.W. (2007). *Negative Dialectics*, trans. Ashton, E.B., New York: Continuum.

Arrow, K.J. (1951). *Social Choice and Individual Values*, New York: John Wiley & Sons.

Barrow, J.D. (1991). "Laws," in *Theories of Everything: The Quest for Ultimate Explanation*, Oxford: Oxford University Press, pp. 12–30.

Blaug, M. (1968). "Introduction: Has economic theory progressed?," in *Economic Theory in Retrospect*, Homewood, IL: Richard D. Irwin.

Bloomberg (2009). "Vatican says islamic finance may help Western banks in crisis," March 4.

Boulding, K.E. (1967). "Evolution and revolution in the developmental process," in *Social Change and Economic Growth*, Paris: Development Centre of the Organization for Economic Co-operation and Development.

Carnap, R. (1966). "Kant's synthetic a priori," in Gardner, M. (ed.), *Philosophical Foundations of Physics*, New York: Basic Books.

Chapra, U. (1992). *Islam and the Economic Challenge*, Leicester and Herndon, VA: The Islamic Foundation: The International Institute of Islamic Thought.

Choudhury, M.A. (1986). *Contributions to Islamic Economic Theory: A Study in Social Economics*, London: Macmillan.

Choudhury, M.A. (2011). "On the existence of evolutionary learning equilibriums," *Journal for Science*, 16, 1: 49–61.

Choudhury, M.A. (2013a). *Handbook of Tawhidi Methodology*, Jakarta: University of Trisakti Press.

Choudhury, M.A. (2013b). "Complexity and endogeneity in economic methodology," *Kybernetes: International Journal of Cybernetics, Systems, and Management Science*, 42, 2: 226–240.

Choudhury, M.A. and Korvin, G. (2002). "Simulation versus optimization," *Kybernetes: International Journal of Systems and Cybernetics*, 31, 1: 44–60.

Coase, R.H. (1994). "Adam Smith's view of man," in *Essays on Economics and Economists*, Chicago, IL: University of Chicago Press.

Dadkhah, K. (2007). *Foundations of Mathematical and Computational Economics*, Mason, OH: Thomson, pp. 288–291.

Edel, A. (1970). "Science and the structure of ethics," in Neurath, O. Carnap, R., and Morris, C. (eds.), *Foundations of the Unity of Science*, Chicago, IL: University of Chicago Press.

Erasmus Journal for Philosophy and Economics (2009). "Cambridge social ontology: An interview with Tony Lawson," 2, 1: 100–122.

Einstein, A. (n.d.). "The laws of science and the laws of ethics," in *Lectures in Physics*, New York: Philosophical Library.

Faruqi, F.R. (1982). *Islamization of Knowledge: General Principles and Workplan*, Herndon, VA: International Institute of Islamic Thought.

Feiwel, G.R. (1987). "The many dimensions of Kenneth J. Arrow," in Feiwel, G.R. (ed.), *Arrow and the Foundations of the Theory of Economic Policy*, London: Macmillan, pp. 1–115.

Georgescu-Roegen, N. (1981). *The Entropy Law and the Economic Process*, Cambridge, MA: Harvard University Press.

Ghazanfar, S.M. (1991). "Scholastic economics and Arab scholars: The 'Great Gap' thesis reconsidered," *Diogenes: International Review of Human Sciences*, 154, April–June.

Gleick, J. (1988). *Chaos: Making a New Science*, New York: Penguin Books.

Gruber, T.R. (1993). "A translation approach to portable ontologies," *Knowledge Acquisition*, 5, 2: 199–200.

Halmos, P.R. (1974). *Measure Theory*, New York: Springer-Verlag.

Hammond, P.J. (1987). "On reconciling Arrow's theory of social choice with Harsanyi's fundamental utilitarianism," in Feiwel, G.R. (ed.), *Arrow and the Foundations of the Theory of Economic Policy*, London,: Macmillan Press.

Harsanyi, J.C. (1955). "Cardinal welfare, individualistic ethics, and interpersonal comparisons of utility," *Journal of Political Economy*, 63, 4: 309–321.

Hawking, S.W. (1988). *A Brief History of Time: From the Big Bang to Black Holes*, New York: Bantam Books.

Henderson, H. (1999). *Beyond Globalization: Shaping a Sustainable Global Economy*, West Hartcourt, CN: Kumarian Press.

Hodgson, G. (1989). "Persuasion, expectations and the limits to Keynes," in Lawson, T. and Pesaran, H. (eds.), *Keynes' Economics: Methodological Issues*, London: Routledge.

Holton, R.L. (1992). *Economy and Society*, London: Routledge.

Ibn Taimiyyah (1982). *Public Duties in Islam* [Al-Hisbah Fil-Islam], trans. Holland, M., Leicester: Islamic Foundation.

Imam Ghazali (n.d.). *Ihya Ulum-Id-Din* (five volumes) trans. Karim, M.F., Lahore: Sh. Muhammad Ashraf.

Imam Ghazali (1997). *The Incoherence of the Philosophers*, trans. Marmura, M.E., Provo, UT: Brigham Young University Press.

Islahi, A.A. (1988). "Ibn Taimiyah's concept of money and monetary policy," in *Economic Concepts of Ibn Taimiyah*, Leicester: Islamic Foundation, pp. 139–143.

Kant, I. (1949). "Critique of pure reason," in Friedrich, C.J., (ed.), *The Philosophy of Kant*, New York: Modern Library.

Kuhn, T.S. (1970). *The Structure of Scientific Revolution*, Chicago, IL: University of Chicago Press, p. 154.

Laclau, E. (1996). "Universalism, particularism, and the question of identity," in Wilmsen, E.N. and McAllister, P. (eds.), *Politics of Difference*, Chicago, IL: University of Chicago Press, pp. 45–58.

Lawson, T. (1988). "Probability and uncertainty in economic analysis," *Journal of Post-Keynesian Economics*, 11, 1: 35–65.

Lawson, T. and Pesaran, H. (1989). "Methodological issues in Keynes' economics: An introduction," in *Keynes' Economics: Methodological Issues*, London: Routledge, p. 1.

Lee, F.S. and Lavoie, M. (eds.) (2013). *In Defense of Post-Keynesian and Heterodox Economics*, Abingdon: Routledge.

Maddox, I.J. (1970). *Elements of Functional Analysis*, Cambridge: Cambridge University Press.

Mahomedy, A.C. (2013). "Islamic economics: Still in search of an identity," *International Journal of Social Economics*, 40, 6: 556–578.

Nelson, R.R. and Winter, S.G. (1982). *An Evolutionary Theory of Economic Change*, Cambridge, MA: Belknap Press of Harvard University Press.

O'Donnell, R.M. (1989). *Keynes: Philosophy, Economics and Politics*, London: Macmillan, pp. 93–100.

Polanyi, K. (1957). *The Great Transformation: The Political and Economic Origins of Our Time*, Boston, MA: Beacon Press.

Popper, K. (2004). *The Logic of Scientific Discovery*, London: Routledge.

Qadri, C.A. (1988). *Philosophy and Science in the Islamic World*, London: Routledge.

Rahman, R. (1988). "Islamization of knowledge: A response," *American Journal of Islamic Social Sciences*, 5, 1.

Resnick, S.A. and Wolff, R.D. (1987). *Knowledge and Class: A Marxian Critique of Political Economy*, Chicago, IL: University of Chicago Press.

Romer, P.M. (1986). "Increasing returns and long-run growth," *Journal of Political Economy*, 94, 5: 1002–1037.

Rousseau, J.-J. (1968). *The Social Contract*, trans. Cranston, M., London: Penguin Books.

Rucker, R. (1982). "Large cardinals," in *Infinity and the Mind*, New York: Bantam Books, pp. 273–286.

Schumpeter, J.S. (1968). "The scholastic doctors and the philosophers of natural law," in *History of Economic Analysis*, New York: Oxford University Press.

Sen, A. (1977). "Rational fools: A critique of the behavioural foundations of economic theory," *Philosophy and Public Affairs*, 6: 317–344.

Shackle, G.L.S. (1971). *Epistemics and Economics*, Cambridge: Cambridge University Press.

Siddiqi, M.N. (2013). "Reflections on Islamic economics," available at http://siddiqi.com/mns/Future_of_Islamic_Economics_2012.htm, accessed April 16, 2016.

Simon, H. (1957). *Models of Man*, New York: John Wiley & Sons.

Spechler, M.C. (ed.) (1990). *Perspectives in Economic Thought*, New York: McGraw-Hill.

Sraffa, P. (1960). *Production of Commodities by Means of Commodities*, Cambridge: Cambridge University Press.

Sztompka, P. (1991). *Society in Action: The Theory of Social Becoming*, Chicago, IL: University of Chicago Press.

Taleb N.N (2007). *The Black Swan: The Impact of the Highly Improbable*, New York: Random House.

Whitehead, A.N. (1978). "Fact and form," in Griffin, D.R. Sherburne, D.W. (eds.), *Process and Reality*, New York: The Free Press, pp. 39–60.

6   Critical realism and Islamic socio-scientific reasoning in the episteme of the monotheistic unity of knowledge

The failure of mainstream economics, its dialectical and evolutionary outgrowth premised in rationalism, and the Islamic imitation of these postulates point to yet another deep-seated problem of studying the critical realism of the socio-scientific methodological worldview. We will now argue that, in the absence of the foundational epistemology of uniqueness and universality, which stands for scientific self-referencing (Smullyan, 1992), and an ontological argument that can be also explained by the systemic closure based on circular causation as the methodical formalism of unity of knowledge, the perceived idea of critical realism runs into problems.

Roy Bhaskar (1978) explains his idea of critical realism underlying the scientific enterprise in a purely reductionist way, premised on rationalism. The substantive realm of knowledge emanating from and returning to the divine premise through the actions and responses in the experiential and discursive world-system is left out by Bhaskar. He writes (ibid.: 195): "Knowledge does not exist in a third world. Rather, it exists in our world, embedded in the scientific community. Without men there would be no knowledge, only its traces. In this sense it depends upon men." Yet Bhaskar does not fully reject the a priori existence of knowledge. However, this reducible character of knowledge is not integrative, as was explained in relation to the problem of Kantian heteronomy.

In this dichotomy of Bhaskar's formulation of reasoning, we find the absence of the integrative function of reasoning, as shown in Figure 6.1. We have re-oriented Figure 6.1. The connection between a priori and a posteriori, transcendental "idealism" and transcendental "realism," is purely empirical in nature and can be explained with human approach to modeling. This kind of methodical inter-relationship is continued indefinitely. Thus inductive, as opposed to deductive, reasoning is emphasized by the force of empiricism and the human modeling of events.

Opposed to the above explanation biased towards empiricism and the induction of the critical basis of realism, the organic relational embedding by unity of knowledge causes endogenous (learning) causality between empiricism, induction, and abstraction, and also deduction, by means of the construction of the epistemic methodology of monotheistic law of unity in being and becoming. This approach interrelates the a priori and the a posteriori, which are now taken up together. Heteronomy is then rent asunder.

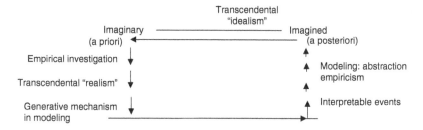

Figure 6.1 The logic of scientific discovery according to the theory of critical realism

In the Islamic monotheistic methodological worldview, with its methodical formal model of unity of knowledge—namely, simulation of the knowledge-induced wellbeing (balance) objective criterion subject to the system of circular causation representing pervasive complementary, participation, and moral embedding—the dichotomy of heteronomy is replaced. Transcendental idealism is replaced by $T = \Omega$ with its mathematical continuous, derived function as S (*functional* ontology) mapping into methodological abstraction as the generation of knowledge $\{\theta\}$ (see Figure 6.2).

These together comprise the deductive domain, $D(\Omega \cap S \cap \theta)$. Next, "*D*" characterizes the world-system, $WS(\theta, x(\theta))$. Thus "*D*" is embedded in $WS(.)$ by a methodical formalism representing the *functional* ontology of unity of knowledge in the world-system. Thus empiricism and abstraction are unified. Finally, the circular causality is continued across evolutionary learning in the emergent episteme of unity of knowledge. Deduction and induction of scientific logic are unified together by abstraction and formalism (methodical modeling and testing) in evolutionary learning rounds of circular causation.

The epistemological foundation of Islamic economics and world-system study

No intellection, explicit or implicit, can be accepted as an Islamic act without the active invocation and utilization of the monotheistic epistemology of *Tawhid* to realize scientific universality, analytics, reasoning, and evidence. Such an intellection would at best remain a rationalist endeavor with an exogenous invoking of *Tawhid*. But the rationalist approach here would mean the same thing as the exogenous treatment of morality and ethics, as in all of economics and finance theories today—indeed in all of science. Choudhury (2006) has pointed out that nowhere among the contemporary Islamic gurus has *Tawhid* been used as the epistemology to develop the socio-scientific order with the divine law and the world-system in light of the endogenous influence of morality and ethics. Islamic economists hold on to the mainstream economic axiom of resource scarcity and accept its central idea of the marginal rate of substitution. Yet this is a most untenable axiom in the *Tawhidi*

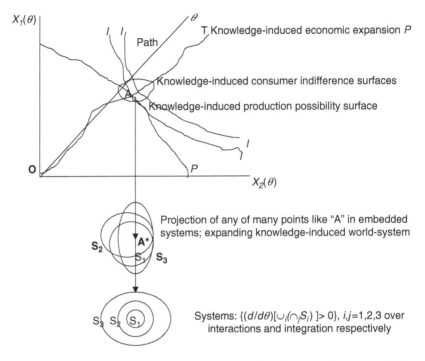

Figure 6.2 Perturbations everywhere in non-optimal and non-steady state conditions of knowledge-induced evolutionary economic surfaces

epistemological worldview under its condition of learning in unity of knowledge and its construction of the knowledge-induced unified world-system. Any conception and its application in Islamic intellection must start and carry on the *Tawhidi* essence of shape and form. As was written by Ibn Al-Arabi, any invocation other than *Tawhid* in Islamic intellection creates only obfuscations.

Unacceptability of the postulate of marginal substitution in mainstream economics and in Islamic economics

How does Islamic argumentation bring into effect the phenomenon of dispensing with the mainstream postulates—principally of rational choice, scarcity, full information leading to optimization, and steady-state conditions of marginal rate of substitution between competing ends? The facts are that a continuously learning world-system in the *Tawhidi* perspective of unity of knowledge, participation, and complementarities between the "good things of life," as ordained by *maqasid as-shari'ah*, causes diversity in unity to extend over increasingly spanning domains of possibilities. The result is the continuous reproduction of output and resources, cooperation and empowerment, distribution, and simultaneity of knowledge-induced events by virtue of linkages between the possibilities as created by knowledge production in the direction of the *maqasid as-shari'ah*. Consequently, this dynamic principle of pervasive complementarities rejects the postulate of the marginal rate of substitution, which is a static idea even if taken across time as datum.

Together with this, the continuous learning in unity of knowledge liberates resources. Thus comes about the end of scarcity. These conditions cause the well-being (*maslaha*) embedded in the *maqasid as-shari'ah* to continuously evolve. Optimization of the criterion function is then logically abandoned.

Yet there are those among Islamic economists who argue that optimization and steady-state equilibrium are constrained by available resources (budget). This is an untenable argument. The presence of knowledge in continuum and the continuous learning in the *Tawhidi* unity of knowledge cause the budget line to shift continuously and permanently. This causes the coefficients of the variables in the wellbeing function to vary along with the learning shifts in the variables. The resource equation then evolves under the force of continuous knowledge reproduction and its inducing effects on the variables. Consequently, no steady-state equilibrium can exist, for the budget line cannot be held fixed on any optimal surface. This is the message of Figure 6.2.

What about the household budget allocation to purchase, say, tea and coffee as substitutes? What about a firm's allocation of its cost of production between the production of tea and coffee as substitutes?

Tea and coffee appear as substitutes because the commercial world has not allowed for the possibility of blending these beverages, as it is done in, say, carrot-and-orange blended juice and the like. Consequently, tastes have not been developed to overcome the scarcity problem driven by the assumed static nature of tastes and preferences. Yet, in a dynamic preference environment of decision-making and choices, it is possible for households to choose complemented goods—such as rice, wheat, and fertilizers—by technological fusion, conservation, and recycling of waste of reproductive resources. Alongside this is the development of complementary technological change that can expand the fertility of land for the complementary production of tea and coffee together, without substitution between them. It is the static preferences and menus linked with assumptions of scarcity and competition of the Western commercial world-system that has perpetuated the scarcity axiom of economics. The result is a marginal rate of substitution between competing ends.

Islamic economists have accepted mainstream assumptions without question by failing to understand the episteme of *Tawhid* underlying the pervasively complementary (participatory), hence diversely unified, world-system under the impact of continuous reproduction of knowledge and learning processes. This is the function in the light of the epistemology of unity of knowledge and its induced, unified possibilities in the choices of the world-system, specifically of economic "possibilities" rather than competing "alternatives."

Thus so-called Islamic economics has not understood the *Tawhidi* epistemological methodology and its dynamics in constructing the Islamic economic, financial, social, and socio-scientific methodological worldview. The *qur'anic* precept of pairing, which results in abundance,[1] as the understanding and pursuit of learning experience proceeds, has not moved the Muslim mind to build the learning universe in the framework of the monotheistic (*Tawhidi*) unity of knowledge and its methodological construction of the world-system.

Towards the construction of the *Tawhidi* methodology in Islamic economics, finance, and the socio-scientific order

From our earlier discussions, it is clear that the dynamics of knowledge is essential in understanding and constructing the *Tawhidi* epistemic worldview of the Islamic world-system. Failure to comprehend this essential and indispensable foundation of the *qur'anic* epistemology has been the root cause of the predicaments of anything that can be proudly called the theory and practice of Islamic economics and Islamic finance for the world of learning. Consequently, no fresh demands of these disciplines have been made. They staggered into disuse and fell prey to the sheer mechanical application of some superficial color of "*shari'ah*-compliance," as opposed to *maqasid as-shari'ah* principles. This was to the sole benefit of the rich man and principal shareholders' interests served by Islamic banks, Islamic financing, and the clamor for interest-free ways of private financing. Despite all these claims, we still find that the participatory real economy linked with development financing instruments has been increasingly abandoned by Islamic banks and financing houses. The focus throughout has shifted to secondary financing instruments and *sukuk* (participatory bonds). These have many *shari'ah* financing debilities in them (Khnifer. n.d; Gassner, 2008).

The emergence of the *Tawhidi* worldview, with the epistemology of unity of knowledge and the world-system induced by such knowledge-flows, is the way in which to understand the logical negation of many of the postulates of mainstream economics and finance theory and practice. Some of these were mentioned above. On the other hand, to understand the substantively endogenous and applied worldview of *Tawhid*, the methodology underlying *Tawhidi* epistemology must be understood.

The general system theory in the light of the monotheistic methodology

We now present such a theory to standardize a general system theory of "everything," premised on the monotheistic methodology. Barrow (1991) used the term "everything" for unification theory in theoretical physics.

The coverage of monotheistic (*Tawhidi*) methodological formalism here is brief. For more details, the reader can refer to many of the works by the author (Choudhury, 2006; Choudhury and Hoque, 2004).

The phenomenology of the circular causation and continuity model of unified reality in the Islamic world-system is explained by the string relation in expression

(6.1–6.13). This is a version of the formal *Tawhidi* knowledge model and is referred
to as the *Tawhidi* String Relation (TSR):

$$\Omega \to s\theta \to_f \{\theta_1\} \to_{f1} x_I\{\theta_1\}$$

(Ω, S) $(\theta_I, x_I\{\theta_1\}) \to$ simulate $W(\theta_1, x_I(\theta_1))$
subject to circular causation
between the variables to bring,
first, their actual state of relations
in the problem under study, followed
by reconstruction to establish
pervasive complementarities between
all the variables determined by the   (6.1)
maqasid as-shari'ah

Recalling (Ω, S)

$$\to_{g1} \{\theta_2\} \to_{f2} x\{\theta_2\} \to$$

Simulate $W(\theta_2, x_2(\theta_2))$
subject to circular causation
as for process 1, etc. $\to (\Omega, S)$
[*Akhira* = the Hereafter]

In expression (6.1), Ω denotes the supercardinal topology (Maddox, 1970; Dewitt, 1992) of the *Tawhidi* stock of knowledge, which is the totality of the divine law (*Qur'an* refers to it as *Lauh Mahfuz umm al-kitab*).[2] Alternatively, it is the complete stock of knowledge of the *Qur'an*. Hence the term "supercardinality" is used. Rucker (1982) refers to such large topological phenomena as having large cardinalities.

Here, S denotes the *sunnah*—the mapping guidance of the Prophet Muhammad. Thus S maps parts of Ω "onto" the conceptual and experiential worlds. The result is the discursive formation of rules and understanding of the nature and functions of the derived knowledge-flows denoted by $\{\theta\}$. The discursive mechanism for deriving $\{\theta\}$ on the basis of the *Qur'an* and the *sunnah*—that is, (Ω,S)—is called the consultative institution of the *shura*. Abstraction and analysis carried out in respect of the problem under discourse in the *shura* reveal the abstraction of the normative world-system for the problem. The emergent relations are constructed by rules derived from the ontology of (Ω,S).

The embedded consciousness of the world-system premised on the problems studied is referred to as *tasbih*.[3] *Tasbih* means also the consciousness of the world in its hidden worshipping of *Tawhid*.[4] Such consciousness marks the intrinsic learning of the world-system in unity of knowledge. The rules derived from the *shura-tasbih* processes of interactive investigation manifest the rules of unity of knowledge in dealing with the unity of the world-system.

The *shura-tasbih* experience—being, first, interactive in terms of the diversity of being and approaches to human intellection of the *Tawhidi* implications of rules— derives consensus through the medium of learned discourse. This is the stage of interactions leading to integration. In the string relation (6.3), the interaction taking place at the level of forming the *primal* $\{\theta\}$ denoted derived rules leads to a consensual knowledge-value denoted by $\{\theta_1\}$ through the discursive medium, here denoted by "*f*" as the *functional* ontology. Advances in the interactive learning in the *shura-tasbih* experience mark the emergence of the *shari'ah*. The *functional* ontology of the *shari'ah* denoted by "*f*" is the enabling medium called the *maqasid as-shari'ah*.[5]

Thus "*f*1" denotes the mapping of the *maqasid as-shari'ah* $f\{\theta\}$ "onto" specific choices of sets of variables and their relations.

The first set of interactions leading to integration is indicated by "1." This set comprises many rounds of interaction leading to consensus or integration in the understanding of rules and guidance derived from (Ω, S), specific to the issues and problems that are subjected to the *shura-tasbih* discursive practice.

Subsequently, at the point of consensus (or majority rule), post-evaluation is carried out to reveal the reconstructed (normative) versus the prevalent (actual) state of the problem under discourse. Now, the wellbeing function (*maslaha*) arising from the *maqasid-as-shari'ah* is simulated in references to the circular—that is, complementary—interrelationships between the variables. Because of the need to restore or improve the participatory (complementary) nature of the *maqasid as-shari'ah* variables, the system of such relations assumes the form of circular causation. The wellbeing function is thus simulated, subject to the system of circular causation relations between the variables.

Following this stage, a new phase of learning process arises at the end of the first process. Now, (Ω, S) is recalled to restart the second process with fresh knowledge-flows denoted by $\{\theta_2\}$. Such an emergence of the new process following the previous one after post-evaluation by the wellbeing function marks the creative evolution in the learning process. Each learning process is an experience of the derivation of knowledge-flows premised on the *Tawhidi* unity of knowledge and its induction of the problems at hand. The interrelated flows of knowledge and the knowledge-induced variables are shown by the *functional* ontologies (the "*f*"-mappings). The domain of the problem under analysis is thus characterized by the wellbeing (*maqasid as-shari'ah*) function and the interrelationships between the circular causation relations.

Learning in unity of knowledge and its induction of the problem under investigation continues on until the Hereafter. The Hereafter is the Great Event mentioned in the *Qur'an*.[6] It is denoted by the ultimate completion of the knowledge stock in the closure of the very large universe. Thus (Ω, S) is once again attained, after proceeding through the continuums of Interactive, Integrative and Evolutionary (**IIE**) learning processes in the world-system. Each learning process is an advancement in unity of knowledge $\{\theta\}$, derived from (Ω, S) and evaluated by the *functional* ontology of the *maqasid as-shari'ah*, which establishes the learning world-system corresponding to such derived and reconstructed $\{\theta\}$-values across learning processes. The resulting reconstructed variables entering the evaluative *maslaha* function comprise the $\{\theta,x(\theta)\}$-tuples in continuums of knowledge, space, and time dimensions.

Let the totality $E \subset \{\Omega,S,\theta\}$ denote the extended Islamic epistemology (E-episteme) at the outset of any round of Interaction followed thereafter by Integration and then creative Evolution. IIE is written down in terms of Ω to signify the supercardinal topological ontology of *Tawhid* in terms of the divine laws, which are preserved in the *Qur'an*. S denotes the *functional* ontological explication (mapping) of the *Qur'an* by the *sunnah*.[7] The *primal* knowledge derivation out of the ontological experience denoted by $\{\theta\}$ signifies the *shura-tasbih* essence of the *maqasid as-shari'ah*. The *maqasid as-shari'ah* thus becomes the functional ontology of unravelling the fundamental epistemology (Ω,S) through knowledge derivation in $\{\theta\}$. (For the idea of functional ontology, see Gruber, 1993.)

Thereafter, $\{\theta_1\}$ knowledge-flows within Process 1 signify the guidance and rule derivation from the basis of the divine laws. Thus $\{\theta_1\}$ carries its *functional* ontological impact on the relations arising from the problem under study. The attributes that generate the functional ontology in action in the knowledge-induced world-system under unity of knowledge as derived from the epistemic premise of (Ω,S) are $A = \{$Justice, Purpose, Certainty, Wellbeing, Creative Evolution,[8] and the beatific attributes of *Allah*, the *Asma*$\}$. In brief therefore, we can write, $\{\theta_1\} = \{\theta_1(A)\}$ in Process 1 followed by its recalling in every subsequent emergent processes of deriving knowledge through the **IIE**-properties of the *shura-tasbih* experience. The primordial reference to the beatific names of *Allah* (*Asma*) signifies the importance of emulating the attributes of *Allah* in the functions of the world-system. Thus the *functional* ontology carries the *Asma* towards consciously understanding and applying the *Asma* to their complex combinations to specific issues and problems under investigation.

The essence of unity of knowledge derived from the epistemic origin of (Ω,S) is simultaneously induced into the *maqasid as-shari'ah* variables, $\{x_1(\theta_1)\}$, using the *functional* ontology of *shura-tasbih* denoted by "f" and "f_1."

The evaluation of the prevalent positivistic relations of the world-system are then normatively reconstructed or improved by estimation of the wellbeing criterion (*maslaha*) defined by the $\{\theta_1, x_1(\theta_1)\}[A]$-tuple.

The wellbeing function objective criterion in the light of *maqasid as-shari'ah*

The *wellbeing function* is represented by $W = W(\theta_1,x_1(\theta_1))$. The estimated value of $W(.)$ is equivalently represented by the estimated θ-relation that appears as one of the circular causation relations with ranked θ-values in general without subscripts. θ-values are ranked in reference to the performance of the $x(\theta)$. Such calculated ranks for θ-values are then averaged across the $x(\theta)$-values. *Rank-values of θ* are not the same as the *primal* θ-value in any emergent learning process. The *primal θ-values* are formed at the moment of the *shura-tasbih* discourse, yielding guidance and rules of the *maqasid as-shari'ah* on the problems and issues under study. Thus $W(.)$ or the estimated θ-relation is the result of the post-evaluation of a normatively reconstructed system with unity of knowledge represented in the reformation of an existing positivistic scenario. The wellbeing function is thus the representation caused by *functional* ontology. Its form, estimated value, and dynamics in the midst of circular causation on extensive complementarities altogether signify the degree to which the system has been unified according to the *Tawhidi* worldview. Appropriate institutional and market ethical transformations, strategies, policies, and the like are derived at the normative (simulated, "as it ought to be") evaluation stage of the *maslaha*.

Thus, following post-evaluation of $W(.)$ in terms of $\{\theta, x(\theta_1)\}$, creative evolution of similar "processual" orders arise. The time variable $t(\theta)$ is subsumed in $\{x(\theta)\}$. Interaction leading to Integration through a set of *shura-tasbih* discourses within Process 1 finally leads to Evolution by recalling the epistemological beginning in subsequent learning processes. Such learning processes perpetuate in the midst of the epistemology of unity of knowledge with induction into the unified world-system. The emergent *Tawhidi* String Relation (TSR) describes how the *impact* of the divine law of Oneness is learnt by simulation in the learning universe of unity of knowledge and the unified world-system.

Since all the inputs and outputs of this learning system are knowledge-induced, therefore, systemic "universal complementarities" are established by means of unification between knowledge and the knowledge-induced variables. The principle of pervasive complementarities signifying the continuously participatory nature of the *Tawhidi* worldview and world-system is the surest measured sign of *Tawhidi* unity of knowledge.

The f's and g's denote mappings signifying the *functional* ontological derivations of rules and guidance from the E-episteme. They are functional ontological forms of ethical endogeneity. Now, the sequences, $P_i = (\{\theta_i\} \rightarrow_{fi} \{x_i\} \rightarrow_{gi+1} \{\theta_{j+1}\})$, $i = 1, 2, \ldots$, comprise the chain of *shura-tasbih* experiences of unity of knowledge. The IIE-properties are thus realized both within these sequences and also across similar ones in extensively participatory types of multidimensional system.[9]

Some economic issues seen from the *Tawhidi* methodological viewpoint

Markets in Tawhidi *reference*

The market system is influenced by exogenous preferences in prevalent Islamic economics and finance. The market is thus a consequentialist venue of ethics and values determined by exogenous individual behavior. This is unlike the endogenous knowledge induction of preferences in ethicizing markets. Islamic behavior in the ideal markets of Islamic economics is a pre-determined prescription. Its forces are not the result of a discursive learning process.

Chapra (1992) for instance, used the concept of a moral filter in the pricing and resource allocation mechanism of Islamic economics. According to this concept, market prices are assumed to be governed by the perfect Islamic baskets of goods and services, to the exclusion of imperfect ones. The filtered output is the ideal

Islamic one and prices are thereby ideal with respect to such a filtered market. The market order is thus segmented into a *shari'ah*-recommended part (*halal*) and a *shari'ah*-impermissible part (*haram*). The moral filter guides preferences towards the prescribed segmented market within such an assumed differentiation.

In all of the above studies on consumer behavior, the role of learning that progressively breaks down the market duality by moral induction is replaced by prescribed behavior. Hence a price-discriminating model is implied between the segmented markets. No analytical explanation is made clear regarding the gradual transition from one market sub-system to another by the force of inter-systemic learning and unification.

Instead, in the *Tawhidi* methodological worldview, markets are progressively ethicized by the selections and choices of goods according to the *maqasid as-shari'ah*. The inherent learning process in such selections and choices as induced by unity of knowledge causes preferences to learn and evolve. Dynamic preferences thereby codetermine the *maqasid as-shari'ah* goods and the progress of the Islamic political economy along the dynamic basic needs regimes of life-fulfilling goods and services. Such was the social market trajectory of Imam Fahruddin Razi in his concept of *ubudiyyah* (see Noor, 1998), Imam Ghazali (n.d.), and Imam Shatibi (see Masud, 1994).

The dynamic learning transformation of embedded markets as multimarkets (*M*) into ethicized ones is defined by the following market topology: $M(\theta, x(\theta), p(\theta), R(\theta); \wp(\theta))$ comprises the system of circular causation relations symbolized by $\otimes$ underlying the IIE-learning processes. The circular causation relations are denoted by $\{x(\theta) \otimes p(\theta) \otimes R(\theta) \otimes \wp(\theta)\}$. All of the properties of simulating the wellbeing criterion and the resource allocation complementarities in the TSR remain intact. Such circular causation underlying $\otimes$ can be represented by

$$[(\Omega, S) \Leftrightarrow \theta \Leftrightarrow \wp(\theta)] \Leftrightarrow [x(\theta) \otimes p(\theta) \otimes R(\theta)] \Leftrightarrow [(\Omega, S) \Leftrightarrow \theta \Leftrightarrow \wp(\theta)] \qquad (6.2)$$

in continuity.

Resource allocation in Islamic economics

We have explained that the resource allocation of neoclassical economics that has entered deeply into Islamic economic methodology assumes the postulate of opportunity cost of "alternatives." Behind this form of resource allocation is the prevalence of competing, rather than cooperating, market behavior. This is the cause and effect of the principle of economic rationality, scarcity, and marginal substitution that altogether characterize both microeconomic and macroeconomic theories of production and economic growth. Thus, although no lateral aggregation is possible from the level of microeconomic decision-making to the macroeconomic level, where decision-making and behavioral aspects of economic agents are absent, nonetheless Islamic economists emulate neoclassical economics to treat the microeconomic and macroeconomic as segmented fields with their separate corresponding perspectives according to mainstream methodologies entrenched in

Islamic economics. Such a perspective leaves void the epistemological foundation of morals and values that otherwise makes all of Islamic social experience a continuous learning behavior premised on induction by the *Tawhidi* episteme of unity of knowledge. In this case, any microeconomic aggregation to the economy-wide level is done by means of non-linear compound aggregation of knowledge-induced variables via preferences in the light of the IIE-processes of complex evolutionary learning in unity of knowledge.

We denote the complex aggregation underlying the economy-wide aggregation of knowledge-induced preferences, acting through the market-system as an example of world-system, by the following topology applying to economy.

Let "*I*" denote interactions; thus *i∈I* is the set of interactions. Likewise, "*j*" denotes integration to come to consensus in choices over learning processes, *j∈J*; "*k*" denotes multimarket systems, *k∈K*. Consequently, the complex interaction and integration dynamics across multimarkets, which defines the economy (*E*), are explained by:

$$E(M(\theta, x(\theta), p(\theta), R(\theta); \wp(\theta))) =$$
$$\cup_i \cap_j \cap_k \{M_{ijk}\{x(\theta) \otimes p(\theta) \otimes R(\theta) \otimes \wp(\theta)\}_{ijk} \tag{6.3}$$

A similar definition of the economy as a topology in the socio-scientific domain has been advanced by Debreu (1959) and Choudhury (1999).

The evolutionary property in IIE-learning processes in this case is explained by:

$$(d/d\theta)[\cup_i \cap_j \cap_k \{M_{ijk}\{x(\theta) \otimes p(\theta) \otimes R(\theta) \otimes \wp(\theta)\}_{ijk}] > 0;$$
$$\theta \in (\Omega, S); \quad \text{for each } (i, j, k) \tag{6.4}$$

The evolutionary ethicized multimarkets and socially embedded political economy in terms of complex aggregation via dynamic preferences are generalized in domains such as S_q, $q = 1, 2, \ldots$ in the multidimensional case.

Money and real economy

This is a topic that is usually studied by macroeconomic methods and models in relation to money and the economy. In the language of the 100 percent reserve requirement monetary system (especially with the gold standard) (Choudhury, 2012), *Y* (real economy output and prices) prevails over the savings environment. Then the interest rate, *i*, prevails in the savings function, having the positive relationship—that is, $S = S(i^+)$. In the Islamic case, the function of money is to finance *Y*. Therefore *S* is then treated as "mobilized funds" from savings continuously converted into its use in generating and sustaining *Y*. The implication is that the function of money (*MN*) is understood simply in terms of its relation with *Y* in the expression $MN = MN(Y)$. Then spending, "*S*," is a connector that brings the monetary sector and the real economy into complementary relationship. This is an example of money and real economy unification via the medium of financial instruments.

Thereby, this money expression (*MN*) can be extended by replacing the rate of interest by a rate of return, $r(p)$, on *Y* as a function of its price, p. Now, $M = M(Y, r(p))$. But the way in which $r(p)$ arises is important to note. By extending to vector variables $(Y, r(p))$, for example including real economic activity (*Y*) and respective rates of return, we write:

$$MN = MN(Y, r(p)) = MN(Y, r, p) \tag{6.5}$$

In this form of the money equation resembling the quantity theory of money and prices, money denotes the total value of spending in *maqasid as-shari'ah* goods and services. Thus the flow of money equals the value of mobilized resources in the directions guided by *maqasid as-shari'ah* and the wellbeing function, *maslaha*.

Furthermore, spending in the *shari'ah*-recommended market activities is found to be the source of economic stabilization, economic growth, and social wellbeing. The last concept was explained earlier in terms of the principle of universal complementarities between knowledge-induced goods and services. In the case of expression (6.13), such complementarities are seen between money, output, and real rates of return (now "*S*" becomes resource mobilization) in terms of exchange prices.

As one example of the form of expression (6.7), the total spending variable *S* can be related to real output by the equation

$$S = A.(Y/p)^a \tag{6.6}$$

where *Y* denotes nominal GDP, p denotes the price level, *A* is a constant, and *a* and *b* are spending elasticity coefficients of output and price level, respectively.

Expression (6.15) is written in terms of growth rates as

$$g_s = a_1.g_y + c.g_u \tag{6.7}$$

where g_s denotes the growth rate of spending, g_Y denotes the growth rate of output, and g_u denotes the growth rate of the random variable.

It is known that the real aggregate demand (spending) function would be flatter than the supply curve of real output; hence $g_s < g_Y$. Therefore the rate of growth of real output growth is expected to be higher than the real spending rate. Consequently, price stabilization is realized.

The continuity of circular causation relations will depend on the formation of preferences of productive spending in accordance with the *maqasid as-shari'ah*— that is, in accordance with the usage of *shari'ah* financial instruments that generate complementary relations between money and the real economy. Such complementary relations bring about linkages in the general equilibrium system by the IIE-processes involving money, real economy, and spending variables in the direction of *maqasid as-shari'ah* possibilities. The dynamic preferences so formed are carriers of knowledge formation in the large-scale general equilibrium system of learning relations. The analytical implications of circular causation relations between *MN*, *Y*, $r(p)$, and *S* all induced by $(\theta, \wp(\theta))$ as outlined above, can be explained.

Some mechanistic developments in heterodox Islamic economics under the monotheistic law of unity of knowledge

The generalized theory of heterodoxy of monotheistic unity of knowledge in meta-science, within which is the study of economics in general and heterodox Islamic economics in particular, has a universality and uniqueness of its own. We have presented the formalism regarding this in earlier chapters. In this section, we will present three further examples to draw out the uniformity of the concept and its integrated application within diverse fields. The three fields we have chosen are theoretical physics, systems and cybernetics, and financial economics. Divergent as the disciplines are, the integrated methodological worldview of unity of knowledge presents a single theoretical formalism, although the methods—but not the methodology—of application in diversity can be different.

Theoretical physics: physicalism and non-physicalism of the universe

The understanding of the structure of the universe is seen in differentiated, partitioned ways by the two great thresholds of theoretical physics. The first is the viewpoint of physicist and mathematician Roger Penrose, who thinks of an inflationary universe that is ever-evolving, having started from a specific Big Bang point. Stephen Hawking views the nature of the universe as collapsing into a Black Hole, even after it has started out of a Black Hole. Such is the Big Crunch universe (Hawking and Penrose, 2010). Such differentiated physicalist notions of the evolutionary universe can be unified by the introduction of non-physicalism as the essence of the nature of the universe or, rather, multiverse. The result, then, is the structure given by the evolutionary learning nature of the multiverse that starts and ends at the same primal ontology of the monotheistic law of unity of knowledge. The evolutionary structure of the multiverse is then the integrated, but convoluted, multiverses of Hawking and Penrose to the limits of the optimal points that are equivalent: one at the beginning and one at the end. In such a shape of the convergent multiverse, physicalism is the cause and effect in a circular causation model of interactive, integrative, and evolutionary learning between unity of knowledge and the knowledge-induced world-system, including in this all of the diversities in knowledge, space, and time dimensions.

The result is also this: The embedding of non-physicalism with physicalism as the nature of the unified multiverse of the monotheistic law of unity of knowledge establishes a unique and unified consciousness about the entirety of the multiverse. There are no singularities in this universe. This is because the monotheistic law, being universal by its "epistemic analytical (mathematical)" nature, encompasses all regions of the multiverse. This renders the Black Hole concept untenable. Likewise, the Big Crunch idea is untenable. Consciousness devolves into the phenomenological consequences of the primal ontology in terms of its overarching functionalism in the construction and measurement of the unified world-system by its generality and particulars. The idea of consciousness in its physicalist meaning is replaced by the permanent continuity of the evolutionary learning universe from process to process of its changing phenomenological capability. The ultimate continual presence of consciousness of the multiverse in knowledge, space, and time dimensions is completed in the large-scale multiverse. This is the final *Closure*, as explained in Chapter 4, with the beginning and the end at equivalent points of completeness, which is the totality of the monotheistic law (*Tawhid*). Then there are smaller closures, followed by their continuities across continuums of open sub-systems as subsets of the large-scale multiverse spanned by evolutionary learning.

The system and cybernetic nature of the evolutionary learning multiverse

The evolutionary learning multiverse, with its intra-processual properties of inter-action and integration, presents a systemic worldview based on organically unified networks. An example is of the transportation network: The better system of network minimizes accidents and thus increases the wellbeing of individuals and public safety. However, the network of such wellbeing must be extensive. Order and net-working for attaining wellbeing in only one sector, say transport, at the expense of the environment sector will increase the diseconomy of scale in this sector. This will subsequently give rise to increases in the social cost and user cost of services. In the interactive and integrative form of systemic model that is evaluated by circular causation relations, the increase in social cost will adversely affect all sectors. The network system will therefore crumble. Otherwise, what sustains the good network system is the interactive integration of all of the related systems taken together with each other and the transportation sector. Such a sustaining of balance of organic relations is the sign of systemic consciousness for the whole system. It is a sign that can be derived only from the principle of pervasive complementarities between the sub-systems in the network system as a whole. Contrarily, the neoclassical theory and similar ideas of resource scarcity, optimality, efficiency, and opportunity cost will result in marginal substitution between the sectors, with transportation network as one, environmental pollution by emission as another. In the end, the system and the cybernetic worldview under the principle of monotheistic law of unity of knowledge is an evolutionary learning reconstruction of organic unification of relations between all interactive and integrative sub-systems by way of pervasive complementarities.

The idea of resource mobilization contra resource allocation in economics

Resource allocation is a mainstream economic idea linked to steady-state equilib-rium, optimization objective goals, and marginal rates of commodity and factor substitution. On the other hand, resource mobilization is the result of continuous circulation and augmentation in resources through the regenerative effect of organic relations that uses evolutionary learning to bypass any steady-state and optimality conditions, and thereby replaces the marginal substitution formulas by different ones that show organic participation or complementarities between learning entities.

Take the case of capital and labor as productive factors, along with the interrelating variable of learning as $\theta \in (\Omega, S)$ in the production function. Resource allocation is realized by maximizing the production function subject to exhausting the production level by payment of productive wages and rents as allocations of resources in their maximal productive states of use. The condition for attaining this optimal and steady-state in factor payments is given by (1) Marginal product labor =Wage rate × Price of output; (2) Marginal product of capital = Rent × Price of output. Thereby, the marginal rate of substitution follows as (3) Change in the use of labor/Change in the use of capital = - rent/Wage rate.

On the other hand, the mobilization of resource $(R(\theta))$ is achieved by increasing any amount of resource by continuously paying factors according to the contract of pervasive complementarities (that is, participation) between them. The wellbeing function now replaces the output maximization objective. The complementary vector of the wellbeing function is $\{Q,K,L\}[\theta]$—Q being output, K being capital, L being labor—and each is induced by the θ-parameter as knowledge that causes complementarities between the variables. Thus $W(\theta) = W(Q,K,L)[\theta]$ denotes the wellbeing function induced by the θ-variable on the basis of their given levels of complementarities. The resource mobilization equation is now given by $dR(\theta)/d\theta = w(\theta).(dL(\theta)/d\theta) + r(\theta).(dK(\theta)/d\theta) + L(\theta).(dw(\theta)/d\theta) + K(\theta).(dr(\theta)/d\theta)$. This assumes a positive value by each term being positive under the technology effect that generates complementarities between the factors. The result then is increasing returns to scale in production. Thereby output augmentation by technological change induces a higher level of resource mobilization to factors of production. The result further increases the resources via the increasing returns to scale under technological change caused by the complementarity effect between factors.

Increasing returns to scale in production, contributing to resource mobilization, is the result of a dynamic basis needs regime of development. In monopolistic competition, it is not possible to attain increasing returns to scale without at the same time sustaining the extensive complementary relationship between factors and outputs. Resource mobilization leading to augmented factor development is the essential condition, created by cause and effect, for sustaining knowledge or technologically induced complementarities between factors and outputs.

Conclusion

This chapter has shown that the discipline of mainstream economics is in serious difficulties as a realist understanding of the world-system that deals with economic problems in the midst of complex embedded moral and social systems. Indeed, this was how the study of economic issues and problems was pursued traditionally. During the times of the Greeks, economics was considered to be the study of family needs. This was an area that could not isolate ethical preferences and discourse from holistic decision-making. The Classical School treated the study of economics as political economy. It was the study of questions of conflict and social resolution in the production, distribution, and ownership of wealth and power.

In more recent times, Boulding (1971) explained economics as moral science that was governed by three kinds of preference: malevolent, benevolent, and integrative. Yet, in all such studies of economics, the field of interactive and dynamic preferences and objectives was not studied by a socially embedded methodology. The field of economics thus remained a specialized, but differentiated, discipline, bereft of moral, ethical, and social phenomena. Specialization at the cost of realism drove the economic doctrines, although that was not the nature of inception of this age-old discipline.

Heterodox economic thinking recognizes this failure of economics. Yet we have noted in this chapter that the methodological development of heterodox economics is still bounded by the domain of materialism. Critically, this excludes the understanding, of the greater reality of the monotheistic methodology of unity of knowledge and its determination of the good things of life. A precise analytical methodology of heterodox economics has not developed. The budding field of heterodox economics, together with its critics (Lee and Lavoie, 2013), has failed to establish a realist and analytical field of inquiry of the broadest field of human inquiry within which economic issues, problems, and reasoning can be placed. This is the evolutionary learning epistemology of interaction and convergence of knowledge between monotheism as the broadest field of intellection and the material world, with its generality in science and society and its particularity in economics.

The challenge to show the new and uniquely universal way in heterodox socio-scientific reasoning could not be taken up with the contemporary pursuit of a concocted term called "Islamic economics." Even after its long years of pursuit, Islamic economics has remained all but a whimper in the world of academia and realism. What we find in the Islamic clamor is a thinking that is fully wrapped up in mainstream economic postulation. No epistemological challenge is born in Islamic economics and socio-scientific thought. This is despite this apt field for studying the discursive interaction leading to integration and evolution in the light of the monotheistic methodology and materiality. The Islamic economic failure is the result of an academic deficiency beyond simply the flare of the financial flourishing of Islamic banks. Yet we see the dying world-nation and community of Islam, the *ummah*.

Is there a possibility for heterodox Islamic economics?

At the end, is there a possibility for Islamic economics as it stands today? No. The impossibility of Islamic economics is the result of its failure to render a universal and permanently entrenched revolutionary worldview. This methodological worldview must emanate from and comprehend the episteme of monotheism within the phenomenology of the world-system. The methodology that so emerges is both *functionally* ontological as well as methodical in its unique formalism.

The possibility of Islamic economics as a particular sub-system embedded within the generality of the world-system lies precisely in the much-needed refilling of the missing epistemic gap. Indeed, this was alive in the original formalism of the great Islamic scholastic thinkers. The epistemology of Oneness of the divine law in its form of the monotheistic methodology (*Tawhid*), together with the emergent scientific and methodical formalism pertaining of generality, particularized to economic issues, is the sure way out. This is a message for the entire world of academia and practitioners; it is not limited to Muslims alone.

Notes

1 *Qur'an* (15:21).
2 *Qur'an* (42:38; 42:49–53).
3 *Qur'an* (59:24).
4 *Qur'an* (42:49–53).
5 *Qur'an* (30:8).
6 *Qur'an* (78:1–5).
7 *Qur'an* 53:1–7.
8 *Qur'an* (27:64).
9 *Qur'an* (13:1–5) draws out the nature of the pairing universe across and between diversities of multidimensional systems. Thus unity in diversity is conveyed in the light of the universality of the divine law.

References

Barrow, J.D. (1991). "Laws," in *Theories of Everything: The Quest for Ultimate Explanation*, Oxford: Oxford University Press, pp. 12–30.
Bhaskar, R. (1978). "The logic of scientific discovery," in *A Realist Theory of Science*, New York: Harvester Wheatsheaf.
Boulding, K.E. (1971). "Economics as a moral science," in Glabe, F.R. (ed.), *Boulding: Collected Papers, Vol. 2*, Boulder, CO: Association of University Press.
Chapra, U. (1992). *Islam and the Economic Challenge*, Leicester and Herndon, VA: The Islamic Foundation: The International Institute of Islamic Thought, Chapter 5.
Choudhury, M.A. (1999). *Comparative Economic Theory: Occidental and Islamic Perspectives*, Norwell, MA: Kluwer Academic.
Choudhury, M.A. (2006). *Science and Epistemology in the Qur'an* (five volumes), Lewiston, NY: Edwin Mellen Press.
Choudhury, M.A. (2012). "The future of monetary reform and the real economy: A problem of trade versus interest," *International Journal of Management Science*, 19, 1, June.
Choudhury, M.A. and Hoque, M.Z. (2004). *An Advanced Exposition in Islamic Economics and Finance*, Lewiston, NY: Edwin Mellen Press.
Debreu, G. (1959). *Theory of Value: An Axiomatic Analysis of Economic Equilibrium*, New York: John Wiley.
Dewitt, B. (1992). *Supermanifolds*, Cambridge: Cambridge University Press.
Gassner, M.S. (2008). "Revisiting Islamic bonds, are 85% of sukuk halal?," *Business Islamica*, March: 22–23.
Gruber, T.R. (1993). "A translation approach to portable ontologies," *Knowledge Acquisition*, 5, 2: 199–200.
Hawking, S.W. and Penrose, R. (2010). *The Nature of Space and Time*, Princeton, NJ: Princeton University Press.
Imam, Ghazali (n.d.). *Ihya Ulum-Id-Din* (five volumes) trans. Karim, M.F., Lahore: Sh. Muhammad Ashraf.
Khnifer, M. (n.d.). "Shocking 21 defaulted sukuk cases in the last 20 months," *Business Islamica*, 4, 6: 24–26.
Lee, F.S. and Lavoie, M. (eds.) (2013). *In Defense of Post-Keynesian and Heterodox Economics*, Abingdon: Routledge.
Maddox, I.J. (1970). *Elements of Functional Analysis*, Cambridge: Cambridge University Press.

Masud, M.K. (1994). *Shatibi's Theory of Meaning*, Islamabad: Islamic Research Institute, International Islamic University.

Noor, H.M. (1998). "Razi's human needs theory and its relevance to ethics and economics," *Humanomics*, 14, 1: 59–96.

Rucker, R. (1982). "Large cardinals," in *Infinity and the Mind*, New York: Bantam Books, pp. 273–286.

Smullyan, R.M. (1992). *Godel's Incompleteness Theorems*, New York: Oxford University Press.

7 Empirical evaluation of Islamic financing instruments across the evolutionary learning trend governed by the monotheistic methodology of unity of knowledge[1]

Objective

The objective of this chapter is to develop a simple approach to "evaluating" Islamic financing trends over interactive, integrative, and evolutionary (IIE) learning processes. To "evaluate" the objective criterion by the IIE model means, first, to "estimate" and, second, to "simulate" through changes of the estimated coefficients. A statistical evaluation of the circular causation model interrelating primary and secondary Islamic financing data is undertaken. This interrelationship proceeds on two sets of observations. If the primary *mudarabah* (profit-sharing data) is compared with either the other primary financing data—namely, *murabaha* and *musharakah*—we note a negative relationship between the primary portfolio of *murabaha* and *musharakah*, on the one side, and *mudarabah*, on the other. Likewise, if the secondary data, including *murabaha*, is compared with the primary data on *mudarabah* and *musharakah*, a negative trend is noted. However, if *murabaha* is included with primary instruments along with the rest of the financing instruments, then there appears to be a complementary relationship between the primary and secondary financing instruments. This chapter will study the implications of these trends and the recommended composition of the Islamic financing portfolio.

Islamic financing in the light of the episteme of *Tawhidi* unity of knowledge

The epistemological tenor of this book rests on the functioning of the episteme of unity of knowledge in its phenomenological embedding with socio-scientific variables. In the field of Islamic financing, the episteme of unity of knowledge is represented by complementarities between all of the diversified instruments, without any sign of marginalism between them. Such a state of financing would be signified by a coterminous increase or positively complementary trend between diversified financing instruments. The instruments may not necessarily be differentiated in the volume of financing. This latter condition would be left to investor preferences to select the kind of financing instruments for their projects. But Islamic banking, non-banking, and financial firms, although they do not, could invoke the ethical consciousness on establishing balance and complementarities between the diversified financing instruments. This would signal a conscious way of realizing the episteme of unity of knowledge that is conveyed by the positive complementarities and balance of use between the various financing instruments in the combined Islamic financial portfolio. This is an example of the principle of *al-wasatiyyah*, meaning organic interrelationship as a sign of balance between financial instruments as a special case.

The attainment of such a complementary state of portfolio would require a teaching environment (*tarbiah*) to induce value and consciousness into the Islamic business environment; this would enable a move towards a portfolio based on endogenous relations of unity between different financial instruments. In turn, this would collect participatory or complementary financing instruments into a pooled fund. Without such an invoking of consciousness, Islamic actualization through financial selection, the failure of the business and investment community, and the business fallacy of Islamic firms will continue unchecked. The world of Islamic business has succumbed to a neoclassical, capitalist position in the face of its drive for competition for market shares and the goal of maximization of shareholders' wealth.

On the side of policy theoretic and strategic effects of the kind already noted, there has been ambivalence in the objective and goal of Islamic financing in connection with the real economic world. For, as we have explained, the episteme of unity of knowledge applied to the economic and financial world implies the ethical reconstruction towards complementarities between money, finance, and the real economy. Such an organic unity of interrelations would reflect the principal objective criterion that reflects the *Tawhidi* type of unity of knowledge. The objective criterion is the well-being (*maslaha*) function. It arises from the purpose and objective of the *shari'ah*—namely, *maqasid as-shari'ah*. Indeed, this prevailing aspect of Islamic economics and finance in conception and application by practitioners has led to sorry results.

Contrary to the goals of *maqasid as-shari'ah*, the so-called Islamic financing agents and their gurus of the *shari'ah* have promoted the catchphrase "*shari'ah*-compliance." The acceptance and practice of *shari'ah*-compliance embraces the rationale and consequences of financing by segregated contracts (*aqd*). This approach of *shari'ah*-compliance does not necessarily abide by the holistic interconnected complementary worldview of inter-instrument causal relations and their complementarities. It is for this reason that we find the erosion of *mudarabah* as a primary financing instrument of profit sharing. *Mudarabah* has been isolated from the Islamic financing portfolio and left to its apparent demise as a result of conception, strategy, and financial policy reconstruction and practice. The reason usually given is that *mudarabah* is a difficult instrument to implement. Such an excuse is untenable when the area of diversified financing menus is viewed from the point of extensive complementarities between the various financing instruments. We will examine this fact below and examine its possible reconstruction.

The cause of ultimate failure in modern Islamic financing

Building on the problems caused by the independently separable contractual aspect of the Islamic financing portfolio under the *shari'ah*-compliance perspective, we note the ethico-economic fallacy in this approach to Islamic financing. We note that this mode of financing weakens the principle of risk and production diversification in a climate of weak endogenous interrelationships or complete exogeneity between the financing instruments (Desai, 1989). For instance, *mudarabah*, as profit sharing, raises its profit shares from the real economy. The real economy prospers by virtue of investment, yield, and stability of risk diversification and production diversification. These are interactively integrated. Investments can yield profitability if liquidity can match with development in the real sectors of the economy. The result of such a matching of liquidity (financing) by industries in real sector development is the result both of the growth of assets and of the activation of the real economy.

Thus complementary circular causation interrelations are established between investment, financing, real economic development, risk and product diversifications, and profitability. The loss of any of these interrelations results in the weakening of the other relations. Therefore the loss of overall complementarities would lead to the weakening of the overall financing structure. On the other hand, the choice of some contractual financing to the exclusion of the other relations would eventually lead to inter-variable marginal substitution by way of competition between real economic activity and financing activity. Islamic financing theory would then return to the neoclassical economic idea of the marginal rate of substitution by way of competition and opportunity cost concepts between real economic activity and financial activity. The opportunity cost and the marginal rate of substitution in such a case is well known to be the rate of interest. Thereby, Islamic financing would fail in its principal objective of replacing interest rates (*riba*) by the rate of profit (for example the profit-sharing rate, rate of return, and yields).

The failure of *mudarabah*, on the basis of it being difficult to implement in Islamic financing, has been a cause of Islamic banks and the academic world of Islamic financing being unable to intellectualize and apply new methods of asset valuation to engender innovative ways of examining the organization and management of diversified portfolios (Choudhury, 2013a, 2013b). This has ethical and social consequences: the participation of variables, institutions, and markets in interactively integrated development along the history of evolutionary learning processes. An example examined closely from the viewpoint of *maqasid as-shari'ah* is the dynamic life-fulfillment regime of participatory development. It brings about and sustains pervasive complementarities between the good possibilities of life to the exclusion of those that compete and substitute each other. The *Qur'an* (102:1–2) declares on this matter of the futility of competition: "Competition in (worldly) increase diverts you until you visit the grave."

Formalizing complementarities between a diversified financing portfolio and the real economy

To formalize briefly the need and possibility of complementary relations in the real economy in connection with the financial economy, the following is a rigorous explanation. Expression (7.1) establishes several implications. First, we note the interactive complementarities through the interflow of relations via the demand and supply of resources, goods, and services. We note the portfolio, risk, and production diversifications, and the cause-and-effect relations between activities. We also note the overall complementarities between such activities in the form of interaction and integration by using circular causation interrelations.

We also note that if the diversified holdings in primary–primary, primary–secondary, and secondary–secondary relations are skewed at the expense of displacement of any one of them, then the structures of assets and capital are also altered. This results in either demand > supply or supply > demand between various financial and real economy activities. The result would then be savings being held up in the financial sector, thus causing interest rates to appear in idle capital leading to lower productivity of capital in the real economy. On the other hand, it is possible that demand exceeds the supply of financial and real economy resources to support overall participatory activities. Consequently, the returns on real activity will remain low. In the end, the participatory process of circular causation is disrupted. All these consequences are contrary to the balanced participatory development (*al-wasatiyyah*) invoked by the *Tawhidi* methodological worldview of unity of knowledge and its experiences.

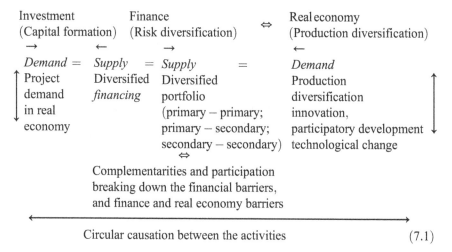

$$(7.1)$$

A financing model of the complementary portfolio

We are proposing here a complementary portfolio of all of the Islamic financing instruments taken up interactively. Such a portfolio would avoid separable contractual financing rule as presently is found to be the case at the expense of complementarities or participation. Instead, we recommend that financial resources move freely between the various instruments. The objective in such a portfolio is to diversify resources between various funds so as to establish a balance of activity in all of them. Strategically, Islamic banks would be able to sell certificates of the holistic financing type. Let us call it the "Pooled Fund" (*PF*).

The composition of *PF* is defined by the holistic complementary relations basket $PF(\theta) = \{M1, M2, M3, S\}[\theta]$. *M1* denotes *murabaha* (cost-plus mark-up pricing). Thus *M2* denotes *musharakah* (equity participation), *M3* denotes *mudarabah* (profit sharing), and *S* denotes the secondary financing instruments. (See Table 7.1 for details under study here.) The epistemic embedding of unity of knowledge is represented by the common induction of all of the variables by the knowledge-flow variable from the *Tawhidi* epistemic origin, $[\theta]$. Therefore "θ," as the knowledge-flow derived from the ontological implication of its primal epistemic source, also initiates the possibility for inter-variable circular causation relations between them.

A formal model of the Pooled Fund (*PF*) in the light of *Tawhidi* unity of knowledge

The formal model of *PF* is the holistic worldview of complementarities between the compositions of the portfolio as shown. The ethico-economic embedding in them is caused by the knowledge variables $\{\theta\}$, intra-systems, and inter-systems of the IIE-processes. Thus θ-values are derived from the episteme of *Tawhidi* unity of knowledge. While the *Tawhidi* episteme forms the primal ontology, the derivation and application of the knowledge-flows $\{\theta\}$ denotes the epistemology. The embedding of $\{\theta\}$ in *PF* denotes the phenomenological (conscious) experience of the episteme of unity of knowledge in the financial instruments as an example of a particular case study. This experience is gained by the evolutionary learning in unity of knowledge and its practice through human experience by their various functional groups of activities.

The entire $PF(\theta)$, in its conceptual and functional form, is studied by the following circular causation model of wellbeing ($W(\theta)$, *maslaha*) in terms of the circular causation relations between the financing variables that are induced by θ:

$$\text{``Evaluate''} \; W(\theta) \; = \; W(M1, M2, M3, S)[\theta] \tag{7.2}$$

$$\text{subject to} \; M1 = f_1(M2, M3, S)[\theta] \tag{7.3}$$

$$M2 \; = \; f_2(M1, M3, S)[\theta] \tag{7.4}$$

$$M3 \; = \; f_3(M1, M2, S)[\theta] \tag{7.5}$$

$$S \; = f_4(M1, M2, M3)[\theta] \tag{7.6}$$

$$\theta \; = \; F(M1, M2, M3, S) \tag{7.7}$$

Expression (7.7) is derived from the implicit function theorem applied to the "similar" functions (7.2) and (7.7), given the continuously differentiable property of all the functions in respect of the variables induced by the θ-variable. The above-mentioned functional forms meet all the underlying meanings of inter-variable and inter-activity circular causation relations explained in expression (7.1).

Table 7.1 Islamic financing by modes of financing, millions of Malaysian ringgit, and percentages, December 2006–2014 and February 2015

Bithaman Ajil Ijara	M1: Murabaha	M2: Musharakah	M3: Mudarabah	Total
	Ijara Thumma	Istisna M1 M2	M3 Other	
2006				
Secondary		M1+M2+M3 = M	REST	TOTAL
29845 + 762.9 + 21470.4 + 509.4		5300.9 + 156.8 + 147.9	15174.9	73368.1
52587.7		**5605.6**	**15174.9**	**73368.1**
2007				
31630.3 + 1153.5 + 25806.1 + 804.1		9681,7 + 374.4 + 109.8	15818.8	85388.6
59394		**10165.9**	**15818.8**	**85388.6**
2008				
35278.3 + 2809.5 + 32275.8 + 1410.4		19556.6 + 854.0 + 326.3	12646.1	108157.1
71774		**20736.9**	**12646.1**	**108157.1**
2009				
42913.6 + 4033.0 + 38953.3 + 1406.5		23022.3 + 2360.3 + 373.6	20354.4	133406.8
87306.4		**25756.2**	**20354.4**	**133406.8**
2010				
53697.4 + 3940.2 + 43497.4 + 1621.0		23296.9 + 3958.3 + 276.8	28924.1	159211.0
102756		**27532**	**28924.1**	**159211.0**
2011				
63211.2 + 4121.6 + 50981.9 + 1466.2		30384.9 + 7307.6 + 251.6	39181.1	196995.1
119780.9		**37944.1**	**39181.1**	**196995.1**
2012				
74280.6 + 4635.7 + 54574.7 + 989.3		40018.4 + 11832.2 + 142.2	40324.7	232797.8
134480.3		**51992.8**	**40324.7**	**232797.8**
2013				
83139.5 + 6373.2 + 62370.3 + 696.2		57026.9 + 16354.2 + 146.0	54799.6	280905.8
152579.2		**73527.1**	**54799.6**	**280905.8**
2014				
79783.2 + 7677.8 + 67253.2 + 1016.7		83842.7 + 23113.1 + 77.3	71417.9	334181.9
155730.9		**107033.1**	**71417.9**	**334181.9**
2015 (February)				
79135.7 + 7863.1 + 68116.5 + 1056.4		93395.8 + 23938.9 + 78.4	73553.6	347138.5
156171.7		**117413.1**	**73553.6**	347138.5

Note: Aggregates by primary and secondary financing instruments.

No fund held in *PF* by any particular instrument is segmented in itself. An open-ended, free flow of funds between the instruments, while being directed into foreign trade, is practiced. In this way, portfolio diversification allows for the channeling of a free flow of instrumental funds into product diversification and innovation. Such activities promote financial and real resource mobilization into the real economy, foreign trade, and development.

The various levels of interaction and integration followed by the dynamic evolution of the interrelationship between the diversified pooled fund in the above-mentioned sense of a diversified portfolio and its linkage with product diversification, technological change, innovation, and participatory development, are as follows.

1   A list of Islamic financing instruments comprises the generic pooled fund portfolio having the characteristic of a free flow of funds between the instruments as deemed necessary to serve the needs of the portfolio return ensemble, but also retaining a critical level of funds in each instrument to sustain its individual survival.

2   The characterization of the suggested mechanism of the *PF* vis-à-vis Islamic financing instruments (M_i, S) and portfolio diversification in respect of serving the foreign trade development target is:

$$PF = \{M_i\}_i, \text{ with } M_i \leftrightarrow M_j; M_i \leftrightarrow S \tag{7.8}$$

$M_i \geq M_i^*$ a critical minimum value for retention in ith instrument; $i,j = 1,2,\ldots,n$.

3   Thus M_i funds are required to diversify *PF* in the direction of risk and product diversifications. In this way, the M_i and *PF* ensemble are maintained by the interflow of returns between them through the passage of production (Q) and unit-risk diversification $(Risk/Q)$. Production and unit-risk diversification are further spread across various sectors $(s = 1,2,\ldots,N)$. Hence $Q = \{Q_s\}$; $Risk/Q = \{(Risk/Q)_s\}$. The diversification bundle (D) is the tuple of production (return) and unit-risk diversification—that is, $D = \{Q_s, (Risk/Q)_s\}$. The organic inter-relations between the participatory variables are shown by:

$$PF = \{M_i \leftrightarrow M_j\} \leftrightarrow D = \{Q_s, (Risk.Q)_s\} \tag{7.9}$$

4   Shares in unit amount (S_{PF}) are sold revolving around *PF* for the purpose of achieving (7.9). Thus S_{PF} is spread over *PF* without it being necessary to identify in which particular S_{PF} component saving is mobilized by specific instruments. Moreover, S_{PF} as financial resources flow freely across *PF* and *D* to sustain the relationship shown in expression (7.9). The IIE interrelations between all the variables are now denoted by:

$S_{PF} \leftrightarrow PF \leftrightarrow D$, i.e.
$$S_{PF} \leftrightarrow \{M_i \leftrightarrow M_j\} \leftrightarrow \{Q_s (Risk/Q)_s\} \tag{7.10}$$

Production, development, and innovation effect are shown by value imputation of a qualitative variable denoted by θ. This is shown to acquire ordinal values in respect of the other variables of the system of interrelations. Expression (7.10) is now written in its θ-induced form as follows:

$$\theta \leftrightarrow [S_{PF} \leftrightarrow \{M_i \leftrightarrow M_j\} \leftrightarrow \{Q_s, (Risk/Q)_s\}][\theta] \qquad (7.11)$$

The "θ-variable" induces all of the variables as shown by cause and effect. It puts the *PF* system in its creative dynamics of participatory interrelations. Because of this primal influence of the θ-variable on all variables, the induced consequences acquire an ethical dimension. Such an ethical dimension comprises the actualization of sustainable development and growth with the equitable distribution of resources across diversely interlinked economic sectors, poverty alleviation by developing microenterprises and training, and small and medium-sized enterprises (SMEs), as well as by productivity and risk-diversification gains. These activities altogether diversify the economy and increase participation in the economy induced by ethico-economic value.The interrelations are implied by $\leftrightarrow$. The origin of a system of organic unity as a learning system of interrelations arises in reference to a certain methodological foundation that fundamentally defines the knowledge-induced function of organic unity. This epistemological foundation is the *Tawhidi* law of unity of knowledge. The *Tawhidi* foundational basis of θ-value is denoted by (Q,S)—that is, $\theta\epsilon(Q,S)$. Expression (7.11) is now extended to its comprehensive form:

$$(Q, S) \rightarrow \theta \leftrightarrow [S_{PF} \leftrightarrow \{M_i \leftrightarrow M_j\} \leftrightarrow \{Q_s, (Risk/Q)_s\}][\theta] \qquad (7.12)$$

In the circular causation system (7.12) of learning interrelations between the variables, every variable, including the θ-variable, is endogenously interrelated. The exception is of $[\Omega = (Q,S)]$, which is solely axiomatic:

$$(Q, S) \rightarrow [\theta \leftrightarrow [S_{PF} \leftrightarrow \{M_i \leftrightarrow M_j\} \leftrightarrow \{Q_s (Risk/Q)_s\}][\theta]] \leftrightarrow$$
$$\text{Repeat the sequence in continuum until} \leftrightarrow (Q, S) \qquad (7.13)$$

Thus (Q,S), through θ arising from (Q,S), actualizes the ethico-economic financing system $[\theta \leftrightarrow [S_{PF} \leftrightarrow \{M_i \leftrightarrow M_j\} \leftrightarrow \{Q_s, (Risk/Q)_s\}][\theta]]$.

5 Underlying the system of circular causation interrelations is the operational function of the real economy with institutions. These comprise the private sector further divided between the urban and rural sectors in order to actualize the developmental effects and social consequences of poverty alleviation. Other categories of sectoral diversification would be finance houses, corporations and microenterprises, SMEs, and industrial sectors. The public sector will comprise the government, central bank, development banks, and organizations. The stakeholders will be both national and international. The above-mentioned categories of sectors will all be sources of gaining participatory holdings.

The conscious Islamic banks, through their evolutionary learning in *Tawhidi* unity of knowledge (*tarbiah*), will act as the practitioners of the idea and generate the synergy relations as pointed out above.

The circular causation system of expressions (7.1)–(7.7) of the complete system of interrelations given by the subsequent expressions is further explained in Figure 7.1.

Statistical facts on the state of Islamic financing: a critique in reference to the episteme of unity of knowledge

The above-mentioned observations overshadowing the grim future for Islamic financing given its present weak consciousness of the true foundations of the Islamic groundwork of the epistemic worldview and its functional applications in the organization of the business world is brought out by Table 7.1. Table 7.1 points out the precarious condition of marginalist relations between primary instruments, and between primary and secondary instruments in respect of *mudarabah* as a primary instrument (see Table 7.2). An adverse repercussion would also be felt on the role of Islamic banks in the rural sector (Pratiwi, 2015). This is empirically established by the case of Islamic banks being ineffective in financing projects in the rural sector in Indonesia and thereby in the weak returns on assets that Islamic banks raise from rural-sector operations.

The statistical results also show that a greater emphasis is placed on secondary-sector financing along with *murabaha* and *musharakah* financing, resulting in the complete neglect of *mudarabah* financing as a key primary instrument. Thus the impact of *shari'ah*-compliance as opposed to the ethico-economic *maslaha* effect of *maqasid as-shari'ah* is seen to have increased Islamic financing. Yet the underlying resource allocation is found to hide the structure of capital formation, risk, and production diversifications, and the ethico-economic effects of balanced complementarities between all the financing instruments of *PF*. An ethical reconstruction based on complementarities and balance between the financing instruments is

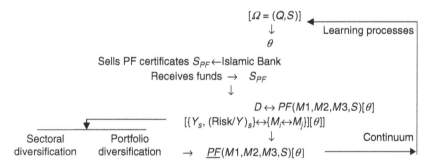

Figure 7.1 Circular flow of resources for sustaining *PF* in the development process

Table 7.2 Percentage distribution of instruments without showing *mudarabah* separately

Year	Financing by type					Total
	Secondary	S%	M	M%	Rest	
2006	52587.7	71.62	5605.6	7.64	15174.9	73368.1
2007	59394	69.55	10165.9	11.91	15818.8	85388.6
2008	71774	66.36	20736.9	19.17	12646.1	108157.1
2009	87306.4	65.44	25756.2	19.31	20354.4	133406.8
2010	102756	64.54	27532	17.29	28924.1	159211.0
2011	119780.9	60.80	37944.1	19.26	39181.1	196995.1
2012	134480.3	57.93	51992.8	22.33	40324.7	232797.8
2013	152579.2	54.32	73527.1	26.18	54799.6	280905.8
2014	155730.9	46.60	107033.1	32.02	71417.9	334181.9
2015 (Feb)	156171.7	46.73	117413.1	33.82	73553.6	347138.5

necessary, so that none of them is found ultimately to disappear from the sphere of primary modes of financing. This effectiveness can be made possible by the *PF* arrangement.

The circular causation relations

Without θ-values as independent variables in the expressions, the estimated relations are as follows.

$$Log(Primary) = a + b.log(Secondary)$$
$$LOG(PRIMARY) = 2.129543 * LOG(SECONDARY)$$
$$- 6.167876 \ (8.847378) \tag{7.14}$$

R-squared = 0.907274

Adj R-squared = 0.895684

F-stat = 78.27610

The elasticity coefficient of primary financing instruments to secondary financing instruments is positive at 2.12943. This implies a positive complementarity between these groups of instruments when *murabaha* is taken along with the primary instruments. This, though, is a moot issue and *murabaha* as it exists today exogenously sets the mark-up instrument. This mark-up is considered by some as tantamount to a shadow interest rate (*riba*).

$$Log(Secondary) = a + b. log(Primary)$$
$$LOG(SECONDARY) = 1.060082* LOG(PRIMARY)$$
$$+ 3.093080 \ (0.426042) \tag{7.15}$$

R-squared = 0.907274

Adj R-squared = 0.895684

F-stat = 78.27610

The elasticity coefficient of secondary financing instruments to primary financing instruments is positive at 1.060082. This implies a positive complementarity between these groups of instruments when *murabaha* is taken along with the primary instruments. This, though, is a moot issue and *murabaha* as it exists today is the exogenously set mark-up instrument. It is considered by some as being tantamount to a shadow interest rate (*riba*).

$$\theta = a + b.log(Secondary) + c.log(Primary)$$
$$LOG(\theta) = 0.371599 * LOG(PRIMARY) + 0.473513 * LOG(SECONDARY)$$
$$- 3.393013 \; (4.660291) \; (2.656154) \qquad (7.16)$$

R-squared = 0.987754

Adj R-squared = 0.984255

F-stat = 282.3097

Although the measured wellbeing function estimated by the θ-value (see Table 7.3) is positively complementary in relation to primary and secondary financing instruments at the coefficients of elasticity values, 0.371599 and 0.473513, respectively, the economies of scale in wellbeing are less than 1 (at 0.845072). This implies that there is still a degree of complementarity to be gained through a gap in the economies of scale in wellbeing. Such a gain can be realized by improving the primary financing with the *mudarabah* instrument.

The rows and column of θ-values are computed in the following way:

θ-values (*s*-column) = $(10/x_{s2013})*(x_s$-values) pro rata

θ-values (*M*-column) = $(10/x_{M2013})*(x_M$-values) pro rata

Avg$\{\theta\}$ = [(θ-values (*s*-column)+ θ-values (*M*-column)]/2

Table 7.3 Computation of ranked "θ"-values

	θ_s	θ_M	Avg $\{\theta\} = \theta$	Secondary (S)	Primary (M)
2006	3.44	0.45	1.94	52588	5606
2007	3.56	0.81	2.19	59394	10166
2008	4.31	1.66	2.99	71774	20737
2009	5.24	2.06	3.65	87307	25756
2010	6.17	2.20	4.19	102756	27532
2011	7.19	3.03	5.11	119781	37944
2012	8.07	4.16	6.12	134480	51993
2013	10	5.88	7.94	192579	73527
2014	9.34	8.56	8.95	155731	107033
2015 (Feb)	9.37	10	9.69	156172	117413

Conclusion

The lesson of risk and production diversifications arising from the ethico-economic premise of unity of knowledge has not been understood by the existing Islamic financial and business world. This may pose serious problem for the objective and performance of Islamic financing in the near future. Presently, the performance of Islamic financing instruments is being supported by rich shareholders' capital. Such evidence is clear from the finance–deposit ratio being higher than 100 percent, whereas this ratio should be near to the value of 1 in the sense of full mobilization of deposit financing from common stakeholders.

The grassroots performance of Islamic finance is not sustainable. This is proved with the government-subsidized Amanah Ikhtiar (AI) program in Malaysia (Al-Mamun et al., 2012). The income-generating capability of AI grant-receiving agents has staggered. Islamic financing through AI has therefore now generated productivity, while dependency on interest-free funds remains with the AI recipients.

Thus, such weak Islamic performances hide many of the *maqasid as-shari'ah* requirements of Islamic finance by wrongly subjecting them to the notion of *shari'ah*-compliance. It is feared that even as *mudarabah* financing has almost all but faded away, so also there is fear that secondary financing instruments, such as *sukuk* (Islamic bonds), may be increasingly revolving around *murabaha* and *ijara* (rents). The result would then be a further scaling down of *musharakah*. A domino effect would then roll over the primary financing instruments. The result at the end would be the skewed rise of secondary financing instruments in the name of *shari'ah*-compliance, which would legitimate the existence of a separable contractual perspective of Islamic financing instruments. Therefore an increase of so-called Islamic commercialism would be witnessed in the name of the *shari'ah*-compliant legitimation of segregated Islamic financing instruments (Alkhamees, 2014).

Note

1 With thanks, the empirical work was undertaken by Dr. Ari Pratiwi, Software Client Architect, IBM Indonesia, and the Postgraduate Program in Islamic Economics and Finance, Faculty of Economics, Trisakti University, Jakarta, Indonesia.

References

Al-Mamun, A., Adaikalam, J. and Wahab, S.A. (2012). "Investigating the effects of Amanah Ikhtiar Malaysia Microcredit Program on their clients' quality of life in Rural Malaysia," *International Journal of Economics and Finance*, 4, 1: 192–203.

Alkhamees, A. (2014). *A Critique of Creative Shari'ah Compliance in the Islamic Finance Industry with Reference to the Kingdom of Saudi Arabia and the United Kingdom*, Ph.D. thesis, University of Warwick, UK.

Choudhury, M.A. (2013a). "Complexity and endogeneity in economic methodology," *Kybernetes: International Journal of Cybernetics, Systems, and Management Science*, 42, 2: 226–240.

Choudhury, M.A. (2013b). "Perturbation theory in cognitive socio-scientific research: Towards sociological economic analysis," *Mind and Society*, 11.

Desai, M. (1989). "Endogenous and exogenous money," in Eatwell, J., Milgate, M. and Newman, P. (eds.), *The New Palgrave: Money*, New York: W.W. Norton.

Pratiwi, A. (2015). *Islamic Banking Contribution in Sustainability and Socioeconomic Development: An Epistemological Approach*, Faculty of Economics, Postgraduate Program in Islamic Economics and Finance, Trisakti University, Jakarta, Indonesia.

8 The *qur'anic* phenomenological model of system

Application to human resource contra human capital theory

This chapter is an application to the building blocks of the scientific research program using the monotheistic law of unity of knowledge as the foundation of meta-science. By its very nature, the scientific research program assumes the study of the system view of meta-reality in terms of its properties of complexity and interactive, integrative, and evolutionary learning processes of unification of nexus of interrelations.

The commencement of any scientific research program of momentous proportions requires an epistemological reference to invoke the body of creative ideas. For Kuhn (1970), this epistemological reference, if belonging to normal scientific thinking, would at best be a paradigm creating simply paradigmatic shifts within the received body of thought. The intellection, its influence on the nature of the world-system, and its general and specific problems under investigation do not go through momentous creativity. On the other hand, Kuhn (1970: 152) writes, on the nature and emergence of scientific revolution "[S]cientific revolutions are here taken to be those non-cumulative developmental episodes in which an older paradigm is replaced in whole or in part by an incompatible new one." This non-cumulative nature of new knowledge in the revolutionary scientific research program meets the great watershed of discursive investigation. These experiences become the beacon of new scientific creativity.

Besides, new scientific revolutions, every time, have been focused on re-thinking the generalized and particular issues and problems contained within the ever-broadening field of human inquiry on impending issues. On this matter, Boland (1989) writes regarding the richer field of inquiry that is built up by higher levels of extensions in human intellection concerning the nature of investigation.

The end result of the reconstructed methodological worldview in such an experience *res extensa* (Descartes, 1954), is to invoke a system and cybernetic perspective of symbiotic analysis. This, in other words, is to understand the scientific theory as process (Hull, 1988). It is by the system and cybernetic nature of scientific inquiry in its framework of revolutionary epistemic discourse that the totality of the issues and the universe in reference can be studied. Whitehead (1978) remarked that the end of science is to weave the complexity of the universe in the form of interrelated relations *res extensa*. Today, Hawking (1988: 15) remarks along similar lines: "The eventual goal of science is to provide a single theory that describes the whole universe." Likewise, Barrow (1991) writes: "The laws of Nature are the dictates of a transcendent God. They enshrine faith in the existence of an underlying order to things."

Some examples of the nature of the socio-scientific universe

Some examples and their critical examination can be mentioned here in the context of the search for—although, hitherto, the failure to explain the universal totality of—knowledge, cognition, materiality, and continuity of the same over the simultaneous occurrence of events in the dimensions of knowledge, space, and time. It appears that the diverse schools of scientists across all socio-scientific disciplines, together with the philosophers of science, have failed to understand events and the universe in reference to this holistic dimensional worldview (Badawi, 1999: 3–13). The limitation of the extent of scientific inquiry has been posed by containing it in the deductive–inductive dichotomous domains of space–time. This is true of both the natural sciences and the social sciences within their dichotomous realities.

Wallerstein (1998: 57) provides a conforming picture for his conception of the occidental world-system:

> For social science, the rise of complexity studies represents an epistemological revolution. On the one hand, it undermines totally the basis of the concept of eternal TimeSpace, while at the same time rejecting that of episodic geopolitical TimeSpace, substituting for it the rules of social processes for as long as these rules are relevant.

Einstein's (1954) relativistic theory of simultaneity of the occurrence of events and the incidence of light at moments of time limits the eventual causality to the interaction between these three primordial elements. They are, namely, Light, Time, and Events. Yet the following question remains unanswered in this relativistic conception: What are the status, explanation, and application of the divine law, and for that of morality and ethics? These kinds of human concerns represent super-luminary objects that cannot be contained primordially in the material limits of the space–time structure. Yet Einstein (n.d.), like all other scientists and philosophers of science, forced such fields of human evaluations to be contained within the space–time structure of scientific analysis that is in space–time structure: "Ethical axioms are founded and tested not differently from the axioms of science."

Economics is another ethics-benign field in the systemic sense. Yet religious reasoning has been forced into economic analysis in the space–time structure of economic reasoning (Witham, 2010). The primordial, yet inter-causal, role of morality and ethics arising from the endogenous nature of knowledge interactively relating with the entire socio-scientific phenomena has not occurred.

The epistemological enterprise to establish scientific cognition in the framework of the primordial, yet inter-causal, relations between knowledge and the world-system, while focusing on the *res extensa* domain of "everything," has remained untapped. The school of heterodox economics has also questioned the problem of the great divide between the antinomy of moral values in the a priori from a posteriori domain of material occurrences, as shown in the Kantian–Humean dichotomy (Kant, 1949). Lawson (1997: 11), borrowing his epistemic questioning from Bhaskar (1978), comments: "While mainstream economists frequently conclude that 'methodology' ... is irrelevant to (progress in) economic science ... these very same economists appear quite unable to refrain from explicit methodological discussion."

Objective

Against the perspective of the extension of the scientific methodological worldview to the *res extensa* of "everything," and thus the creation of the evolutionary learning objectivity of science as system, we now state the objective of this chapter. The chapter identifies that the great watershed of human knowledge that has been left out of scientific discourse and analysis in the epistemic project of the totality of relations is the divine law. Yet, because of the substantive scientific nature of monotheism in the epistemic totality of "everything," we refer to such an understanding and treatment of monotheism in the systemic methodological worldview as analytical monotheism. The *Qur'an* presents this model of the Oneness of God, called *Tawhid*. By holding on to the logical formalism of such a way of interrelating knowledge by means of analytical monotheism and the domain of emergent causation, we erect the formal nature of the phenomenology of knowledge in this context.

The chapter explains the details of the *qur'anic* phenomenological model of analytical monotheism and the world-system in its generality and particular subsystems. In such methodological formalism, this chapter launches the theme and resolves it. This is the theme of the universality and uniqueness of the monotheistic law of unity of knowledge. The epistemological basis of the monotheistic law becomes the foundational praxis of the systemic view of reality in the framework of epistemic oneness. Such is the derivation with its ultimate epistemological roots in the *Qur'an*.

The chapter finally presents the example of studying the meanings of human resource contra human capital in the *qur'anic* phenomenological model. It forms an example of how the phenomenological model of *qur'anic* unity of knowledge is used in the socio-scientific case.

Epistemology and phenomenology in constructing the system orientation of science

Epistemology is well known to be the theory of knowledge. But, beyond such a narrow definition, this chapter inquires into what is the ultimate source of knowledge, the function of knowledge in the cognitive and analytical formulation of the world-system, and the universal and unique properties of the emergent world-system in the dimensions of knowledge, space, and time. Such a total formalism reflects the universal nature of the monotheistic law.

However, taken in its emergent sense of derived unity of knowledge and its use in the evaluation and moral and ethical reconstruction of the world-system in its generality and particulars, one cannot bypass the relations that are developed in the inter-causal nature of the world-system. This is to suggest that phenomenology is the study of consciousness in relation to knowledge that is causally interrelated in the world-system.

Nonetheless, the meanings of episteme and phenomenology are not the same. Episteme conveys the totality of emergent knowledge-flows, not its knowledge-induced logical formalism in relation to the world-system and the inhering issues. Episteme explains the net result of the totality of classifications of knowledge. Phenomenology explains the details of simulating knowledge through the structure of thinking, formalism, and application in the total methodology of knowledge in relation to the world-system and its continuity across knowledge, space, and time as processes evolve.

The meaning of episteme does not lead to a construction of the knowledge-induced systemic worldview. The phenomenological methodology based on the epistemology of unity of knowledge does construct the system-oriented worldview of unity of knowledge.

In logical sense, we can write as follows:

$$\text{Episteme}: \theta = \{\theta_1, \theta_2, \theta_3, \theta_4, ...\} \tag{8.1}$$

where θ_i $i = 1,2,3,4, \ldots$ denotes classifications of knowledge forming the sequentially staged aggregate vector "θ" of such classifications. In this form of the definition, there is no special demand for extracting the epistemology from the monotheistic roots. We refer to this ultimate root of knowledge in the *Qur'an* as Oneness of God, termed as *Tawhid*, or the unity of the monotheistic law. In its functional form, it is denoted by the absolute origin of the monotheistic law of unity of knowledge.

The absolute ontological beginning of knowledge is considered to be the unbounded and non-compact super-space of knowledge.[1] We denote this super-cardinal space in its ontological form by the notation, Ω, such that for any functional derivation G, $G(\Omega) = \Omega$. And for any Ω' with $\Omega' \supset \Omega$, $\Rightarrow \Omega' = \Omega$ identically.

Thus Ω in this form is like the *Dasein* of Heidegger (1988), detached from creation. Therefore Ω by itself does not form the methodological worldview of analytical monotheism; it is necessary for knowledge to be extracted from Ω by the tenets of the monotheistic law of divine Oneness. This extraction is done by the discursive medium. It is mediated by the worldly perfection of the Prophetic mission, called the *[s]unnah* in Islamic terminology. We write this case of extraction of unity of knowledge from the monotheistic law by the medium of S as $\Omega \rightarrow s$. The result of this extraction is the first-level worldly knowledge-flow by the learned ones on the exegesis of the *Qur'an* and the *sunnah*. This phase of knowledge is denoted by $\{\theta^*\}$ and is extracted by $\Omega \rightarrow s$. Yet $\{\theta^*\}$ does not involve details of interpretation and application of the *Qur'an* and the *sunnah*, now together denoted by (Ω, S). However, guidance towards further particular discursively evolved understanding remains clear via $\{\theta^*\}$.

We now write the three first levels of primal knowledge derived from the ontological roots by $(\Omega \rightarrow s : \{\theta^*\})$, or as (Ω, S, θ^*). In this sense, the monotheistic law (Ω)

has become functional through the extractive function of (S,θ^*). The totality of functional extracts from (Ω,S,θ^*) forms the *functional* ontology of the monotheistic epistemology.

The emergent knowledge-flows and the phenomenological configuration involving the unified world-system are denoted by "θ." It denotes the epistemic classification of levels of knowledge-flows and their induction of the emergent world-system—that is, knowledge-flows are now simulated through the events denoted by $\{\theta,x(\theta),t(\theta)\}$, with any $\theta \in U_v[(\Omega)\cap(S)\cap(\theta^*)] \neq \phi$. Here, U_v means the relational combinations of guidance and rules arising from the integrated premise of $[(\Omega)\cap(S)\cap(\theta^*)]$. The socio-scientific theme under study and as induced by the epistemology of unity of knowledge is denoted by $\{x(\theta)\}$, with any θ derived as explained above from the monotheistic epistemology. The event is configured at time $t(\theta)$.

Phenomenology

While we define Episteme in the *Qur'an* by

$$\text{Episteme}: \; \theta = \{(\Omega, S, \theta^*), \theta_1, \theta_2, \theta_3, \theta_4, \ldots\} \tag{8.2}$$

where $\theta_i \, i = 1,2,3,4,\ldots$, we define [p]henomenology, P, in reference to Episteme as a subset:

$$P: [\{U_v \cap_u \{\theta, x(\theta)\}\}, \; W(U_v \cap_u \{\theta, x(\theta)\}\}] \tag{8.3}$$

Here, $W(.)$ denotes the positive monotonic functional transformation of $\{\theta,x(\theta)\}$ on its own diverse relations governed by unity of knowledge as complementarities between the component variables of the vector. We refer to $W(.)$ as the wellbeing evaluation function. It denotes the measure of the degree to which unity of knowledge exists or is constructible in the world-system with respect to specific issues and their combinations.

Rationalism in the phenomenological model of the monotheistic law

Yet again, by the same properties, the phenomenological explanation for other than unity of knowledge, as for rationalism, holds true by the same definition of P by redefining knowledge-flows now for the space of rationalist consequences. In other words, we replace knowledge-flows by "de-knowledge-flows" (Choudhury, 2000). "De-knowledge" arises from the epistemological premises of rationalism, methodological individualism, and competition instead of participation, unity, cooperation, and social integration. Thereby, the world-system so constructed emulates the properties of "de-knowledge" and responds to this. The order of relations is thereby maintained in "de-knowledge."

The epistemological origin is still uniquely premised in the divine law. That is because the well-defined notions of truth and falsehood are to be found in the universal nature of the monotheistic law.[2] Yet the definitions of phenomenology, in respect of their differentiated episteme and separate world-systems, present opposite kinds of properties. They define the dynamics of their different socio-scientific processes and orders. These are procedurally similar, but substantively different. We note these as follows.

P *(phenomenology of unity of knowledge: monotheism)*

$$P: [\{\cup_v \cap_u \{\theta, x(\theta)\}\}, \ W(\cup_v \cap_u \{\theta, x(\theta)\}\}], \text{ given the properties}$$

$$plim[\theta \rightarrow \theta^{**}; x(\theta) \rightarrow x^{**}(\theta^{**})][\{\cup_v \cap_u \{\theta, x(\theta)\}\}] \neq \phi \qquad (8.4)$$

Expression (8.4) persists across evolutionary learning processes regenerated continuously by the episteme of unity of knowledge. Thus θ^{**} denotes continuous the process-oriented probability limits of the learning epistemic vector, and $x^{**}(\theta^{**})$ denotes the corresponding probability limit of the socio-scientific vector that is endogenously induced by the knowledge variable continuously across evolutionary learning processes.

Also, in this case,

$$plim[\theta \rightarrow \theta^{**}; x(\theta) \rightarrow x^{**}(\theta^{**})][(d/d\theta)W\{\cup_v \cap_u \{\theta, x(\theta)\}\}] =$$

$$plim[\theta \rightarrow \theta^{**}; x(\theta) \rightarrow x^{**}(\theta^{**})][\{\cup_v \cap_u (d/d\theta)W\{\theta, x(\theta)\}\}] > 0 \quad (8.5)$$

Expression (8.5) means that evolutionary learning wellbeing functions are continuously differentiable both as intra-processes (denoted by $u = 1, 2, \ldots$) and as inter-processes (denoted by $v = 1, 2, \ldots$). The continuous differentiability of $W(.)$ explains the moral, ethical, and social transformation that is simulated across the evolutionary phenomenological experience in the dimensions of knowledge, space, and time. The time variable, merely reading the occurrence of events, can be bracketed as $t(\theta, x(\theta))$. The mathematical differentiation with respect to "θ" implies that learning, process, causality, and change are caused by changes in knowledge-flows. Time merely records such changes.

Expression (8.5) also implies that, in both the general (inter-process aggregation) and the particular (intra-system) senses, the effect of evolutionary learning on the moral, ethical, and social transformation remains positive in perpetuity of knowledge, space, and time.

P *(phenomenology of "de-knowledge" in the monotheistic worldview)*

Next, consider the case of "de-knowledge," which is characterized by the systems of rationalism, methodological individualism, competition versus participation, inter-causal complementarities, and systemic differentiation versus social embedding.

The following properties hold for phenomenology according to "de-knowledge." We re-interpret all the symbols in terms of their induction by "de-knowledge":

$$P: [\{\cup_v\cap_u\{\theta,x(\theta)\}\}, W(\cup_v\cap_u\{\theta,x(\theta)\}\}], \text{ given the properties}$$
$$plim[\theta\to\theta^{**};x(\theta)\to x^{**}(\theta^{**})][\{\cup_v\cap_u\{\theta,x(\theta)\}\}] = \phi \qquad (8.6)$$

$$plim[\theta\to\theta^{**}; x(\theta)\to x^{**}(\theta^{**})][(d/d\theta)W\{\cup_v\cap_u\{\theta,x(\theta)\}\}] =$$
$$plim[\theta\to\theta^{**}; x(\theta)\to x^{**}(\theta^{**})][\{\cup_v\cap_u(d/d\theta)W\{\theta,x(\theta)\}\}] = 0 \quad (8.7)$$

Expression (8.6) implies the convergence of optimal systems towards methodological independence and hence the occurrence of non-learning states. Shackle (1971) remarked on such states, whereby the mainstream economic models end up losing their novelty of learning. Expression (8.7) implies the probability limiting case of optimal "welfare" functions, as opposed to the continuously evolutionary learning character of the "wellbeing" function of expression (8.5). Such consequences of optimization are found in both the microeconomic (intra-system) and the macroeconomic (inter-system) cases. The result is likewise carried over into public choice theory, social choice theory, welfare economics, and rational expectations hypothesis (Buchanan and Tollison, 1972).

When expressions (8.4) and (8.5) are contrasted with expressions (8.6) and (8.7), then the properties of the knowledge-induced and the "de-knowledge"-induced cases over a short term will yield negative comparative values. Over the long term, the two systems will become independent of each other. The monotonic positive nature of the knowledge-induced system will prevail over the dimensions of knowledge, space, and time. The non-learning nature of the "de-knowledge"-induced world-system will prevail almost everywhere in knowledge, space, and time. But since "de-knowledge" optimizes the system to its terminally non-learning state, "de-knowledge" therefore becomes dysfunctional. Time is then taken as the cause of change. This consequence is contrary to the way in which knowledge, space, and time is inter-causally treated in the case of the monotheistic epistemological worldview.

Systemic worldview

According to the evolutionary learning worldview governed by unity of knowledge, a system is characterized by the following properties: inter-variable and inter-entity interaction. This is followed by integration signifying relational unity between the interacting agents. Hence pervasive participation and complementarities arise in this attained state of integration. We will refer to this property as interaction leading to integration. From the state of interaction leading to integration by the relational epistemology of unity of knowledge emerge the processes of moral, ethical, and social transformation by continued evolutionary learning. Taken altogether, these properties form the permanent characteristics of evolutionary learning systems under unity of knowledge and hence the monotheistic methodology. We refer to the emergent learning processes as the IIE-processes.

The objective criterion of measured unity of knowledge: wellbeing

Besides the IIE-process-oriented systemic worldview, the system described by epistemic unity of knowledge has its corresponding objective criterion to attain. We denoted this by the wellbeing function. It provides the evaluative measure of the degree of unity of inter-causal or participatory organic relations between the good things of life. This property is also explained by pervasive complementarities between the good things of life. Such an analytical property of the wellbeing function was explained by expressions (8.4) and (8.5). The essence of morality, ethicality, and social embedding of systemic variables and their complementary relations inheres in the monotheistic law of such epistemic oneness.[3]

A system with its IIE property and objective wellbeing function, to measure the degree of unity and the transformative simulation towards attaining greater degree of unity by organic complementary and participatory relations, must have its quantitative method. By the principle of pervasive complementarities between all the variables, the wellbeing function is evaluated using the circular causation relations in the complementary variables. Such a system of circular causation relations explains the dynamic organic relations of unity of knowledge. Thus the wellbeing function is evaluated, meaning "estimated," with real data and then "simulated" by constructing targeted degrees of complementarities between the variables as would be explained by the simulated values of the coefficients. Thereby a new set of variables is obtained. These explain the transformed structure of inter-variable causal relations that ought to be attained to simulate the wellbeing function to achieve better degrees of complementarities between the variables of the good things of life.[4] Such complementarities between the good things of life mark the measured sign of unity of knowledge. The quantitative index of such complementarities is the result of the simulated wellbeing function intra-system and inter-system across IIE learning processes.

The phenomenological system of *Tawhidi* (monotheistic) unity of knowledge

The comprehensive epistemological embedding of the concepts of phenomenology, episteme, and system are now brought together to establish the phenomenological model in Figure 8.1. The inherent analytical nature of the imminent model establishes the methodological understanding of analytical monotheism.

We formalize the moral, ethical, and social embedding of the above-mentioned concepts by expression (8.8):

$$\text{Evaluate } W(x(\boldsymbol{\theta})) \tag{8.8}$$

subject to the circular causation relations, $x_i(\theta) = f_i(\boldsymbol{x}'(\theta),\theta)$, where $i = 1,2,\ldots n$ and $\boldsymbol{x}'(\theta)$ denotes $\boldsymbol{x}(\theta)$-vector without $x_i(\theta)$.

The last equation, which represents the evaluative index of unity of knowledge is,

$$\theta = F(x(\theta)); (\Omega, S, \theta^*) \ni \theta \rightarrow x(\theta) \equiv \theta, x(\theta)$$

Note that $W(\theta)$ and θ-functionals are monotonic transformations of each other.

Therefore we proxy $W(\theta)$ by θ, a linear approximation.

Such an approximation suggests that only $\theta = F(x(\theta))$ needs to be evaluated ("estimated" and "simulated"). Yet $W(\theta)$ is important for studying its conceptual worth as the wellbeing criterion in terms of *Tawhidi* (monotheistic) unity of knowledge.

The analytical model of circular causation summarizing the conceptual and empirical nature of monotheistic oneness as epistemology is now summarized.

Evaluate ("estimate" and then "simulate") the system:

Inter-process continuity

$$x_i(\theta) = f_i(x'(\theta), \theta) \text{ where } x'(\theta) \text{ denotes the } x(\theta) \text{ without } x_i(\theta);$$

$$i = 1, 2, \dots n; \text{ and}$$

$$\theta = F(x(\theta))$$

Intra-process $(\Omega, S, \theta^*) \ni \{\theta\} \rightarrow \{x(\theta)\} \equiv \{\theta, x(\theta)\}$ (8.9)

Qur'anic phenomenological model

The phenomenological attributes of monotheistic unity of knowledge as explained above are now brought together in the *Tawhidi* String Model in Figure 8.1.

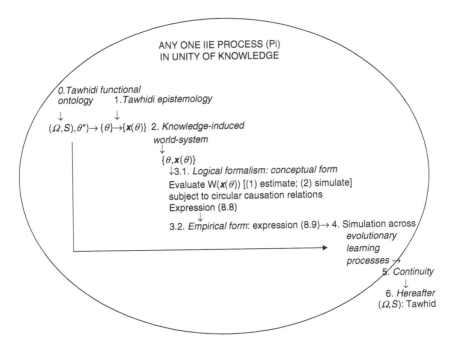

Figure 8.1 Generalized form of the *Tawhidi* String Relation (TSR) of monotheistic phenomenology

The whole P_i surface manifests the complete *i*th IIE-process, $i = 1,2,\ldots,$ proceeding on until the Hereafter, the final *Closure* of a self-actualized evolutionary learning universe of "everything."

Interactions leading to integration occur everywhere, except in the foundational functional ontology part (Ω,S), in reference to socio-scientific study. IIE properties are derived from the *Qur'an* to mean *tasbih* (the worshiping world-system) or *ayath Allah* (signs of God). Institutional discourse in respect of *tasbih* is referred to in the *Qur'an* as *shura* with *ijtihad*.

(Ω,S) is continuously recalled at the beginning of every new "*i*th" process. These can be continuous intra-system and inter-system processes, as in social and natural phenomena. They can also be discrete, as in the case of observational and learning lags.

Evolutionary learning in IIE processes continues until the end in the Hereafter, when all knowledge is optimized. The explained universe of everything self-actualizes.

Summary of the generalized model

IIE-processes

Tawhid → {Knowledge-flows, World-system} → *Tawhid*: Universal *Closure* without bounds in knowledge, space, and time

The *Closure* is carried over the continuous sequences of finite closures in every IIE-process. This enables evolutionary equilibrium to attain—but there is no optimum except at the points of *Tawhid* where knowledge is full, perfect, absolute, and exogenously endowed in their supercardinal spaces.

A particular case:

Knowledge-flows $\{\theta\}$: invoking consciousness in the epistemology of unity of knowledge
Socioeconomic variables: human capital $(x_1(\theta))$; human resource $(x_2(\theta))$; other pertinent variables $(x_3(\theta))$
Wellbeing Function, conceptual version: $W(x_1(\theta),x_2(\theta),x_3(\theta))$
Circular Causation relations (Empirical Evaluation):

$$
\begin{aligned}
x_1 &= f_1(x_2,x_3,\ \theta)[\theta] \\
\{x_2 &= f_2(x_1,x_3,\ \theta)[\theta]\} \\
x_3 &= f_3(x_1,x_2,\ \theta)[\theta]
\end{aligned}
\tag{8.10}
$$
$$\downarrow$$

$\theta = F(x_1,x_2,\ x_3)[\theta]$: empirical version of Wellbeing Function.
$[\theta]$ means common induction of all the inner bracketed variables.

Episteme: determination of aggregate average $\boldsymbol{\theta}$: (θ^*(point 0), θ_1(point 1), $\theta_{3,2}$(point 3,2), θ_4(point 4).

These points represent the evolutionary learning surfaces of the phenomenological model (Figure 8.1).

The theory of human capital has turned out to be a socially bereft acquisition of assets that serves the ends of methodological individualism. All economic theory, within which is located the postulate of rational choice, considers education to be a competing good with other social ends in its objective criterion of maximization of utility function with scarce resources competing for allocation between education treated as a private good and as a social good.

In the social sense of education that embeds it in the joint acquisition of social and economic security, social and economic empowerment—and the participatory nature of self and society—become most important. The economic prospects are not left out. So also social effects are not diminished. Human resource now enters front stage to acquire a more meaningful concept of economic and social capital. The two are complemented by the medium of continuous resource reproduction via its regenerative abundance. The structure of the life-fulfillment regime of development prevails in sustaining the complementary effects of resource abundance. Organization and institution play their significant role in instilling the epistemological foundation of the emergent form of the world-system, with human resource as the conjoint social and economic good.

The idea of human resource now assumes its meaning contrary to human capital as a neoclassical economic concept. The respective organizational and institutional meanings are thus invoked in social policy formulation. The economic consequences of ownership and the distribution of income and wealth arise.

The following expressions formalize the contrasting meanings of human resource by knowledge-induction to the neoclassical definition of human capital:

1   Human resource (HR) : $HR = HR(\theta, x(\theta), \wp(\theta, x(\theta))$ (8.11)

wherein $dHR/d\theta > 0$ implies that $\partial HR/\partial\theta + \Sigma_i(\partial HR/\partial x_i).(dx_i(\theta)/d\theta) + d\wp(\theta, x(\theta))/d\theta > 0$, identically.
This result thereby establishes the principle of pervasive complementarities between the variables, $\{x_i(\theta)\}=x(\theta)$, $i = 1,2,..,n$, when they are induced by the foundational θ-values. HR becomes the derived knowledge artifact, which is then driven by the corresponding force of institutionalism in its own epistemic unity of knowledge.

2   In neoclassical human capital (HK) theory, the institutionalization of derived θ-value is premised on the pervasive marginal rate of substitution (that is, the postulate of opportunity cost). Preferences are datum (constant). We then have the following result in the optimal resource allocation state of the neoclassical world:

$dHK/d\theta = 0;\ \partial HK/\partial\theta = 0$ and $\Sigma_i(\partial HK/\partial x_i).(dx_i(\theta)/d\theta) = 0$ (8.12)

identically by individual terms.

In this case, $\partial HK/\partial x_i > 0$, $\partial HK/\partial x_j > 0$. Consequently, $dx_i/dx_j < 0$, owing to the postulate of marginal rate of substitution. Furthermore, by the grouping of partially complementary variables such as $\Sigma_i x_i$, $\Sigma_j x_j$, we have, $d(\Sigma_i x_i)/d(\Sigma_j x_j) < 0$.

Expression (8.10) implies the evolutionary continuity of resource regeneration with the episteme of unity of knowledge determining this property of abundance everywhere. On the other hand, expression (8.11) points out the ultimate scarcity of resources resulting in the trade-off between HR and HK.

Along with $x(\theta)$ are included the variables of poverty alleviation, technology, and production and consumer choices. Such variables, being governed by the episteme of unity of knowledge, also determine the evolutionary learning preferences. The dynamic preferences are causally interrelated with the dynamic basic needs regime of development.

The basic needs regime of development and the organizations that operate in such a development regime simulate the episteme of their institutionalism in the light of the primal Islamic epistemology in the Islamic case. Thus the dynamic basic needs regime of development is the essential nature of organization of markets, economies, development, life-fulfillment choices, and learning institutions.

Conclusion

In this chapter, we have dealt with the important theme of developing a scientific research program based on a systemic understanding of the phenomenology of the theme left out in scientific research. These are the *res extensa* and *res cogitans* domains of the monotheistic treatment of socio-scientific phenomenology. The result is to extend the domain of the limited socio-scientific experience to its completeness as discovered in reference to the monotheistic epistemological worldview.

While the derivation is from the *Qur'an* in order to determine the analytical content of the socio-scientific project of monotheistic oneness of knowledge, the conclusions based on it are twofold: First, the emergent phenomenological model is universal in nature; second, the underlying methodology is of a unique type. On these issues we simply state here the basis of the aforementioned formalism, without proving it, owing to lack of space in this chapter: The unified perspective, as the conceptual-empirical methodology of "everything" combined with the circular causality between deductive and inductive reasoning along evolutionary learning processes, bears the character of both universality and uniqueness of the monotheistic law and its dynamics. The domain of conceptualization, formalism, and explanation forms the totality encompassing the dimensions of knowledge, space, and time.

Furthermore, the *Qur'an* presents the systemic unity of knowledge through evolutionary learning by causing reality to be increasingly separated from truth and falsehood. The separation in this respect occurs with the final optimization and completion of knowledge in the Hereafter.[5]

Notes

1 Rucker (1982) terms such overarching super-space with large cardinality as the super-space. According to the *Qur'an*, the supercardinal space of knowledge comprises the monotheistic law in its relational form of generating worldly knowledge-flows through observation, interaction, and integration, followed by creative evolution by continued learning in unity of knowledge and its induction of the unifying world-system in general

and particular. Because God is full in knowledge and is non-corporeal in any extant of cognition, therefore the super-space is inexhaustible; hence *res extensa* across everything. The totality of such super-space generates relations in the framework of unity of knowledge reflecting monotheistic oneness. Such relations thereby reflect pervasive pairing and extensions in the form of organic relationalism. On the subject of organic relationalism, one can refer to Imam Ghazali's (n.d.) theory of knowledge.

2 *Qur'an* (25:1): "Blessed is He Who has sent the criterion (of right and wrong) to His slave that he may be a warner to the *a'lameen* (world-system)."
3 *Qur'an* (36:36) on the dynamics of pairing: "Exalted is He who created all pairs— from what the earth grows and from themselves and from that which they do not know."
4 *Qur'an* (42:38): "Those who hearken to their Lord, and establish regular Prayer; who (conduct) their affairs by mutual consultation (participation and complementarities); who spend out of what We bestow on them for Sustenance (the good things of life)."
5 *Qur'an* (83:7, 18): "Nay! Most surely the record of the wicked is in the *Sijjin*.";"Nay! Most surely the record of the righteous shall be in the Illyin."

References

Badawi, M. (1999). "Universe," in *Man and the Universe*, Amman: Wakeel Books, pp. 3–13.
Barrow, J.D. (1991). "Laws," in *Theories of Everything: The Quest for Ultimate Explanation*, Oxford: Oxford University Press, pp. 12–30.
Bhaskar, R. (1978). "The logic of scientific discovery," in *A Realist Theory of Science*, New York: Harvester Wheatsheaf, Chapter 3.
Boland, L.A. (1989). "On the methodology of economic model building," in *The Methodology of Economic Model Building*, London: Routledge, pp. 39–63.
Buchanan, J.M. and Tollison, R.D. (1972). *Theory of Public Choice*, Ann Arbor, MI: University of Michigan Press.
Choudhury, M.A. (2000). *The Islamic Worldview*, London: Kegan Paul International.
Descartes, R. (1954). "Discourse on method," in Commins, S. and Linscott, R.N. (eds.), *Man & the Universe: The Philosophers of Science*, New York: Pocket Books, pp. 163–220.
Einstein, A. (n.d.). "The laws of science and the laws of ethics," in *Lectures in Physics*, New York: Philosophical Library.
Einstein, A. (1954). "The problem of space, ether, and the field in physics," in Commins, S. and Linscott, R.N. (eds.), *Man and the Universe: The Philosophers of Science*, New York: The Pocket Library, pp. 473–484.
Hawking, S.W. (1988). *A Brief History of Time: From the Big Bang to Black Holes*, New York: Bantam Books.
Heidegger, M. (1988). "The thesis of modern ontology: The basic ways of being are the being of nature (*res extensa*) and the being of mind (*res cogitans*)," in *The Basic Problems of Phenomenology*, trans. Hofstadter, A. Bloomington, IN: Indiana University Press, pp. 122–224.
Hull, D.L. (1988). *Science as a Process: An Evolutionary Account of the Social and Conceptual Development of Science*, Chicago, IL: University of Chicago Press.
Imam Ghazali, (n.d.). *Ihya Ulum-Id-Din* (five volumes), trans. Karim, M.F. Lahore: Sh. Muhammad Ashraf.
Kant, I. (1949). "Critique of pure reason," "Critique of judgment," in "Reason within the limits of reason," and "Idea for a universal history with cosmopolitan content," in Friedrich, C.J. (ed.), *The Philosophy of Kant*, New York: Modern Library.
Kuhn, T.S. (1970). *The Structure of Scientific Revolution*, Chicago, IL: University of Chicago Press.
Lawson, T. (1997). *Economics and Reality*, London: Routledge.

Rucker, R. (1982). "Large cardinals," in *Infinity and the Mind*, New York: Bantam Books, pp. 273–286.

Shackle, G.L.S. (1971). *Epistemics and Economics*, Cambridge: Cambridge University Press.

Wallerstein, I. (1998). "Spacetime as the basis of knowledge," in Bordo, O.F. (ed.), *People's Participation: Challenges Ahead*, New York: Apex Press, pp. 43–62.

Whitehead, A.N. (1978). "Fact and form," in Griffin, D.R. Sherburne, D.W. (eds.), *Process and Reality*, New York: The Free Press.

Witham, L. (2010). *Marketplace of the Gods: How Economics Explains Religion*, Oxford: Oxford University Press.

9 Conclusion
From meta-science to ethico-economics

In this concluding chapter, the theme of the entire book is summarized in the light of the episteme of the monotheistic law of unity of knowledge as the origin of meta-science. The monotheistic law is also equated with the Oneness of God in the form of the perfect law. It is referred is to as *Tawhid*. The *Qur'an* is a divine book of knowledge. It presents knowledge as the divine essence of the Oneness of God, referred to as *Tawhid*. This word is derived from the generic *qur'anic* term, *ahad*, meaning divine Oneness in the sense of there being no equality in partnership with God in any shape, form, or implication, either directly or indirectly. *Tawhid*, as the ultimate reality of the Oneness of God, also means God's absolute, complete, and perfect state of knowledge as law that creates, governs, and prevails over all the universes. Thus the *Qur'an* refers to that perfection of God's attribute in terms of His creatorship and sustenance of the universes in the verse:

> Verily this is a Revelation from the Lord of the Worlds: With it came down the Spirit of faith and truth – to thy heart and mind, that you (Muhammad) may admonish in the perspicuous Arabic tongue.
>
> *(Qur'an, 26:193–195)*

In this regard, *Allah* also refers to Himself as the Light of the Heavens and the Earth (*Qur'an*, 24:35).

The *Qur'an* and the knowledge-centered worldview: briefly delineating the praxis

Qur'anic *world-systems*

The complete, perfect, and absolute nature of divine knowledge, never changing, but ever enriching the universes of self and others, over which the Creator sublimely rules, is the meaning of the unity of knowledge in its primordial form. From this stock of knowledge emanate knowledge-flows. These knowledge-flows then determine the *qur'anic* world-systems (*a'lameen*) that invigorate life, existence, and comprehension. In this sense, such knowledge-flows are causally linked with human cognition, comprehension, intellection, and, thereby, relations and inferences. While the acts of comprehension, intellection and inference are commands of the human order, the relational functions are existences of human, animate, and inanimate orders. It now takes the human mind to search, discover, and unravel the inner depths of animate and inanimate relations, as well as those that fill the human domain.

Thus the primal existence of a divine stock of knowledge creates universes that remain permanently premised on this fundamental divine unity of knowledge. From this primal premise of knowledge appear knowledge-induced worlds, their entities, systems, domains, and relations. Such processes and entities learn pervasively within and across their own and other interrelated world-systems. An extensively relational order is thus born out of such learning on the framework of unity across the diversity of systems and relations, actions and responses. Such a framework of unity of knowledge is conveyed by the epistemology of *Tawhid* as the essence of oneness in perfection, completeness, and the absolute nature of divine knowledge as law. (For studies on Islamic epistemology from a historical Islamic perspective and in terms of a *qur'anic* lexicographical approach, see Bakar, 1991; Al-Edrus, 1990.)

The *Qur'an* points to such overarching learning and relational processes that span all systems of creation in terms of unity across diversity. Knowledge-flows and their induced systems and relations are causally bound together by the unique law of divine Oneness, *Tawhid*. We have the following verse from the *Qur'an* in this regard:

> And in the earth are tracts (diverse though) neighboring, and gardens of vines and fields sown with corn, and palm trees – growing out of single roots or otherwise: watered with the same water, yet some of them. We make more excellent than others to eat. Behold, verily in these things there are Signs of those who understand!
>
> (*Qur'an*, 13:4)

One can also refer to the chapter of *Nahl* (the *Bee*) that expounds on instilling depth on the meaning of relational orders caused by the conscious invocation of divine Oneness as the epistemology of learning worlds with diversity and complementarities within and among themselves.

On the theme of submission of will by the animate and inanimate worlds to divine will—that is, to the law of unity—the *Qur'an* says:

> Do they not look at God's creation, (even) among (inanimate) things,—How their (very) shadows turn around, from the right and the left, prostrating themselves to God, and that in the humblest manner? And to God pays obeisance all that is in the heavens and on earth, whether moving (living) creatures or the angels: for none are arrogant (before their Lord). They all revere their Lord, high above them, and they do all that they are commanded.
>
> (*Qur'an*, 16:48–50)

Furthermore, the *Qur'an* (30:11) says on the divinely conscious process of creation: "It is God Who begins (the process of) creation; then repeats it; then shall you be brought back to Him."

The creative nature of knowledge-centered world-systems

The implication of the creative process emanating from and returning to the ultimate source of oneness is of a continuous nature over knowledge, space, and time dimensions. The same process also establishes the closed nature of the learning universes in terms of the ultimate reality, which is the Hereafter (*Akhira*) and is equivalent to *Tawhid* in terms of completion of knowledge. The *Qur'an* equates the Event of the Hereafter with faith and refers to it as the equivalent part of the purpose of creation in Truth. The Event of the Hereafter (*Akhira*) is thus referred to as the Great Event (*Naba ul-Azim*) (*Qur'an*, 77) or the Sure Reality (*Al-Haqqa*) (*Qur'an*, 69).

Being premised on the same theme of the intrinsic and conscious nature of unity in creation, the intellection of human faculties is invoked through reflective contemplation (*tafakkur*). Such contemplation extends over the entire creation beyond mere human domains of reflection. The *Qur'an* says in regards to the intrinsic consciousness of *Tawhid* in inanimate creation:

> Moreover He comprehended in His design the sky, and it had been (as smoke): He said to it and to the earth: "Come you together, willingly or unwillingly." They said: "We do come (together), in willing obedience."
>
> (*Qur'an*, 41:11)

With regard to reflective contemplation and the observant disposition of the human world to *Tawhid*, the *Qur'an* says:

> Behold! In the creation of the heavens and the earth and the alteration of Night and Day,—there are indeed Signs for men of understanding,—men who celebrate the praises of God, standing, sitting, and lying down on their sides, and contemplate the (wonders of) creation in the heavens and the earth, (with the thought): "Our Lord! Not for naught have You created (all) this! Glory to You! Give us salvation from the Penalty of the Fire.
>
> (*Qur'an*, 3:190–191)

A comprehensive understanding of this verse extends its meaning to the entire fold of human cognition, intellection, and reflective empiricism while being centrally premised and causally determined by divine knowledge. It also links both the episteme of divine knowledge and the experiential creative order with the proof of purpose in all of these. This purpose is then brought to relate to the ultimate reality of the Hereafter (*Akhira*). Thus the meaning of extensively unifying interactions among various domains of realities under the premise of the divine unity of knowledge is induction of all such realities or entities by the signs of God (*ayath*). The meaning of *qur'anic* world-systems (*a'lameen*) is thereby derived under the praxis of the divine unity of knowledge.

The above brief discussion in this introductory section initiates the nature of the inquiry, which is about searching and discovering a methodology of the grand and permanent, unique and universal praxis of unity of knowledge as the epistemology of *Tawhid* that is uniquely explainable in all world-systems. This absolute and unique essence of the *Tawhidi* episteme that brings about the fundamental role of divine unity into the experiential world and makes this reality explainable in the framework of unity across diversity of material being can be explained in different ways by the process of unraveling through evolving knowledge-flows.

Knowledge-flows and their induced forms in *qur'anic* world-systems commence and continuously return to the divine source of unity across processes. Between these periods of commencement and return, there is the intellectual process of creative learning in the ensuing unifying world-systems. Such a process is a vastly relational and unifying order across the diversity of domains, relations, and systems. The process of forming such interrelationships and realizing their evolution by the advance of the knowledge of unity in experiential domains reflects the dynamics of knowledge-flows in such universes, once they are derived from the source of *Tawhid* and continuously return to the same episteme.

The *Qur'an* refers to this dynamic knowledge-induced movement, the repetitive re-origination in the framework of unity and unification of knowledge, as *khalq injadid* or *khalqa summa yueid*. These *qur'anic* phrases mean creatively re-originated orders arising by the command and will of God, thus premising such evolutions on the unity of the divine law. The *Qur'an* (29:19) says in this regard, "See they not how God originates creation, then repeats it: truly that is easy for God."

The dynamic process of discovering unity in world-systems after commencing from the *Tawhidi* epistemology and configuring the world-systems (domains and systems) on the basis of that very epistemology for confirmation and assertion forms a total phenomenological order. The resulting evolution of knowledge-flows over the totality of space–time, both revealed and hidden, culminates in the Hereafter at the very end. This is also a meaning of the *qur'anic* reference that our ultimate return is to God in the Hereafter. It means the culmination of all universal knowledge-flows back to the stock from which they continuously emanate in living experience. The stock is ever spending, but never spent. The *Qur'an* (30:11) says in this regard: "It is God Who begins (the process of) creation; then repeats it; then shall you be brought back to Him."

The thought process and the world-system derived from the organization of such a knowledge-centered worldview together comprise the unique praxis of all systems of life and thought. Such knowledge-centered systems convey the *qur'anic* meaning of worlds or world-systems, which is the *qur'anic a'lameen*. Now, there remains no distinction between the praxis of the natural sciences, social sciences, and human sciences. They are all unified by this fundamental epistemology of unity. The principle of unity of knowledge pervades all systems and thus unifies them uniquely by this epistemology. Upon such unification process rests the ultimate purpose of existence and reality.

A process-oriented systems view of qur'anic *praxis*

A system view of pervasive interrelationships among the tenets of the *Tawhidi* worldview now emerges. The tenets of such a system are, first, the epistemology of the fundamental unity of knowledge. Second, there occurs an emanation of knowledge-flows for the construction of the knowledge-induced world-system along with the associated thought processes, reflective action, and response in and through such diverse, but unified, world-systems. Third, there is the process of creative evolution of the same knowledge-centered order to its cumulative, full, and optimal realization in the Hereafter.

These systemic interrelationships are borne out in many ways and are well explained by the interaction, integration (unification), and creative evolution (*khalq in-jadid*) caused by circular interrelationships among the three *qur'anic* tenets. These are, namely, the premises of the Supreme Truth. This is also the epistemology of *Tawhid* (*haqq ul-yaqin*). Next to follow is the domain of knowledge-flows within world-systems emanating from that epistemology (*ilm ul-yaqin*). These are followed by the use of the two tenets in the organization of *qur'anic* world-systems as being unified and creatively evolutionary, while enabling reflective empiricism and inferences to arise as creative responses once they are premised on the truth actions of the knowledge-flows (*ayn ul-yaqin*).

Such a circular interrelationship maintains *haqq ul-yaqin* as the exogenous, permanent, and immutable invariant in every sub-process caused by this epistemology in developing continuously relational creativity between *ilm* and *ayn* of the *Tawhidi* worldview. The processes of interrelationships remain permanently endogenous in nature. The only exogenous position is given to the singularly complete essence of *Tawhid* as the fundamental epistemology in all kinds of *qur'anic* world-systems.

The complex nature of *qur'anic* world-systems

Since the circularly repeating endogenous interrelationships among *ilm* and *ayn* are creatively dynamic and diversely evolutionary in form with the immutable centricity of *Tawhid* as *haqq ul-yaqin*, the interrelationships in this systemic order are therefore of a complex nature. Order, harmony, balance, and equilibrium are all maintained, but only within the non-linear meaning of complexity. Complexity is bestowed by the ever-widening function of knowledge-flows in initiating the emergent knowledge-induced unified forms as caused by interaction and integration among such knowledge-flows and forms. Even in Heaven (*Jannah*), the creative evolution stabilizes and continues on in a knowledge-induced continuum.

The above forms of endogenous interrelationships among *ilm ul-yaqin* and *ayn ul-yaqin*, with the singularly exogenous epistemic centricity of *haqq ul-yaqin* (*Tawhid*), are explained in Figure 9.1. Figure 9.1 is to be understood as a cross-sectional view of a conical evolution of the base comprising *ilm ul-yaqin* and *ayn ul-yaqin*, while the vertex of the cone, *haqq ul-yaqin*, remains invariant. This geometry is not commensurable in essence, owing to the immeasurable nature of divine knowledge as stock. Hence the vertex is explained here by the "open" point belonging to a supermanifold topology.

Topology is a non-dimensional method of pure mathematics that is used particularly for explaining relational forms. These may be entities or otherwise. The method

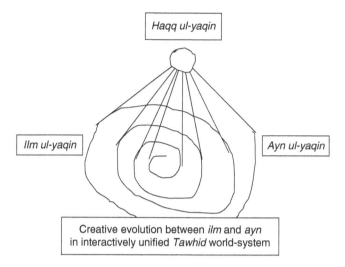

Figure 9.1 Evolutionary interrelationships in the *qur'anic* world-system

of topology is chosen here over other mathematical methods in order to appropriately address the non-dimensional, but pervasively creative, nature of *Allah's* essence (*fitra*) as the monotheistic law in the order of things that come about simply by the intervention of divine laws.

Supermanifold is a hyper-topology in which numerical measurability is replaced by relational mappings of "complete" types that span all possible world-systems. Hence if the world-systems can be delineated by topological spaces and mappings, then a supermanifold, as the diverse combination of such spaces and mappings, belongs to the nexus of all of them. When such a nexus of inter-relationships is comprehensive, then it is also mathematically complete. The limit of the supermanifold is reached. Completeness across the diversity of relation-ships across all possible combinations among such pervasive interrelationships is possible only in a perfectly unified world-system that evolves in its own unique praxis. This is the *Tawhidi* worldview. But this same episteme also determines the "mathematical opposite" space of relations. This is the domain of "de-knowledge." It must also belong to the supermanifold by way of reinforcing the ineluctable proof of the unity of knowledge as truth in the *Tawhidi* worldview by virtue of its contrast with the falsehood of disintegrative rationalism found in the mathematical opposite of truth, which is "de-knowledge."

Certain outstanding questions

Even while we are delineating a worldview premised on *Tawhid*, certain outstanding questions need to be addressed. Such questionable areas follow: How can the *Tawhidi* praxis become the epistemology of a world-system that is distinct from the scientific philosophy of the heteronomous world-system? Is not much of the clamor of modernity, science and technology, power and prowess taking place in the Occidental order? These are questions that must be addressed in the light of the kind of interactively unified evolutionary knowledge-induced world-system projected in Figure 9.1. They are then to be taken up in relation to a variety of conceptions, systemic diversity, issues and problems, analytical details and applications that arise in and through the *Tawhidi* methodological worldview. Such realizations represent combinations of interrelating tenets of a knowledge-centered worldview that is fired by reflective empiricism. The continuity between knowledge-flows and their induced forms enables actions, responses, and the creative dynamics of evolution to move into more of the same kind. Such organisms of the *Tawhidi* world-system remain endogenously interactive in reference to the epistemological permanence of the monotheistic law of unity of knowledge.

Further questions arise: Is there reason to believe in the permanence of modernity, and its scientific validity, that has appeared in the West over the last 200 years? Is there a serious critique of received philosophy of science in terms of essentialism rather than rationalism? Is there reason to be skeptical of the emergence of a truly integrated science and society that is a socio-scientific order, which can be premised on the *Tawhidi* epistemology after these 200 years of science, technology, economics, and political power in the West? In other words, was *Tawhid* not always permanently entrenched within the diverse problems of mind and matter—except that we see its *conscious* resurgence as a distinct civilization process that came with the advent of Islam and subsequently delineated the age of Islamic scholasticism? Can such a worldview again mark the human future?

We are then led to ask the resulting question: What will be the future threshold of such a new global transformation? Will this be determined by a continued show of scientific and technological feats and their global transference, or will it be determined by addressing the great and impending moral and social issues on which the wellbeing of humankind and the world truly rests?

We are now led to assert that the means of addressing the future and the total environment of humans both morally and ethically would implicate a new methodological conception, understanding, and application of economics, science, and technology. Within this very unique praxis will come about the interactive unification of these disciplines across a diversity of systems, and this will make the methodological approach creatively dynamic between actions and responses spanning all human experience in relation to the unified world-system (*a'lameen*).

Thus the concept of a *socio-scientific* order is a domain of intellection that interactively integrates (unifies) diverse issues and problems by a unique methodology. Such a unifying methodology becomes the praxis of all verities of world-systems—economics, science, technology, and the human order, with its extensive ecological and cosmological meaning and relations with each other and with other domains. Such is the meta-function of the knowledge-centered world-system premised on the fundamental unity of knowledge as the epistemology of a coherent and unique praxis in the study of the relational order involving God, man, economics, environment, science, and society.

The last 200 years of Western modernism is to be questioned on the premise of this singular praxis of unity of knowledge. The survival of the Occidental mind and its acceptance of a posteriori reasoning as the sole human source of operation is also to be questioned on the same grounds.

Behind these affirmations relating to the inevitable consequences of Western mind–matter relationships that have remained insensitive to the endogenous role of ethical and moral forces is the recognition that the unitary worldview is permanently entrenched in reality. Yet it has been rejected by a distorted culture of economics, science, thought, social action, and response.

Briefly contrasting the *qur'anic* worldview with rationalism

This book has taken up this substantive topic to highlight the relevance of the development of meta-science in the moral, ethical, and human perspective of the monotheistic law of unity of knowledge. To understand the background and past and future prospects of the culture of economic, science, technology, and society, and the treatment of the mind–matter dichotomy in Western thought, actions, and responses, a brief summary of Occidental thought is presented here. It is contrasted with the *qur'anic* epistemic worldview of unity of knowledge.

At the outset, we have noted in this work the exogenous nature of the universally determining role of *Tawhid* in all experiential relations. The law and inherent relations are endogenously pre-determined by *Tawhid*. To discuss this topic, we must first carefully define the place of Reason in the understanding of Truth. The question begs serious consideration. Is Reason a primordial entity that is required to understand *Tawhid* and the role of divine law (*sunnat Allah*) in creation? Contrarily, is Reason as natural essence a created quiddity that is realized spontaneously at the *moment* when a relational complexity ensues through interactions between the divine law and the consequential events? In the *Tawhidi* world-system, such a consequential and relational outcome would be of the interactive, integrative, and evolutionary (IIE) type. We have explained this phenomenology throughout this work.

The emergence of the Western mind in Greek thought

In reference to the subject matter of this whole work, it was sufficient for us to have an overview of the divine law and the world in Greek thought in which both the Muslim rationalists—and subsequently their heirs, the Occidental world—had their epistemological roots. The details of life, such as economy, society, and science (the physics of the Greeks), were tied intrinsically to a peculiar connection between God and the world (Vermont, 1995).

To the Greeks, God was earthly born as required by human need. Hence it was an earthly God of needs and thus remained relative in the scale of functions. This gave rise to many gods, each taking domain over a particular function of human relations as they exist and evolve over space and time. Yet there was an unbridgeable distance between God and the world in terms of a relational law. Such limitations as sickness and weakness, joy and defeat, and the ups and downs of life's variegated patterns did not affect the Greek gods as they did the humans. Yet the Greek gods were relationally tied to human actions and relations. This is a conception of gods as pantheistic in nature and multiple in corporeal origin.

The Greek concept of morality, ethics, and values in mundane affairs emanated from a perfect order of the gods. This kind of concept took an earthly meaning of the relations assumed to exist between particular gods in their domains and consequent human affairs. In this way, human relational order in the picture of a god-centric Greek universe took up a rationalist fervor. Divinity was relinquished to such a relativistic understanding of God as divine and in terms of His relationship with human actions and propensities.

The pantheism and material relativism of Greek thought was a forerunner of the evolutionary dynamics of a rationalist mind, which became part and parcel of the Western dialectical culture. Likewise, the banishing of God as the substantive lawgiver, so that divine law does not act upon the world, assuming an exogenously numinous existence, is the continued message of Western socio-scientific epistemology. It was also inherited by the Muslim mystic rationalists and carved into an unacceptable orientation of *qur'anic* exegesis and fundamental knowledge.

The mingling of Greek thought, Muslim rationalism, and the Western mind is therefore not difficult to understand. Each of these, by choosing a rationalist orientation to divine origin, made the divine order either non-functional in a numinous epistemological sense or left it to pantheistic conceptions. None of these approaches can be any part of the *qur'anic* worldview, wherein God is One, everlasting, and the creator and sustainer of the universes. God is the ultimate lawgiver above the limitations of the created worlds. The emergent worldview created by divine law is thus natural and consistent, unmarred by fault. They are explainable and remain as organic relations to world-systems. God is above earthly attributes. Yet He is the lawgiver, whose divine law is the essential part of reality and around which world-systems are established, organized, and evolved.

The opposing character of systems in the *Tawhidi* worldview and rationalism

Although rationalism and the *Tawhidi* worldview of the unity of knowledge both prescribe a systems-based, process-oriented methodology, the above inference points out an entirely different construction of the theories of man, machines, science, technology, economy, and society, and the cosmos between the two polar praxes. Polarity between the two kinds of understanding and sensation is expressed emphatically in the words of Capra (1983: 302), who wrote:

> Detailed study of ecosystems over the past decades has shown quite clearly that most relationships between living organisms are essentially co-operative ones, characterized by coexistence and interdependence, and symbiotic in various degrees. .... This insight is in sharp contrast to the views of the Social Darwinists, who saw life exclusively in terms of competition, struggle, and destruction. Their view of nature has helped to create a philosophy that legitimates exploitation

and the disastrous impact of our technology on the natural environment. But such a view has no scientific justification, because it fails to perceive the integrative and co-operative principles that are essential aspects of the ways in which living systems organize themselves at all levels.

To consider more deeply the methodology of *Tawhidi* unity of knowledge, this methodology totally rejects the place of economic competition within organic categories premised on the unitary epistemology. Competition is seen as the attribute of a differentiated world-system. In the perpetual conflict between truth and falsehood, the rule is not one of competition between truth and falsehood; rather, it is to pursue the fixed goal of the truth paradigm. Thereby, the two trajectories of truth and falsehood evolve in evolutionary world-systems in distinct ways of their own kinds. They remain permanently polarized to each other, given, however, that they are both explained uniquely by the dynamics of the *Tawhidi* methodology, as referred to above (Choudhury, 2000). These realities cannot be explained by any of the heteronomous paradigms of economics, society, and science.

This point of singularity between the two polar and opposing praxes of life is brought out both in the *Qur'an* and the *sunnah*. Regarding the uncertain rambling of rationalist thought, even in its most tempting form, the *Qur'an* (51:10–11) says, "Woe to the falsehood-mongers,—those who (flounder) heedless in a flood of confusion."

Also, there is the verse:

> And they worship besides God things that hurt them not nor profit them, and they say: "These are our intercessors with God," Say: "Do you inform God with that which He knows not in the heavens and on the earth?" Glorified and Exalted be He above all that they associate as partners with Him!
>
> (*Qur'an*, 10:18)

Furthermore, the *Qur'an* says:

> Say: "I have been forbidden to invoke those who you invoke besides God— seeing that the Clear Signs have come to me from my Lord; and I have been commanded to bow (in Islam) to the Lord of the Worlds."
>
> (*Qur'an*, 40:66)

Although this verse refers to the mission of the Prophet Muhammad, by the principle of universality of *qur'anic* verses it is extended to apply to all believers in general. Yusuf Ali (1942) commenting on this verse, writes: "When we bow to the Real and Everlasting, we are automatically saved from falling victims to the false and Evanescent."

In a *hadith* (a saying of the Prophet Muhammad) on these matters, narrated by Abu Huraira, a companion of the Prophet, the people of the scripture used to read the Torah in Hebrew and then explain it in Arabic to the Muslims. *Allah*'s Messenger said (to the Muslims): "Do not believe the people of the scripture, nor disbelieve them, but say, 'We believe in *Allah* and whatever is revealed to us, and whatever is revealed to you'" (Sahih Al-Bukhari, Vol. 9, *Hadith* No. 460).

Also (narrated by Abdullah, a companion of the Prophet) the Prophet said: "Whoever dies while still invoking anything other than *Allah* as a rival to *Allah*, will enter Hell (Fire)" (Sahih Al-Bukhari, Vol. 6, *Hadith* No. 24).

There is this and much more evidence from the *Qur'an*, the *sunnah*, and the *hadith* to unequivocally establish the undiluted purity of the *Qur'an* in establishing its meaning and worldview by referring to itself about the Oneness of God. This is the challenging methodology of self-referencing in socio-scientific theory and practice. This topic was covered in this work. It is to be found nowhere else in received Occidental and other philosophies of socio-scientific thought.

A summary outlook of the theory of meta-science for socio-scientific thought

The generalized methodology of meta-science emanating from the monotheistic law of unity of knowledge in socio-scientific thought that is developed in this work is summarized as Figure 9.2.

Final words

This work was concerned with discovering the methodology shown by the *Tawhidi* knowledge-centered worldview of the *Qur'an* in a way that can be explicated to form a unique epistemological foundation of the *qur'anic* praxis for explaining all socio-scientific phenomena. The *Tawhidi* knowledge-centered worldview emerges as a substantive methodology of a nature quite contrary to the epistemology of all received bodies of thought in the natural and social sciences. The *qur'anic* methodology so derived has been shown to apply uniquely in a logical way to both the

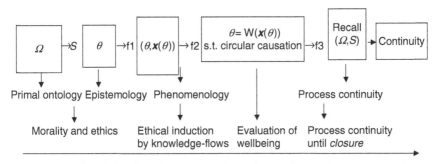

Figure 9.2 The generalized structure of meta-science and the birth of heterodox Islamic economics and a new theory of ethico-economics

natural and social sciences. Thus the terminology of the *Tawhidi* knowledge-centered foundations of the socio-scientific order is used.

While establishing the *qur'anic* knowledge-centered worldview by referring principally to the *Qur'an* with due reference to the *hadith* and *sunnah*, and claiming its uncompromising distinction from a rationalistic philosophy of the sciences and human behavior, an extensive study of received philosophies of the sciences has been undertaken. Within this critical approach, real problems of human thought and experience were addressed. Some of these issues and problems are of a mundane nature. They explain the nature of the *qur'anic* world-systems conceptualized and applied to the generality and particulars of the socio-scientific world-system.

While developing a general system outlook of the *qur'anic* worldview, central methodological questions were made to revolve around the praxis of the *Tawhidi* methodological worldview. Upon this praxis, this work pointed out rules and explanations after researching the principal Islamic epistemological sources. These are, namely, the *Quran,* the *sunnah*, and learned discourse with moral consciousness (*shura* with *tasbih = tasbih-shura*).

References

Al-Edrus, S.M.D. (1990). *Islamic Epistemology: An Introduction to the Theory of Knowledge in al-Qur'an*, Penang: Secretariat for Islamic Philosophy and Science.

Ali, A.Y. (1942). *The Holy Qur'an: Text, Translation and Commentary*, New York: McGregor & Werner.

Bakar, O. (1991). *Tawhid and Science: Essays on the History and Philosophy of Islamic Science*, Kuala Lumpur: Secretariat for Islamic Philosophy and Science.

Capra, F. (1983). "The systems view of life," in *The Turning Point*, London: Flamingo.

Choudhury, M.A. (2000). "The *qur'anic* model of knowledge: The interactive, integrative and evolutionary process," in *The Islamic World View*, London: Kegan Paul International, Chapter 3.

Vermont, J.-P. (1995). *The Greeks*, trans. Lambert, C. and Fagan, T.L., Chicago, IL: University of Chicago Press.

Index

References to illustrations are given in italics